7·13·78

FOR THE MILLIONS of men and women who have been brought up to date on how to dress for success, who have been made over and shaped over, have learned to design their faces and have run themselves into Olympian condition, now here is the single book that goes that essential step further—the book that reveals how to put it all together and *live with style.*

And no one does it better than ROBERT L. GREEN, who for a quarter century has been one of America's reigning arbiters of style, fashion, and manners. In this wise, witty, and entirely engaging book, this veritable renaissance man not only shares a lifetime's experience, but offers his discerning insights into the fine art of attaining a superior lifestyle—how to entertain, decorate, socialize, and develop the flair to *live* as well as you look.

A cornucopia of invaluable information, this is the ultimate guide if you are eager to . . .

- make your mark socially,
- dress with imagination and up-to-the-minute fashion flair,
- impress business associates with your glittering circle of friends,
- learn how celebrities, from Bill Blass and Oscar and Francoise de la Renta to Polly Bergen and Vidal and Beverly Sassoon, entertain, and pick up their tips on decorating and entertaining,
- shine on the country weekend circuit, either as host or guest,
- entertain your friends with elegance, verve, love (and without undue stress on purse or psyche).

ROBERT L. GREEN'S LIVE WITH STYLE will prove the passport to a world of gracious living you may have glimpsed, but never before imagined could be yours.

Robert L. Green's

1928 · 1978

COWARD, McCANN & GEOGHEGAN, INC.

LIVE

WITH

STYLE

Coward, McCann & Geoghegan, Inc. New York

Acknowledgments

I have adored doing this book, but it would never have been born if George Friedman had not insisted that he wanted to live with style. After one breakfast (good food—bad service) and talk at the Plaza about style, George announced that I must do a book. An agent and a publisher all happened because of him.

I am happy to have shared the experience with Elaine Louie, Betty Cornfeld, Elaine Kussack, Patricia Brehaut Soliman, Ron Bernstein, Angelo Donghia, David R. Taylor and my assistant and good friend, Lon Smith.

"Thank You So Much, Missus" by Cole Porter, copyright © 1934 by Warner Brothers, Inc. Copyright renewed, all rights reserved. Used by permission.

Portions of Chapter 2 appeared in the July-August, September, and October, 1977, issues of *Architectural Digest*, copyright © 1977 by Knapp Communications Corp.

A version of "The New Etiquette" in Chapter 4 appeared in the May, 1977, issue of *Harper's Bazaar*, copyright © 1977 by The Hearst Corp.

A version of "The Picnic—A Pleasure Party in the Open" in Chapter 9 appeared in the July, 1976, issue of *Review*, copyright © 1976 by East West Network, Inc. Used by permission.

Versions of "The Fast Feast" and "The Joy of Giving" in Chapter 9 appeared in the November 20, 1977, and the December 4, 1977, issues, respectively, of *The New York Times Magazine*, copyright © 1977 by The New York Times Company.

Library of Congress Cataloging in Publication Data

Green, Robert Lamont.
 Robert L. Green's live with style.

 Includes index.
 1. Entertaining. 2. Cookery. 3. Success.
4. Fashion. I. Title. II. Title: Live with style.
TX731.G69 642'.41 78-9457
ISBN 0-698-10920-1

Contents

ONE: Let Me Entertain You

My biggest break in life was that I came from a broken home. In my father's family, it was called paté; in my mother's family it was chopped liver. This schizophrenic pattern taught me to depend on myself very early in life, and made me realize that if I were to have a meaningful existence, I would be forced to invent myself. That is how I became Robert L. Green, fashion editor, designer, teacher, cook, gardener, TV talk-show guest, raconteur, and partygiver to the world. I suppose that I have aspired to some form of Renaissance personality, because every society and every age produces people who come to the realization that, like Oliver Twist, they want some more.

This book is for those who would be led to the table to partake of the feast. Writing it has been another adventure for me. It is an opportunity to go to the next plateau, perhaps to teach a little, but most of all to indulge my passion to entertain. If I were suddenly told that my life was going to end, I would have no exhausting regrets such as "I wish I had, I wish I'd said, I wish I'd done." Memorable experiences have accumulated in the course of my life, and I hope that others will find them as dear and warm and delicious as they were in the living. I have enjoyed my life, been rewarded by it, been proud and pleased by it, and now I'd like to share it.

Recently I was asked to give a lecture at the Fashion Institute in New York. I was told that I could take a few days to think about a subject. "No need to think about it," I said. "I would like to talk about the 'educated eye.'" And I think that is what this book is all about. There are various gradations of quality that can be applied to one's life: inferior, mediocre, good, and best. If you really care about yourself, then you owe it to yourself to give yourself the very best. Most of the prominent people in the world today were once unknown, shy, and uncertain. Yet, somehow they broke through, and made their lives glamorous creations. As I look at my students at the Institute, and wonder which of them will "make it," I am reminded that there are perhaps only twenty-five top designers in the world today. If I am going to help them succeed, I must make them aware of a personal style that will express their talent. I must train them to educate their eye, so that they can more fully appreciate the extraordinary palette of joys the world has to offer.

It would be presumptuous of me to say that this is the definitive book on style, taste, or manners, or that these are the rules. First of all, I think we've reached the stage where we are not so much interested in rules as in alternatives—different ways of doing things. I, of course, have a point of view, which has made my life reasonably happy and successful, and one which you are free to reject. In the process of rejecting, however, you will be forced to crystallize your own thinking and find out what you really feel. If you know what you really feel, you are very close to knowing who you are.

I suppose that the moment Eve offered the apple to Adam, she became the world's first hostess. There is a tendency to dismiss the role of the host or hostess, or characterize them as trivial or frivolous, when actually they perform a vital function in society. If you examine the history of entertaining, you will discover that it has served as an important process of education and communication. It was a way of giving comfort, aid, and love to early travelers who were dependent for survival on the kindness of strangers. Odysseus, as he traveled in his quest to reach home, spread news of the larger world to those who had never left their firesides. And since there were no laws to regulate international affairs, an elaborate tradition developed between travelers and their hosts. Hosts were expected to protect their guests from harm, and guests had the responsibility not to betray their mentors. The Trojan War was actually caused by a breach of faith on the part of a guest, Paris, who was visiting Menelaus, a Greek king. Paris seduced Menelaus' wife, Helen, and ran away with her to Troy. The Greeks retaliated by sending the most famous bread-and-butter gift of all time, the Trojan Horse. That romantic country weekend practically changed the course of civilization.

Today being invited to the right parties can serve as entrée from one class structure to another, as well as further one's economic interests. Making the proper contacts at a party can save a thousand frustrating phone calls to William Morris. A social situation is certainly the most comfortable environment in which to pursue one's cause.

If you are reasonably content with your lot, are willing to settle for the kind of food you eat, the sex you have, and the income you earn, then by all means close the book. Not everyone has to live with glamour, with excitement. But, if you believe you are meant for something more meaningful, that you are not ordinary, then you must adopt a behavior pattern that is based on a higher level of your belief in yourself. Belief in yourself is the common thread that exists among the great achievers of the world. I saw it in a dying Scott Fitzgerald. I see it in Jimmy Carter, and I see it in myself. It is this belief that will support your confidence. It doesn't preclude your having fears or doubts, but I think, in a funny sort of way, your belief in yourself is your destiny.

Determining *what* you want is the primary factor in achieving success. In many ways it will dictate what happens to you. If you are convinced you cannot function unless you drive a Mercedes or wear designer clothes, you must mobilize your resources so that you can acquire them. I suspect that if I were a woman who felt strongly enough about having beautiful clothes, I would buy a sewing machine on time and a collection of designers' patterns, take lessons, and learn to sew.

If you dress the part you would like to play, and then support your image with intelligence, you will develop both the look and the sound of authority. Once you achieve the look of the authority, people will invest you with it. Originality and individuality are qualities people envy and talk about. It takes a unique person to adopt an individual stance on the way he or she dresses, writes, or behaves. If your are brave enough, you might become a legend.

Next, examine what your life is all about. Look at the job you have. Do you like it? You may discover that you don't want to live in the city any longer. Why can't you move to the country? Think about your relationships! Are they based on compromise, accommodation, and adjustment? Is your life a ritual of pasta every Wednesday and sex every Saturday night whether you need it or not? Have you arrived at the stage in your marriage where it is no longer the beauty of an earned silence but simply that you no longer have anything to say that makes you sit and stare at each other? Would you come alive if another person came into the picture? Perhaps now is the time to take the positive steps that are going to make things happen for you. Face up to the fact that you hate gardening, that you loathe barbecues, that you no longer get a bang out of attending the Bahai temple. Regroup and begin a new lifestyle.

My childhood fantasies are largely responsible for the life I have carved for myself. My mother was a divorced Ziegfeld girl and had to work to support me. Because of the demands of her career, I was not able to live with her and was farmed out to a variety of foster homes. But I managed to turn a rather bleak childhood into a plus factor. Rather than spend my time breast-beating and feeling paranoid, I found some positive solutions. The key questions I asked myself were: "What do I have in my life? What do I want in it? How do I go about getting it?" Yousuf Karsh, the famous photographer, remarked on a recent talk show that he would like to photograph my face. Apparently, in the space of the brief half hour that we were together, he could sense my feelings of self-fulfillment and contentment. As has been said, "Before thirty-five you have the face you were born with. After thirty-five you get the face you deserve."

Since I was not in the usual parent-child situation, I had choices as to what and to whom I would relate. It was too dangerous to make exhausting transferences to the people I was living with, because there was always the possibility that it would all inexplicably disappear. So I discovered that it was wise to place importance on things that could not suddenly be taken away—the memory of a play, the excitement of a film, the value of a book.

Good writers, like good performers, always crystallize the best of whatever they are communicating. I learned far more about manners and style from writers and performers than I did from the people who were paid to take care of me. My family became the great actors and actresses of the American theater; the movies became my secret finishing school. It was the combination of movies, theater, and books that gave me the sense of constantly changing fantasies, enabling me to decide who I was and who I hoped to be. I have always felt an enormous sense of gratitude that I wasn't limited to one set of words, one set of values, one set of accents.

My teachers were the best in the business: Laurence Olivier, Noel Coward, Gertrude Lawrence, Fred Astaire, and the Lunts—the most urbane, witty, and stylish forebears a fledgling sophisticate could have desired. I wanted to be like them all. (Johnny Carson once asked me whether I was British. "No, just affected," I replied.) What need had I for real parents when I could assimilate the dry wit of Robert Benchley and the hysterical sense of timing of Tallulah Bankhead? That's a very important question. All of it fed me and imbued me with the realization that I could be all things. Every experience taught, inspired, and motivated me to develop a talent for living.

All those extravagant movie sets that were done for the Astaire movies—elegant, marvelous, white satin—were for me extended fantasy realms that had nothing to do with my mundane world. But they kindled in me a desire to find all the new, exciting places the world had to offer. My home today is actually a far cry from a 1930s movie set, and Fred Astaire would experience difficulty performing his magic among its eighteenth-century furnishings. However, Fred Astaire dancing on those Saturday afternoons at the movies was an influential encounter with a world larger than my own. His sense of style is one that I directly identified with; his wonderful simplicity—of silhouette, drape, manner. To this day I am a frustrated "gypsy" and yearn to tap-dance down the street like my idol in *Top Hat,* but I must be content to do those magnificent tap steps only in my head. My only real talent is my talent for being alive, the ability to create my own rewards. To always think positively and influence others to do the same.

Ina Claire made an art of taking off her hat and it made a life-long impression on me. She did it so well that it soon became her trademark on the screen. She would shake her head and every hair automatically fell into place. I remember thinking that one day I would find a barber to cut my hair like that. I have yet to find him.

Kay Francis, who started her career by being elected "Miss Beautiful Back" in 1922, had a glorious back and wore clothing marvelously. She earned her fame by always entering a room backward. It was her sense of personal authority that came through to me. It was at this stage of my development that I learned, that the poor always look at the buttons on their jackets as they button them; the rich never do. Perhaps the answer is that suits that are finely tailored do not have buttons that fall off. These are the little things that determine who you are, and how you are looked on by others.

My substitution of movie people for my own family members knew no limits. I never thought of Katharine Hepburn as a parent, but she certainly would qualify as a marvelous aunt. Needless to say, I desperately wanted Walter Pidgeon for my father. For my mother, Greer Garson—in the role of Mrs. Miniver, was top choice. Perhaps it was the promise of a rose garden.

Ronald Colman influenced my voice. For weeks I walked around playing Sidney Carton in *A Tale of Two Cities*. "It is a far, far better thing I do," I would repeat, breathing heavily, driving my friends insane. My philosophy was formed at the moment the guillotine started its descent toward Ronald's implacable expression. I decided that if I had to be executed, I would do it with that same style. It was another important lesson for me: In the inevitability of disaster, make it a positive moment for whoever is watching, as well as yourself. I try to accept defeat as well as the rewards of success with style.

I also identified closely with Osgood Perkins, Tony Perkins's father. Tony is intense, but his father had a loose sophistication and a long, lean quality that unfortunately is not my genetic fate. I loved all those people whose manner was supported by the trappings of wealth—the clothes of wealth, the beauty of wealth.

The world of the movies and theater so completely immersed me that it pervaded my reality from my earliest childhood. When I was eight, I was placed on a train from Boston to New York in order to visit my mother. Already I felt like a boulevardier, old enough to take care of myself. A note was pinned to my jacket giving my name, Boston address, and phone number and also my mother's vital statistics in New York. Even then I enjoyed thinking of myself as someone who traveled a lot—and the thought of being regarded as a child who needed a note pinned on his jacket was abhorrent. I sat across from a kindly lady who looked like Spring Byington and who was most concerned about me and my welfare once the train stopped in New York. I told her confidently that I was visiting my parents who were meeting me. At that point, I looked out the window at 125th Street and saw a billboard reading "Alfred Lunt and Lynn Fontanne in *The Guardsman.*" I proudly announced to her with absolute conviction that my parents were in the theater—that they were, in fact, Alfred Lunt and Lynn Fontanne. I pronounced it "Fontanney."

Years later when I met the Lunts, I told them the story. Somewhat later during World War II, I returned to New York on leave from the Army and went backstage to see them when they were appearing in *O Mistress Mine.* Lynn saw me in my uniform from her dressing room and called to Alfred in her extraordinary voice, "Alfred, our boy is home from the army!"

In my lifetime I have met many famous and near-famous people. The ones who affected me most were those whose humanity and standards of personal behavior overshadowed their concern with social status or other materialistic considerations. I was fortunate enough to be influenced by several outstanding human beings who made me reach out for new goals, new attitudes and new ways of thinking. One was no less than Alexander Woollcott. As he watched me rescue a defenseless child from a sadistic nanny in the lobby of the Waldorf, he informed me later that he was taken by my imperiousness. I was crossing the hotel's lobby when I saw a French governess dragging an obviously exhausted child up the stairs. I grabbed the boy, lifted him quietly, turned to the governess, and demanded to be taken to her mistress. She could, of course, have called the police, but instead she took me to her employer who accepted the child with graciousness and a great deal of confusion. As I was leaving the hotel, the bell captain touched my shoulder and informed me that there was a gentleman who wished to see me.

"The gentleman" was unmistakably Woollcott, who was sitting in the lobby reading an English magazine. In his strange, wonderful, ridiculous voice, he asked, "Do you know who I am?" I nodded. "I saw what you did," he continued. "It was a nice thing to do. What is your name?" I told him my name and address and he wrote it down. Then he went back to reading. I continued to stand there, gaping at my first celebrity. Woollcott suddenly looked up. "Don't dawdle, young man. Go away. I'll contact you." I considered myself dismissed.

True to his word, and much to my amazement, Woollcott did contact me. We met frequently to have lunch and talk. My relationship with Alex created a secret world I kept for myself, and it allowed me to play a role that had nothing to do with the rest of my life, or my family. With him, conversation was not a lost art, but a found profession. He made me realize you could create with words and weave a whole marvelous environment, as well as set the stage for a life that is adventurous. Woollcott alerted me to the fact that I had something very valuable—presence. "You are not the most patient man in the world, or the most sympathetic, and I doubt that everyone will like you, but I do think you can achieve what you want," he informed me. I'm not sure I understood him at the time, but he continued to play teacher. He would give me things to read, to develop my insights and perceptions. And because he functioned in a world of competitive wit, whatever wit was in me rose to the surface, and was sharpened. For a long period of time, I used it like a rapier, and hit out a great deal.

Once Woollcott invited me to a luncheon with Hope Williams, Gertrude Lawrence, Noel Coward, and Moss Hart. I was only eighteen and still very impressionable. And when I came out of that lunch, I honestly could not decide who I wanted to be, Noel Coward or Gertrude Lawrence. I wished I could be a bit of both; that was probably my plunge into androgyny.

Judy Holliday was another dear, close friend. Her integrity, intelligence, and talent were only minor qualities compared to the aura of goodness she conveyed. It seems rather silly to say it, but there was something almost holy about her and I wanted nothing more than to earn her respect. I watched as she affected people as varied as Leonard Bernstein, Betty Comden, Adolph

Green, and certainly me. She was not conscious of her power over us, but her mystique and her dignity engendered a desire for her approval from all of us.

Judy had an astronomically high IQ even though her public image was based on the character of Billie Dawn in *Born Yesterday*. Billie Dawn, the dumb blonde who really was a smart cookie as well as a sexpot. I never thought of Judy personally as being sexy, but I did find her interesting, knowledgeable and aware. Most of all, she cared, and was thus involved in a myriad of human relationships.

Harry Cohn bought the film rights to *Born Yesterday* for a million dollars, then proceeded to test the most unbelievable people for the part of Billie Dawn. Cohn's perception of Judy was that she was a fat Jewish broad who nobody would be interested in. He tested everyone from Rita Hayworth to Susan Hayward, and it wasn't until Katharine Hepburn came out batting for Judy that Cohn considered her. Hepburn went backstage to compliment Judy on her remarkable performance, and wondered why she was not doing the film. Kate arranged for her to be given a role in her next picture, *Adam's Rib*, and Judy received an Oscar nomination. Harry Cohn reconsidered his casting and finally gave Judy the part.

I like to think that I was able to be of help to Judy Holliday in some of the more important moments of her life. Oddly enough, it was my knack for fashion psychology that helped her to win two major battles. On the evening that she was to go out to dinner with Cohn to negotiate for the part, we discussed strategy— what to wear and how to perform. We decided to play it against character and present the *real* Judy Holliday. What she revealed that evening was a very bright, intelligent, pulled-together lady with a sharp mind. We recognized that a dumb blonde was just another "broad" to Harry Cohn, but a brilliant lady was probably a rarity. Obviously we made the right choice, because he was finally able to appreciate Judy Holliday's uniqueness.

When Judy was called before the Congressional Investigating Committee, she made exactly the opposite presentation. "What you *don't* want to appear is intelligent," I cautioned. "Think of who you are publicly to those Congressmen and their wives. You represent a mistress, an absolutely darling piece of fluff. I would dress in dark clothes, a little sexy, but not too trashy. They'll think you're Billie Dawn. How can they take you seriously as a political figure?" The lawmakers adored Judy and they were almost embarrassed to think that this charming, irresistible, dumb broad could be a threatening subversive. It was probably her finest hour as an actress.

Of course, we would all like to be thought of as brilliant, handsome and possibly the nicest person in the world, but I think we must always be able to assess our own strengths and weaknesses and also keep that very special human ability to laugh at ourselves. Two women came up to me at a charity affair at the Boutique Noelle, told me how much they enjoyed me on television, and how brilliant they thought I was. I, of course, was charmed and flattered. Everything was just wonderful until they were about to leave. "Keep up the good work, Mr. Susskind" was their farewell.

Even as a teenager I realized that a sense of humor could be one of my most valuable assets. Looking at my eyes in the mirror, at the time, I thought, well, they are neither blue nor brown, but no matter what, they cannot be changed. I decided that it was foolish to waste a lot of energy worrying about what could not be changed. My mother's description of me when she was asked if I was good-looking was, "No, I would not describe him as good-looking. I think he has a lot in common with Abraham Lincoln." I suppose what she meant was that I would get better-looking every ten years, and that if I lived long enough I would possibly become a very distinguished-looking man.

Well, there was some validity to that because, while I could not be described as handsome, I was certainly interesting-looking. I became aware that if you were not good-looking you had to develop other things. The key is to discover some quality in yourself that *you* find interesting, and then find the opportunity to present yourself in such a way that the package is appealing.

Humor, the way you speak, your vocabulary, your timing, are all talents that can be worked on. If you are as gifted as Henry Higgins, you can transform yourself from the proverbial flower-girl into a duchess. My voice is not the product of manipulation, since the same stentorian tones were in evidence at the age of three when mother wheeled me across the Boston Commons. I don't think I can advise anyone about how to develop his or her voice, but I do know that what makes something arresting is the unexpected. If you listen to an evangelist or gospel singer who is capable of really stirring people, you will discover that it is because of the sudden changes in their timbre. The voice goes up, the voice goes down; the voice suddenly booms, then it is tender and kind. Listening to voices you admire is one way to improve your own.

Wit is the winning ticket, because most people are not very amusing. I can't tell you how to develop wit because it may be genetic, but you can certainly improve your ability to articulate. Look up words in the dictionary and use them effectively! If you read writers who have imagination and style, you can learn to describe ordinary things so appealingly that they create a moment of delight. There is no reason why you cannot take a simple experience, such as the fact that your eight-year-old has been chosen to play Snow White, and relate it in a way that not only holds interest, but amuses and captivates others. Enhance your own charm through the use of language; words, like legs, never lose their original youthful character until the day you are buried.

Develop your assets to their fullest. Assess your wit, your charm, your appearance, your talents, and then package yourself as attractively as possible. Most important, take the shackles off your mind. Dare to think big! What separates the Beautiful People from the rest of society? One simple fact: they refuse to lead regimented, commonplace lives. They take risks. They don't worry about the possibility of being embarrassed! Let my own experience serve as an example that life can be an adventure, filled with fascinating associations.

If you are a wife and a mother of two, living in the suburbs, scanning Suzy's column over your morning coffee, and reacting with an irresistible urge to be one of the elite, let me direct you so that you can be a Beautiful Person in the best sense of the word. If you are a man who desires to be "center stage," to be noticed for yourself rather than for the job title you currently possess, here are some concepts and advice that will help you become a "star" in your own right. If you are just out of college, in the city on your first job, and suffer from the great fear of doing something that will mark you as not being urbane and sophisticated, you will find in these pages many ideas that are long on style and short on cash.

For those of you whose great moment of pleasure comes when your bitchy next-door neighbor reacts to you with a case of terminal envy, let me give you some invaluable tips, to keep her perpetually green. Your table setting, service, or party concept can be something her superior bank account can't buy, if your eye is educated to superior style. If your motive is to produce a party, send a gift, please a guest, or entertain so that your invitations are on the "much-wanted" list, I have lots of hints for you. If you are a guy or gal who is on the verge of credit collapse because of your penchant for Vuitton, Gucci, or Yves Saint Laurent fashions, let me show you how to find your own identity.

Have you spent your life entrenched in traditional patterns of living, and do you now feel that something is missing? Are you aware the old rules no longer apply? Let me offer you a fresh look at the changing values of the new etiquette. Or, if you want only the joy of being in touch with the ever-changing world, I may be able to give you some new perspective and insight. You will achieve success, if you learn how to take full advantage of the opportunities you encounter or create for yourself.

No matter how old you are, the important thing is to make your life an exciting, exhilarating experience. You can create a world where your influence dominates because you are a good cook, a good hostess, a charmer, a wit. It is not necessary that you function in the best of all possible worlds—only that you make your own world the best possible.

Whether it has been as a host, or in any other role I've played, I've tried always to prepare to learn daily. What I aspire to, now that I am past fifty, is probably more ambitious than anything I have ever done before: I have begun a whole spectrum of new careers. Arlene Francis interviewed me recently, and said that every time she turned around I was doing something entirely different. "The truth is," I told her, "before you're fifty, you think you are immortal. Once you pass fifty, you realize that you don't have too many friends who are a hundred, so you may as well live to the hilt!"

One of the most destructive prevalent notions is the hanging sword called retirement. The word is dated and has little to do with today. In the past, retirement marked a person as finished as a contributor. Passive enjoyment was supposed to be his or her reward. "Lucky you, without a care in the world," was the familiar cry, and for many the absence of cares eliminated caring so that they just gave up.

Each period of change in our lives represents a transition, a passage from one reality to another. You leave school and get your first job; no one regards that as retiring from school to the work force. You get married or live with someone, you go back to your home town or to an urban center; or just the reverse, you become an activist, when you grew up a conservative, or you adjust your radical liberalism and take a moderate stand. You change from reclusive absorbtion in science, test tubes, and research animals and become an extrovert, who gets turned on by people instead. None of these changes, or others in your life, is thought of as retiring from one phase to another; so it follows that when you take another step and move out of one area of the work force and on to other activities, you do not give up or doubt your worth or embrace boredom, or accept a living death. Do not retire from living, but welcome the changes as just one more transition to another set of actions and priorities.

Four years ago I decided to get up from the soft Fashion Director's chair at *Playboy* after almost twenty years. Here is my answer to the dread notion of "retirement." With a garden in Bucks County that has a hundred and twenty thousand daffodils and fifty thousand lilies, a beach house in Malibu, a villa in France, a much-photographed eighteenth-century farmhouse, a Greenwich Village Federal townhouse (a luxurious converted bakery), I could have been temped to lie on a chaise longue and shovel in the Godiva chocolate calories. But what made that leisure unattractive was my "big list"—a compilation of all the things I'd always wanted to do. I suddenly realized that life is not a commutation ticket and, by God, if I was ever going to realize the visions on my list I'd better do it now.

I had the choice and so do you. Don't fool yourself into promising yourself tomorrow, for there is none. Tomorrows will all disappear and become another today. Make out your own list of the things you want to do, the things that will make you happy.

—13—

Enjoy one today after another, and do it with your own personal style. Allow yourself to entertain and be entertained. Life really is a banquet and there is no reason for anyone to be on a diet.

Here are my current activities; they were all a part of the original big list:

DESIGNER: After thirty years as a fashion arbiter/editor, I was ready to admit to being a frustrated designer. Flying back from Los Angeles to New York I sat next to Richard Segrin, now *Vogue* Patterns Fashion Director. We started talking about gifts and he asked directly what anyone could give me. Rubbing my knee, I explained that I had planted five hundred tulip bulbs the preceding weekend in the cold, cold ground and what I certainly could have used was a gardening pad. My first commercial design effort was born. From the first gardening pad and apron to a cooking apron and gloves on to casually elegant menswear to great-looking designer clothes for boys, I found myself a Butterick pattern designer. Edith Head once told me that the key to designing clothes for the movies was to make them move a little away from current silhouettes, avoid fads, embrace classics, and your movie clothes would last the expected three-year viewing of a film. I did the same for my patterns. They are now number three on the list of best-selling patterns—important enough to justify a coast-to-coast TV tour, showing what the "Singer" crowd is really up to.

On his television show Merv Griffin asked me what the most complicated problem for me to solve in decorating my home had been. Because I wanted to slightly startle with the unexpected I announced that I had been exhausted in the search for the right wallpaper. The samples in the books look terrific, until you actually saw the pregnant rose or the witty elephant all over your rooms—enough to make you wish you lived in a cave. There are people out there watching and listening, and weeks later when the tape was aired in New York, my phone rang. It was Angelo Donghia, the Leonardo of the home-furnishing and interior-design field, asking if I would permit him to see the wallpapers I did have in my house. I asked him to tea and we toured my "bakery." He remained pleasantly polite and as we returned to the tea table he said warmly, "Every paper in this house is from my own company." I had no idea—for unless one owns Chinese paper from Haddon Hall, most people don't remember the name of the wallpaper company. My phone rang and it was a publicity person from Butterick asking me if I would do a personal appearance at B. Altman's in the sewing department. I'm no Debbie Reynolds snipping my threads at my Singer and said that unless there was a fashion show during which I could comment, I would be at a dead loss. Angelo overheard and invited me, now that he discovered I designed, to design a collection of wallpaper for & Vice Versa. We are into our third collection and there are ten papers done in fifty color combinations plus my Barnaby Thumper paper and fabric. Zandra Rhodes brought me a charming rabbit as an Easter-brunch present and it stirred the Walt Disney in me. I immediately dubbed him Barnaby Thumper. The first collection was inspired and created at the farm. The underside of a hanging kitchen basket, a small display of blue-and-white Canton China, my fields of iris and blooming lilies and detail from an eighteenth-century Lowestoft teapot, and the edge of a seventeeth-century chair. I saw all these with the "educated eye" of an editor with long experience in transposing his ideas from one medium to another. So I was able to transform these design ideas into wallpapers. Barnaby followed me around the kitchen and it seemed only fair to give him his own paper. He has it in silhouette, and he follows his own shadow across the paper in an endless parade. I used it last year to wrap Easter presents for local farm children and local city grown-up children. Barnaby thinks his paper belongs to the ages, one can hear him say, *I am a legend in my own time.*

I spoke with Arlene Francis of my own interest in double gifts—for scarves pushed into an oversized brandy snifter; for a book on the ballet with two ballet tickets to a major performance as a book mark. This was just talk, but I soon found myself designing a collection of gift watches for ladies and gentlemen packaged in a leather wallet. Style and attitude in gift-giving became reality with the Robert L. Green Watches for Nastrix which now appear everywhere. I wanted to give Rex Reed a clock as a gift; we are both managed by the Keedick Lecture Bureau in New York and on separate occasions we have suffered at the hands of forgetful innkeepers who were not wide awake enough to respect our wakeup calls. The Town Hall lecture crowd arrives on time and they expect the speaker to do the same. An alarm travel clock seems necessity rather than luxury, yet most of the clocks available look like something you would give to a retired English nanny. They had all the dignity of the Queen Mother and none of the charm of the Prince of Wales. So a new clock collection from Nastrix linking function and wit was produced.

The design world talks a lot and I was approached by John Kornblith, who heads up Inter-Continental Apparel, the company that produces Cardin men's clothing in the United States. Twenty years earlier I had once rescued John from the embarrassment of hiding in his own room because he could not manage to tie his black tie. It was in San Francisco—see how the little things can change your life. If your bow tie frustrates you, just close your eyes and pretend it's a shoelace and tie it; it's exactly the same principle. Of course, if you still can't tie your own shoes, then do not accept formal invitations. Inter-Continental added Robert L. Green for Gentlemen Clothing separate and executive gifts to its clothing line. Ralph Destino, President of Cartier, and I lunched and he liked the concept of a gardener and cook designing a series of gifts for the weed and paté crowd. Sterling silver trowel, anyone?

EDITOR AND ARTICLE WRITER: Hugh Hefner, the ultimate playboy, has made it possible for me to enjoy my piece of the *Playboy* cake. There is a page each month, and once a year an eight-page designer spread that I produce. With my new freedom I could choose other articles I wanted to write. I have now become a regular contributor on all subjects touching on style to *Architectural Digest, The New York Times Magazine, National Lampoon,* and *East West Network,* the airline magazine publisher. After so many years of writing on nothing but men's fashion, the third item after "Designer" on my list expanded to include free-lance articles on anything where I felt my point of view was worth putting on record.

ACTOR: A revived career that is not without some risk. I

stepped into an elevator in the Empire State Building and looked at the other passenger, a lady with the face of a sentimental madonna painted by Murillo. A friend passed by and we exchanged a few words; no sooner had the elevator doors closed, than my lovely lady began pounding me with her purse. Her clothes, her jewels, and her voice all reflected quiet taste. Her well-modulated voice repeated, "How could you, How could you?" I got off at the first stop and she followed. As I held her at arm's length, not knowing whether to be amused or angry, she suddenly stopped. Her apology was energetic but embarrassed. The night before, the CBS "Mystery Theatre" had broadcast a show in which, as the villain, I murdered Celeste Holm. My voice, as I talked to my friend, had made her vividly recall the horror she had felt as she listened to the show. It was the first show I had done in forty-two years. My early career was from eight to fifteen in Boston where I played a revolting but eager brat called Bobby White in a show sponsored by the R. H. White Company Department Store. Any wonder I bristle when anyone calls me Bob or Bobby? I do the CBS shows some six times a year, typecast as a villain who resembles Clifton Webb in *Laura*—a sardonic but smooth meany whose self-confidence makes headwaiters nervous. I also do a large number of TV and radio shows a year and have the joy of sharing my point of view on them.

PROFESSOR AND LECTURER: Long a contributing teacher at the Fashion Institute of Technology, I knew I wanted to set up a lecture series for students at the Town Hall level. The spring semester sees me introducing, as chairman, such major designers as Pierre Cardin, Bill Blass, and Rudi Gernreich. The questions of the students teach us all so much.

There is no end to one's list—it grows as you do. I want to design—from ashtray to zither and everything in between. I want to turn my barn into a showcase theater for young and established talents to perform and experiment. I want to create an important annual fashion show for students who are selected from competition across the country. I want to design clothes for a movie and produce products from Tollgate Farm. I tell you, my raspberry jam and smoked ham spread do not pale before any other jams or spreads. Years of cultivating these two specialties have brought them to their true potential and individuality. They are both examples of the personal and are ready to be enjoyed by everyone.

AUTHOR OF PLAYS AND BOOKS: Inside every raconteur there is a play trying to get out. I ache to free mine. I still revel in the daydreams and fantasies that are often the testing grounds for reality. I continue to live a cookbook entitled, *Courage in the Kitchen,* and ride my tractor in the back forty with my head reworking the plot of an unborn novel with the working title of *A Country Weekend.* I read the *National Enquirer* and reread Proust, I am totally curious.

And above all I wanted to share my point of view—and my years of happy experience—in a book on entertaining. So, "Let me entertain you."

TWO: Style, Glamour, and Chic

No one is born with any of it. It has to be learned; it has to be longed for; it demands self-discipline and it is unrelenting in its search for perfection. And you can have it if you really want it. The basic secret of having style is having confidence—you exude it and people assume that everything you do is not only fashionable but chic. Prepare yourself to be copied, criticized and envied. People who have style have it, regardless of what it costs. Everything they do, from dressing in the morning to setting the table in the evening, from writing a card to a sick friend, to choosing a gift, will have style. You may not be able to define it, but you can always recognize it. Muhammad Ali, the Sarah Bernhardt (and didn't she have it all over her contemporaries?) of the fight stage, makes claim to have more of it than anyone else. Gertrude Stein, Josephine Baker, Coco Chanel, made a career out of it. Zelda and F. Scott had an abundance of it. Poor pink-shirted Jay Gatsby never really had it, because he went out and bought it, which has very little to do with possessing it. Halston, Peter Frampton, Joel Schumacher, and Angelo Donghia are as well known today because of it as because of their creative efforts. Barbra Streisand, David Bowie, Mick Jagger, Elton John, and Farrah Fawcett-What's-her-name have developed a surplus of it. All of them have packaged it to the ultimate advantage. William Buckley and Gore Vidal are polls apart politically—but apart from brilliance, the thing they have in common is style. It isn't always a class act—stop, shudder, and savor the knowledge that Bette Midler, Mick Jagger, and Billy Carter have developed more than anyone should have of it.

Don't confuse style with taste. Taste is proven and it is very safe, full of the proven conformities. Taste resists change and regards style as a prime threat to existing and accepted values. Taste is concerned with carefully cultivated and broad lifetime progress. It never commits errors. Style, which is individualistic, reckless, and aristocratic, moves by jerks. I find style something to be admired. True style is often iconoclastic—springing from the best kind of human pride, which often brings on the urge to fight and destroy the rigid trivialities that attach themselves to our lives. Style explores creativity constantly and, like everything else in life including good conversation, is subject to imitation by inferiors. But for me the dazzling sparks of style will always light the way.

Style is so free that you can look as feminine in a man's football jersey as you can in a lace-trimmed tennis dress. I see a strong move away from the complete focus on oneself to a fresh focus on one's surroundings. Style is reflected in the ability to create better personal environment and a rewarding selection of friends. It is all in your attitude. Leave yourself open to the fresh, the original, and the new. Your interests will range from an amusing cocktail party dip, to a haircut, to a work of art, to avant-garde slang. You will always believe in yourself, always have the courage of your convictions. You will ignore the banal and the superficial will be avoided. There is an emptiness in the canned chic some designers and decorators offer in clothes and rooms. Being chic today is truly a state of mind, a kind of ingrained instinct for leadership. And it is truly personal—your clothes, your rooms, not the designers' or the decorators.' Your likes and dislikes become the likes and dislikes of others—they will follow you.

The chic possess the knack of being able to do something new with the same old money, space, or bodies. They are able to change the old because they are able to invent. Chic is not for the weak. It demands a strong personality. To be glamorous, one must be mysterious about the past, aloof about the future, and alert to the present. Glamour calls for a revived appreciation of refinement in living. Dom Perignon in cut crystal is eminently preferable to prebottled Sangria in dixie cups. Ethel Merman belts out a song and it is thrilling, but Mabel Mercer whispers one and it is glamorous. Jackie O. glamorizes anything she touches. Romance and sex appeal are, perhaps, the two most important ingredients in the image of glamour. Romance includes courage, imagination, and adventure. Sex appeal, for most people, tends to be associated with what is currently described as "good looks." Cynthia Gregory and Mikhail Baryshnikov offer glamour as make-believe, a sensation of beauty at the ballet.

You can express your love of living through flowers, plants, lighting, color, fabrics that make any space more delightful and appealing to the eye. You can do the very same with yourself. Take a piece of chiffon and twist it into a belt for the 1920s diamenté belt buckle you found in a thrift shop, or combine an authentic ethnic piece of clothing with your well-loved wardrobe—use an item like an exotic spice to tart or sweeten your image. The personal twist that makes active sports clothes (soccer, baseball, riding, hockey, motorcycle, football, tennis, skiing, lacrosse, etc.) amusing to wear every day is taking them out of context of their particular sport and adapting them to your whims. Put together a baseball shirt with a wide seersucker skirt and wrap it all up with a wide, soft leather belt. Put a sleek, slim, perfectly fitted leather motorcycle jacket over a body-clinging Halston silk dress. This is the height of both a fashion and sexual nonchalance. This is style. Go to museum exhibits and look at period paintings, tour gardens, enjoy displays in advertising art. Read shelter magazines, browse in book stores over travel, photography, food and cooking, and interior-decorating coffee-table books. You will copy, adapt, and adjust and you will learn.

Don't just look at people and things as you go through your day, but make yourself *see* them. Personal style is what life is about now. Nobody knows better than you what you should wear or how you should look. The crux of chic is learning to put things together for the person you imagine yourself to be, and even when you achieve a personal style, there is a striving for perfection that means you will keep seeking, learning, replenishing, and enjoying. Occasionally you will fail, struggle in chic's turbulent seas, but you will survive. If the outfit, the setting, the meal, the party doesn't work, keep yourself flexible so that you can easily move and work with what you have learned from the experience. Continue to take risks—accusations of "bad taste" may just turn out to be figments of someone else's paranoia.

Style, chic, and glamour are part of the entertainment of living. Keep an awareness of our time, live it, we are only human; we deserve to enjoy.

THREE: How to Make Your Mark Socially

If not being invited to a party can cause you to break out, to lie viciously, to flee the country or contemplate suicide then you are part of the disappearing breed called the social climber. But if you have been recently divorced, widowed, retired, relocated to an unfamiliar city by your corporation or profession, left home or college and entered the urban work force, inherited enough money to significantly change your lifestyle, or suddenly realized that your youngest sounds like a Dead-End Kid and suburbia is calling—if you are any of these, you belong to a steadily increasing group who face major social adjustments.

Each change, no matter how painful, offers fresh opportunities to reestablish your priorities. Examine what you like about your life and what you would like to change. New circumstances will allow you to stop playing the role that you no longer have to or want to play. Forget the brainwashing that convinces most people that genuine growing is something that only takes place during childhood. On this new plateau it is possible to become more oneself than ever before. Don't lie around and agonize about yourself; the same energy can work to getting yourself together and organizing your life. Find the joy for you. Until you learn to please yourself—to free yourself from all those "must and shoulds"—you can offer little genuine pleasure to anyone else. Start by changing everything you don't like about yourself.

One: Lose or gain weight by going to a doctor and dieting intelligently.

Two: Consider a posture class, an exercise gym, or yoga lessons to teach you how to control your body. Being a schlump (a shlep who slumps) is attractive to no one—not even to another schlump. Make a positive statement about your life by standing up straight.

Three: Develop a fresh approach to the way you dress and comb your hair. Unkempt, dirty, frizzy hair can defeat the best of looks. If you hate the gray—dye it (anything but black, it always looks like dead shoe polish). Or let the gray grow and re-style it so the color looks "premature." Check and see if you have been frozen into an image just because it once worked for you. Don't date yourself by complaining, "It's all I look good in." That kind of talk is empty, lazy and defensive nonsense. There are endless ways to wrap your person in clothes. The fashion magazines and fashion shows will show you how to stop being a conformist and to avoid stereotypes. You must learn how to make a difference between you and others in your world. Whether clothes are a reflection of a new negligence—everything loose and gently crumpled as though you took a nap in them—or classically elegant enough to influence a snob *maître d'*—it is you who has to add the most important ingredient—a hell of a lot of attitude.

All this has little to do with how much money you spend. A perfect fit can make the least expensive find look supremely elegant.

Four: If you look ravishing with makeup and ravished without it then learn how to use it properly. If one of the makeup wizards is unfolding his tent in your local department store, go and put yourself in his hands. Learn from the experience and take away what makes you look and feel good.

Five: Don't be defeated by imperfections; slightly buck teeth, the imperfect nose, a generous backside, a too-full lower lip, or runaway freckles—accept them and so will everyone else.

You have now packaged yourself, since you reflect your own personal style.

Six: Will a member of the opposite sex find you sexy? Yes, if *you* think you are. You must provoke by the way you move, the way you use your eyes to look at others, the way you send sexual signals. Be open enough to admit what turns you on and use the same to turn someone else on.

Seven: What do I do about my shyness? People feel shy with strangers at parties because they are convinced they have nothing to say that anyone else would care to hear. Remember, most initial party conversations are about as scintillating as a second mortgage. It is also the fear of rejection that makes people shy. There is no way to completely avoid rejection or you will never meet anyone. Flattery, honestly given, can work miracles in lessening the chance of rejection. Compliment her on her outfit or him on his tie. Open with a remark that will deliberately make the person talk about himself and what he thinks. Your opening gambit may not be memorable or quotable, but it will not fizzle into uncomfortable silence if it sincerely says, "I would like to know you."

Eight: Leonardo da Vinci and Edith Wharton notwithstanding, you can't all be all-knowing. But we can fool some of the people some of the time. Therefore, it is not impossible to become an authority on some subject that interests you. Not only does your learned expertise impress other people, but it also serves to give you confidence in yourself and your potential. Read all the books of a particular author who intrigues you or bone up on a certain school of art or a period of music. Take a course, join a political party, attend museums and concerts. Subscribe to a lecture series or guided tours. Just make sure the subject interests you, because it will afford access to people of the same interest. And if the subject bores you, then the people involved will, too, which will totally defeat your original intention. Be selective about the people you get involved with. Proximity is no insurance that you and your neighbors are destined to be friends. Make your own judgment as to your feelings about your work, your professional colleagues and classmates, but give yourself time to evaluate their place and yours in the new scheme of things. You don't want to be saddled with the local bore or unwittingly identified with the loser. Be flexible enough to absorb the differences between where you came from and where you are. What is acceptable in one crowd might be considered outrageous in others. You will do best if you are open, direct, and warm. Unjustified pretention or unskilled adaptation is a real no-no. Do not rush into changes just because it means doing something new. Fads can be very demanding and expensively temporary.

Nine: If you meet people you like at your activities, don't wait for them to include you in their social scheme. Be creative and decisive and include them in yours. Invite them, with ample notice, to attend your theater party and a review of an off-Broadway play. Or to join your food safari for a native supper party in Chinatown or any other ethnic section or specific restaurant. Thai food, anyone? You add up your acceptances, buy your tickets, and make your reservations. Select a TV program on your public broadcasting station that would interest your group and invite them to watch and eat.

Helen Lawrenson in an article, "The Woman," outlined the Clare Booth Luce technique of casting the party with celebrities she did not know. She would call, for example, Constance Bennett, getting the telephone number from the office files or from a friend and say, "This is Clare Booth of *Vanity Fair* and I'm giving a little party for Maurice Chevalier and he suggested that I ask you." Then she would call Chevalier at his hotel and go through the same routine. "I'm giving a little party for Connie Bennett and she suggested that I ask you." It usually worked, and although it seems a little dishonest to me, it does show how to invite someone you don't know to a party to honor a personality who is admired. This is to be done only after the person has agreed to be honored. It is another use of flattery. Everyone from a political candidate, a touring author, a guest lecturer, a columnist or TV host, editor or music teacher, coach or principal, director or designer or actor may well be delighted to be an honored guest.

Ten: Aim for the top, whatever you do. Don't assume that anyone is too important, too handsome, or too rich for you. More often than not your assumption of equality will be interpreted in exactly that way. You may be accepted out of surprise and even curiosity or with joy and gratitude. Don't take it for granted that people at the top are always busy. It is not so. Often they are pleased to be invited; whether they will come, again, will depend on you.

In the late forties I was living in Washington, D.C., and there was not a lot of good restaurant food there. On Sundays the situation was desperate for transients and noncooks. I set Sunday afternoon from five to eleven P.M. as my "at home" time. I made foods of the season but always had cold meatloaf, Boston baked beans, and bread—good bread. It soon became an established time when old and new friends would drop in and be sure of a bite to eat and some biting and good talk. I would call book authors on tours, casts of plays, and guest artists in town. Within a couple of months it was a salon. A salon is the most convivial and intellectually uplifting social arena available and it has all but been abandoned. You can begin by collecting your friends for an evening. Make it the same every week so that that night becomes identified with your soiree. Serve a U.S. vin ordinaire and cheeses or make a kettle of chili and interesting breads.

Eleven: There is no dowager out there capable of opening or closing society's door in your face. Big-city department stores have replaced the dowager as social pace-setter. In New York Bloomingdale's invites you, Bonwit's feeds you, Lord and Taylor photographs you, and Bendel's greets you personally. These American institutions are devoted to assuming the dowager's role by tying up charity fundraising, cultural activities, and fashion worship. You can keep yourself completely busy by going from one to the other. No one else has the space, the staff, or the money to give parties on their scale anymore.

Twelve: Select your own charity or cause—a problem that you are really concerned about—and get involved. You will start by having something in common with the others in the group. Volunteer work takes time and energy and seems always to involve out-of-pocket spending. Only volunteer what you can handle or you will fail yourself and the needy. If you are good at it you will get far more out of it than you give.

You can be creative in your choice of volunteer work. Why not consider reading or recording for the blind, directing a play at a retirement home, involving yourself in the preservation of historical landmark houses in your town? Produce a cookbook of dinners-for-one for all the singles in town. Organize a showcase house with leading decorators (amateurs or professional). Redo the rooms of an empty mansion. Create a gourmet gala by inviting the best cooks in your area to a "cook-off" and award ceremony. Set up a hobby fair, help the local athletic fund via a father-son, mother-daughter vaudeville show. Or reproduce the famous flea-market of Paris in the parking lot of your church.

Today making one's mark socially means finding new friends. And to find new friends you have to be one. Don't deny yourself any part of living. Start right now to do what you really want to and you will never regret what you could have done and didn't do. One sure-fire way to begin enlarging your horizons is by giving a party.

FOUR: The Party Master Plan

I look at the parties I give as a professional performance, no different from the performance of actors, athletes, lawyers, and other professionals. All these people take pride in what they do, as do I. Advance planning is the basis for successful entertaining. It's a kind of social engineering that allows you to function, as housekeeper, cook, and hostess. You start by choosing the date and making a list of the guests. It is vital to put the right mixture of guests together. To mix people of various ages, interests, and opinions, to mix the menu with different flavors, textures, and colors.

What you put on the table is less important than what you put on the chairs. Everything about a party should flatter the guests. The temperature should be pleasantly cool, the flowers important but not dominating in color and scent. Your pleasure in and affection for your guests should be seen by everyone. Don't handle last-minute invitations vaguely—be direct, because without some explanation guests may well think they were not part of the original plan. "I just heard from the Fields. They're only here for two days and are longing to see you. Can you come to dinner, tomorrow, at eight o'clock? Just wear a sweater." And if you did not include the guest originally, just be frank. "Can you rescue me from the spot I'm in. The DeMarcos were coming for dinner tomorrow night, but have been called out of town. Be an angel and fill in for me, I promise I owe you one."

Count the forks, spoons, glasses, plates, coffee cups, the serving equipment. Adjust the guest list to your equipment or arrange to borrow. Your oven or deep-fryer can work for only so many dishes. Often you can make do with any combination of silver and china you have. Mixed patterns of dinner plates, salad, and butter plates work. If your honored guest's fork is not the same pattern as yours, he won't notice.

I have not sent a printed invitation in years. The telephone gives you an instant yes or no. If you get a no from the first four guests, you obviously have selected the wrong date. Wait a few days, choose another date, and start telephoning again. Keep your guest list next to the telephone to take down acceptances, regrets, who will be late, who will need directions or is on a diet, or has a transporation problem. I always reassure guests that each will receive a reminder about the party. A correspondence card that says "To remind you that Robert L. Green expects you for dinner to celebrate Donald Brooks's birthday, January 10th, 8 o'clock, 297 West 4th Street, black tie."

Plan the menu so that you are serving food appropriate to the season. Think through what is available in the market. If you repeat your menu too frequently to the same guests, you become a food bore. No matter how well it works, or how delicious your stroganoff, friends will become disenchanted. Everyone wants new experiences and it is much better to keep a record of what you served to whom. Save your party menus together with the guest and shopping lists. Make notes of special preferences such as a new friend who doesn't take coffee but will finish his own pot of Sanka, or the guest who longs for a particular sweet liqueur after dinner.

Prepare for unexpected guests by increasing the proportions of your main dishes rather than adding an extra one. Check your list of staples, flour, sugar, butter, and so on. But even more attention must be paid to the spices, herbs, the extra eggs or heavy cream, the oyster sauce or fresh ginger, chutney or saffron required for your recipes. Plan the party in advance to the last detail: (a) menu; (b) equipment; (c) service; (d) timing. Do it with a pad, paper, and pencil. Think it all through and make concise lists. Be sure that your party menu does not demand the impossible of one oven. There is no way you can broil a steak, bake potatoes, bake popovers, toast the top of a casserole, all at the same time. If you are going to have extra help at the party, be thorough enough in your pre-planning so that the help can be directed simply. Avoid the exhausting "I would rather do it myself" syndrome, while your "help" stands, stares, sulks, and gets in your way. Don't make any assumptions, because they can't guess what you plan to flambé or where you keep your good platters. Just pretend for a moment that *you* are the help and set down on paper what you would ask or need to know. Having your after-dinner coffee interrupted because no one in the kitchen seems to know where the dishwasher detergent is kept can challenge your look of gracious self-confidence.

Don't try to keep the menu all in your head. Write it out on a sheet of paper and hang it somewhere in the kitchen. This makes it impossible to forget to serve the salad or heat the rolls. Don't stain your cookbooks by trying to use the recipe while preparing the foods. Copy it out on a separate sheet and use that as your cooking guide. Plan the menus so that you are not serving foods that call for careful, last-minute watching in the kitchen. Eliminate any dish that turns to rubber, falls flat or becomes cold unless whisked from the stove to the table with laser speed. Don't do more than one critical dish that requires you to be away from your guests. Undivided attention is required for soufflés, zabaglione, and either should be done by dependable help in the kitchen or skipped for buffet parties.

Small dinner parties can include one dish that leaves the hostess absent, behind the scenes. Any more and guests begin to feel guilty or compelled to apologize for causing so much trouble. Repeated kitchen exits and entries by a nervous hostess interrupt the flow of the party. There is a preoccupied, harassed look that seems to accompany repeated forays behind-the-scenes. Guests should not be concerned for one moment about the kitchen mechanics. They won't be if you are not. It is unwise to spend more money on the party than you can afford. It is wiser to offer a bowl of chili, a great bread and fresh fruit than to try a Beef Wellington and a major wine, chocolate mousse, and international coffee. Delicious to the taste, but disastrous to your budget. Hospitality isn't a contest. It is sharing the best you have.

ABOUT DRINKS: I always plan for unexpected guests and that means liquor as well as food. Unless your friends are all lushes you will not need a bottle of liquor (a fifth) for every four people.

That is based on four hearty drinks for each guest and, I think, is unrealistic. I plan on two cocktails for each guest for dinner or three to four drinks at a cocktail party. There are always a few who will down more but they are always balanced out by those who will nurse one drink all night or do not drink at all. I use a one-and-a-half-ounce jigger for each drink and after years of entertaining here is my list:

BEFORE DINNER

8 guests	16–24 drinks (2-fifths)
12 guests	24–36 drinks (3-fifths)
20 guests	40–60 drinks (4-fifths)
40 guests	80–100 drinks (6-fifths)

AFTER-DINNER BRANDY OR LIQUEURS

8 to 12 people	one-fifth
12 to 20	two-fifths
40	three-fifths

It would be rare for anyone to take more than two or three drinks after dinner.

TWO-HOUR COCKTAIL PARTY

8 guests	24–32 drinks (3-fifths)
12 guests	36–48 drinks (4-fifths)
20 guests	60–80 drinks (6-fifths)
40 guests	120–160 drinks (1 case)

The amount of liquor that will get you by will depend on the tastes and habits of your guests. Lots-of-parties later I realized that gin, scotch, and vodka are the big choices in New York. Bourbon is very big in the South, Southwest, and California. Blended whiskey is an East Coast choice from Maine to Florida.

For some reason Pennsylvanians are mad for it. Friends from Minneapolis, Madison, and Chicago are into brandy. Californians overwhelmingly favor vodka.

After the liquor and the friends you will need ice. Plan on more than you think you will need. I figure about four cubes to a drink. If your party is not too big, you can store up enough ice from your own refrigerator. Here is how I do it. Empty the ice-cube trays into plastic baggies and put them into the freezer. This way you can take the bags from the freezer, one at a time, as you need them. You can then set the bags in a Scotch Cooler by the bar. For a larger party buy the ice from a vendor. Be sure to check your liquor store. Sometimes they will supply ice along with your liquor purchase. Check your ice bucket to be sure your lid is tight. With the right guests, enough liquor, and more than needed ice, your party is off to a good start.

Wines for Dinner

I plan a direct allowance of three ounces for a serving of an aperitif wine, sherry or port. For my table wines, including champagne, I pour in four-ounce portions. This does take a wide-bellied wine glass.

Remember, there is a difference if you are serving one (red or white) wine during dinner, or whether you are raiding the cellar for several wines to be served with individual courses. You can count on two or three glasses per person if a single wine is served throughout the dinner. However, if several wines are poured, count on one or two glasses of wine per person.

APERITIF WINES, SHERRY OR PORT

8 guests	8–16 drinks (2-fifths)
10 guests	10-20 drinks (3-fifths)
20 guests	20–40 drinks (5-fifths)
30 guests	30–60 drinks (8-fifths)

A SINGLE RED OR WHITE DINNER-TABLE WINE:

6 guests	12–18 drinks (3-fifths)
8 guests	16–24 drinks(4-fifths)
10 guests	20–30 drinks (5-fifths)
12 guests	24–36 drinks (6-fifths)
20 guests	40–60 drinks (10-fifths)
30 guests	60–90 drinks (15-fifths)

TABLE SETTINGS. Table settings are an immediate reflection of your style. Avoid the ritual perfection that can lead to over-coordinated boredom. There really is no unbreakable rule; set your table any way you choose. Just as our manners change, so do table-setting traditions. It was all very logical to follow Emily Post when every dinner party consisted of the proper seven courses that proper hostesses served. All the flatware was arranged in order of use and everything was geometrically spaced so that the staff would have well-defined directions. I consider all that a holdover from the nineteenth century. Today, the way to set a table depends on the nature of the occasion and what is going to be eaten. Napkin-placement errors used to be unforgivable. And the fear of committing a gaffe was the reason for the dictatorial rule of etiquette. What you do with your napkin now is based on the total look of the table. It is an accessory, as is everything else on the table, and your personal style determines how you will use it for each dinner party. Here are just a few options: the napkin can be folded as a rectangle or a triangle, or go dramatic and you can turn it into a flame shape. Easy to do by first forming a triangle and then rolling the napkin so that the ends interlock, then standing it upright on the plate. Pleat the napkins and stand them like fans in a goblet or a mug. For buffet dinners fold the napkins so that a serving of flatwear is contained in each. Make your napkin become a lapkin by doubling its size—great for buffets. I use lapkins at table when I am serving shellfish to be cracked. Napkins in rings (wood, ivory, silver, jade and plastic) are very effective, decorative accessories. The texture of the fabric, the design of the pattern, and the color involved all add up to a versatile use of the napkin as keynote on your table to set the style.

Traditional candles and tall flowers will always work but I prefer a more personal expression. Use things already in your home as fresh focus at the center of the table. Anything you collect—from paperweights, boxes, porcelains, figurines, and so on, can be worked into an attractive display. Try a basket filled with fresh vegetables or a tray covered with small pocket ferns of different heights.

If your party has a guest of honor, use something associated with him as the basis of your visual statement. At a party I gave for a writer I used antique inkwells and Williamsburg reproduction pen quills sitting on a sheet of parchment paper. When a chemistry-major friend finally got his PhD I made the centerpiece beakers of various sizes and shapes from a laboratory supply house, filled with colored water (food coloring) lit by votive candles. The combinations of shape, size and reflected beauty are endless.

Everything can be used. For example, ordinary red clay flowerpots filled with green grapes and limes set on two-step platforms of ordinary housebricks. A flat mirror edged in greens and leaves with a narcissistic cat figure admiring its image or looking longingly at a school of tiny jade fish floating on what appears to be a miniature pond. Spray a shallow basket gold and fill it with a treasure of glass, diamonds, rubies, emeralds, sapphires, and pearls (purchased from a wholesale hobby house). Contrast in display can be exciting. I once scrubbed six Idaho potatoes and arranged them in the center of my bare, but highly polished, dining table and draped over them an Indian turquoise silver belt. Take a piece of the blackest cannel coal and set it smack in the center of your table with scotch tape fastened to two of the whitest gardenias or any other exotic flower you can find. For me, the only rule is *you should never be afraid to take a chance.* Use your imagination, be brave. Just decide on what mood you want to create—sophisticated, elegant, or carefree and fun, dramatic or understated, shining and crisp, or soft and subdued.

Change your candle pattern from the tall tapers to the short, stubby ones. Buy some new glasses, search out some antique ones, it doesn't take a lot to make a difference. Table-color directions can come from nature and fashion. Both Mother Nature and those in fashion are not afraid of the unexpected and thrive on change—overmatching produces lovely boredom. Mix what you have so that it pleases your eye. Guidelines can be found in the layouts of magazines and the style of advertisements and the windows and interior displays of journals and stores that reflect your own lifestyle. Your table is a short-lived work of art that *you* create. Don't hesitate to alternate antiques with contemporary pieces. Just remember that holding on to the gentility and elaborate codes of the nineteenth century has little to do with the way we live now, or what our guests would really enjoy today.

LIGHTING: Don't ignore the lighting—too bright lights can be unkind to the guests and the food; too dim lights irritate and create discomfort. There is a balance between the antiseptic glare of the surgery and Hernando's hideaway. Lighting should not spotlight anyone, nor should it hide anyone.

PARTY PLANNING: Take care of whatever you can the day before, the morning of the party, or anytime in advance, so the party doesn't become less exciting or more exhausting for you. Set out your clothes, accessories, and so on so that as you step out of the bath into your party clothes, you will look and feel as though the upstairs staff were devoted to you.

Be specific to yourself and your guests as to the time you will sit down to dinner. Plan the party so that your guests will have an hour to arrive, drink, chat, freshen up, and have a drink before sitting down. If you are new to an area, check with an established hostess as to when you can expect your first guest to arrive after the invitation time. In New York some seem to interpret an eight o'clock dinner invitation as meaning an eight-thirty arrival. You, however, should not count on any rigid pattern but be ready to receive your guests ten minutes before the time of the invitation. If, for any reason, guests arrive too early, ask them to amuse themselves until you can join them. Don't attempt to play active hostess while the water is still filling the tub or you are in the middle of dressing. Normally when the first guests arrive you should be able to greet them as though you could hardly wait for the party to start. The hostess with that distracted, far-away look in her eye instantly signals trouble to the guests.

For the "hostess," Elsa Maxwell says, "duty begins the moment the door opens." I suspect if you are feeling a sense of duty rather than pleasure in your relationship with your guests you're already in trouble. The only reason for giving a party, other than for professional purposes, is to do it for the joy of it. Of course there is a responsibility, but as I said earlier, I think you should regard it as a performance in which you take pride. Your technique, your style, your approach are uniquely yours, but everything should be put together with great care. It is an excellent idea to examine your game plan for the evening, from the guests' point of view. I always ask myself, as I prepare to entertain, whether my guests will have derived enough pleasure from the evening to justify the trip from uptown down to Greenwich Village. If you are formal with your guests when they arrive, they are immediately going to take on that posture. If you are over-protective of their feelings or careful of language, you will quickly establish in the minds of your guests a false tone for the evening. Open your door and spray your guests with tension and you have lost control of the evening.

On a recent evening I asked some friends what they considered the primary prerequisite for giving a party. Their response was unanimous. Never plan an affair which requires that you remain in the kitchen rather than being with your guests. Glasses don't get filled, hors d'oeuvres don't get passed, people don't know what is happening. Later, when the host or hostess finally materializes from the kitchen, a perfectly delightful supper may be served. Unfortunately, the damage has already been done. It's better to develop a repertoire of excellent menus that can be prepared the night before, usually consisting of a casserole, a cold mold, and a salad.

There is a maddening breed of well-meaning but exasperating women who consistently manage to make their guests miserable. I call them "guilt-provoking" hostesses. If their guests don't eat everything in sight they are accused of hating the food. Rather than being victimized by this type of hostess (or host) the aware guest usually gorges in order to avoid a scene. If he is brave enough to say simply, "I don't drink," he is flagellated with an instant replay of "I'll Cry *Tomorrow*." A real understanding of this onerous syndrome can be of service to all of us.

As a guest I plunge quite forcefully into conversation, as a host I assume a more passive role. If things are not going well, however, I will tell a story to start things moving. For instance, I flew to Australia as a guest of some wool growers. It *does* seem a million miles away, and you arrive with your body in Sydney and your mind in San Francisco. I got off the plane in a jet-lag daze and was ceremoniously whisked off to the TV station to be part of Australia's "Tonight Show." The act that went on before me was a 52-year old Weight Watcher-dropout singing with a six-foot-seven exhausted baritone, and the songs were rerun Jeanette MacDonald and Nelson Eddy. Suddenly it was my turn. I listened to the introduction and was appalled. The TV host was rather snidely resenting that anyone from *Playboy* or the States was going to talk about Australian fashions or taste. I was brought on with unveiled hostility. "Here he is now. Just what we have been waiting for. The big-shot fashion critic." The audience just stared as I sat down. The host plunged in and demanded to know what conclusions I had reached since I arrived "down under." Considering that the sum total of my exposure to the country had been the inside of a car and the saddest duet I'd ever heard, what could be said? I stared directly into the camera and announced: "If London and New York had a child, they would have to name it Sydney." The audience roared its approval, the next morning it was a newspaper headline and the Aussies took me in. Party guests hearing this are reminded of their own travel stories, TV or lecture appearances, anecdotes, jet-lag mishaps, or Australian jokes.

If your party is not going as you wish, *don't panic*. So you are not perfect. If one of your guests is a certified dud, don't tear your heart out over the deathly pall that is setting in over the dinner table. You have got to stop worrying. This is only one night in your life. Some people are beyond redemption, and it is not your duty to do social rehabilitation. Putting up with bores is sometimes the price one has to pay for an extensive social life. I'm sure that no one prefers to be a bore, but unfortunately some simply do not know they are. They probably think that they are scintillating, because in most cases they are well informed. The problem is that they don't converse, they lecture. Statistics and endless details are their stock in trade, but by the time they have decided whether it was the third or fourth Sunday in June, or whether Hannah or Harry arrived first, you feel that you have not only been invited to the party, you have been sentenced to it.

THE NEW ETIQUETTE: You can always trust Cartier to know the correct form for a wedding announcement. But who knows the correct wording for a we-used-to-live-together-but-now-we've-broken-up announcement? You may have graduated cum laude from both Emily Post and Amy Vanderbilt only to discover that in the world of the "new etiquette" you are socially retarded.

In Victorian times and even in the early days of Emily Post the underlying goal of etiquette was to behave in such a way that other people thought well of you. In today's era of "live together," "be yourself," "do your own thing," we understand that self-respect is infinitely more important than what others think. So the goal of manners is to maintain your own self-esteem and permit others that same right. Throughout history social amenities grew out of reality and experience. They should make life easier, not more complicated.

There were kings and queens who told everybody how and what to do, from what to eat to how to hold a fan. The Chinese aristocracy invented etiquette, always ate brown rice until they learned how to polish the grains pearly white. From that moment on the upwardly mobile lower classes adopted the nonnutritious stuff because white was socially right. As the accepted social rule is dictated, so the masses followed.

Sixth-century Japan developed a court etiquette based upon the folded and painted fan. At court only the emperor could open his fan, symbolizing the bestowing of prosperity and happiness upon his admiring courtesans. To show their modesty the hoi polloi kept their fans closed. When they walked they tucked the fans in the sleeves of their kimonos and when they sat they placed them behind their backs, an accepted but dangerous practice if the damn things slipped. Louis XV fiddled with fan etiquette but let his queen establish the rules. Nobody but the queen was permitted to open a fan when he was present. If she dropped a glove, her lady-in-waiting deftly retrieved it for her on a half-open fan. In hot weather courtiers couldn't actually use their fans, for this would imply that members of the royal household did indeed sweat.

America, to its credit or dismay, has never had a blood royalty. We have always been highly individualistic—or terribly unsure—Ben Franklin and Thomas Jefferson hold the distinction of being our first socially accepted celebrities abroad, and lord knows how *they* were tortured. Despite the tremendous strides we have made economically and militarily, several generations of Americans have suffered from social paranoia, lying awake at night worrying about their latest social blunders. Confronted with more than one knife, one fork, or one spoon—or worse yet a princess—we panicked. And so, sensing the crying need, Amy Vanderbilt and Emily Post became our self-appointed arbiters. Americans loved and bought their books by the millions. These two gals were surely in the right place at the right time. They identified a "gap" in the market—and filled it. Once Americans got beyond the bread-and-butter level of survival they needed some ground rules to guide them on their upwardly mobile trek. Emily Post's book illuminated the way for the children of the nouveau riche and was given along with the family Bible at birth. The Kennedys, and of all people, the Beatles, were the battering ram that started the downfall of neo-Victorian rules of etiquette. Joan Kennedy wore a mini-dress to the White House. Debutantes and their dates did the twist on our television screens. The Beatles thumbed their noses at the Queen. The sex, music, and drug revolution made new "royalty" out of artists, decorators, entertainers, and fashion designers—people who *worked* for their money and based their reputations on their own personal styles. These were the trend-setters who might keep a copy of Vanderbilt or Post around just in case they had to address an invitation to Henry Kissinger or because they could never remember if the shrimp fork was placed inboard or outboard of the grapefruit spoon. Basically, however, they were men and women who trusted their own social instincts rather than rely upon some obscure set of rules or upon a social heritage that never existed. It was no longer where you came from but *what you did and how you did it* that set you apart. Polly Bergen was just a girl from Tennessee, Angelo Donghia's father was a tailor, my step-father sold ties.

It is now the late 1970s, when people discuss multiple orgasms at dinner parties. You are your own Amy Vanderbilt or Emily Post. If you are talented, energetic, and charming, you can create your own rules of etiquette. Nowadays, rituals are a bore. For instance, it is always best to do the easiest and simplest thing in directing people to their seats at a party. If you start with a lady simply say, "Carla, will you sit there and Earl next to you, then Molly," I prefer this to the dated rule of seating the ladies first, which leaves all the men standing around uncertainly. The amenities should be observed only as long as they simplify your life; if they complicate it, dump them. In the past, when a single woman was entertaining another woman and two men, she placed the woman opposite her. If she placed a man opposite her it implied that he was officially involved with her and had become the host. Today *you* make the decision of whom you want to face. Is there really anyone left who would judge a seating placement as an official announcement of interpersonal relationships?

Alternating men and women is usually the pattern and it is easy to set up. If you are a single woman and ask any of your guests, married or single, to play host, don't ask him to carve or assume other duties, unless you have checked it out with him beforehand and privately. This has nothing to do with relationships or how it might be construed, but has a lot to do with work. The title "host" is no imposition but the work is. Don't try to carve at the table. It may look baroquely festive to carve the rib roast or the roast goose in front of your guests, but it means lukewarm servings with all eyes staring at the carver in utter fascination. It is no wonder that anything less than a professional carver leaves the food a mangled mess. If you have more than six guests, skip exhibiting the masterpiece and the center-stage bows as you milk the applause, and precarve the roast behind the scenes.

THE GUEST LIST: The only rule to follow when making up your guest list is to invite the people you like. The chances are that all your friends won't like each other anyway, so you might as well please yourself. Since people are the most important element in giving a successful party, however, plan a provocative, but nonantagonistic mixture. The atmosphere should crackle—but not explode. Think yin-yang when you invite your guests. I don't mean balance the sexes, just the personalities. You want an equal number of flamboyant wits and an equal number of listeners. If you invite guests with only gently flowing personalities your dinner party will wind up like a Librium commercial; put a lot of lunatics together and it is *Marat/Sade*. Don't invite too many performers at once; they tend to compete and you get cacophony. You can mix wits with noisy people or slightly funny people, fey people with raconteurs, mimics with gigglers and experts with interested admirers. Mix your party by ages as long as your guests' interests blend. A party is like a salad, you can toss in an endive with mushrooms or spinach with bacon but you wouldn't mix a scallion with a strawberry.

If you mix your guests with thoughtfulness and care, your party will be richer, more unpredictable, and fun. The only criterion should be that they can relate to each other. They must share some mutual interest, otherwise sheer eclecticism will create total chaos. And while it is exotic to have Brazilians, Frenchmen, and English ladies at a party, make sure they have at least one language in common—preferably English. You shouldn't have to play interpreter, unless for some reason you are considering running for an important post at the United Nations.

Remember, These Days an Escort Is a Sometime Thing

I never insist that my guests be accompanied by an escort. In fact, unless I am aware that there is a special relationship existing between two people, I would prefer that my friends all arrive solo. In the late 1970s escorts can be like lace doilies—extraneous, anachronistic, and stifling. From the point of view of your guests, coming alone to a party these days can be positively desirable. It is unfair to put someone in a position of having an obligation to drag someone along just for appearance sake. Today's smart young woman, whether she is young or old, married or single, straight or gay, has figured out that if she can clamor for her rights, do her own tax return, fly an airplane, or race a horse, she can surely go to a party alone. In the case of my unattached friends, if I have balanced my guest list carefully, a dinner party can be more exciting than an exclusive singles club. Why should they want escorts to cramp their style? If a potential lover wants to get close, an escort can only muddy the social waters.

Many of my married, career-oriented friends are not always at home together and are frequently free to go out on their own. The savvy host or hostess, such as Betsy Bloomingdale, asks, "Are either of you free on Saturday night?" Then there is the wife, husband, or lover who actually hates some of his or her partners, business acquaintances, or friends. Knowing this, it would be sheer stupidity to jeopardize an entire relationship for the sake of a social obligation. If the couple is mature they will acknowledge each other's personal likes and dislikes and suffer (or welcome) the occasional separation.

Gay couples should be accorded the same respect as other married couples. They should not be forced to bring "cover" girls or guys. It is a great insult to ask them to hide what they are and to treat them as if their relationship was shocking or illegal. Invite nonmarried partners (homo or hetero) by sending two invitations or by addressing one to both. You may create a ticklish situation when you invite one and do not include the roommate. If you want to invite one as an extra person or if the occasion is an expensive, highly organized wedding reception or business affair, you may respectably ask only one. They can decide whether to go alone or decline the invitation. Live the wisdom of Beverly and Vidal Sassoon: "A couple is a couple. Ask Noah."

Eleanor Lambert, the public relations doyenne of the fashion world, says escorts are permissible for bringing the guest of honor, the very elderly or the utter stranger, who would otherwise get lost. A widow since 1959, she has gotten over her need for an escort: "Bill Blass, Geraldine Stutz, and Jerry Zipkin invited me to parties to make sure I brought myself out of the doldrums. They always sent escorts for me and I always worried that maybe the escorts wouldn't come. One day I decided that I would not be dependent. I now have a hired car instead of an escort. It gets me there, it doesn't plump up pillows needlessly, it doesn't talk back and it takes me home."

Kenneth J. Lane always invites a few witty and sexy extra men to his dinner party. He believes in inviting pretty people just for prettiness's sake. If they are clever, even better. Sometimes someone who just wears beautiful clothes is the center of attraction. "It's amusing and naughty," he says. "My extra people are always men and never women—because men are seldom jealous of other men." Women don't like ravishing strangers unless they are in an entirely different age range. An older woman is not threatened by a 20-year-old beauty. Instead she is threatened by a contemporary who is free at the moment.

DRESS: Most people really prefer to know the correct level of dress for a party. Rather than make them uncomfortable and feel that they have to call you, tell them what it is up front. No one wants to be embarrassed or gauche or arrive in an ensemble that is completely out of step with the tone of the evening. Sometimes my guests are confused about what to wear to my parties, probably because I'm a part of the fashion industry. When entertaining I usually prefer an informal mode of dress because I live in Greenwich Village and enjoy relaxing after my day's hectic pace. There are occasions, however, when I feel there is someone in my life who is important enough to honor with a black-tie party, or sometimes I just enjoy giving my guests the opportunity to dress up.

Many people are very concerned about dressing and actually refuse to attend parties when they don't feel they can afford to dress appropriately. I think this is something we should all take into consideration when we plan an affair. I learned my own lesson when I continually asked a friend to dinner and the theatre, and he kept refusing. Eventually, I stopped calling him, thinking he was somehow angry with me. One day I ran into him on the street and asked him to join me for lunch. All the warmth and friendliness reappeared, and finally I asked him why he had refused my invitations. He admitted he had been out of work for a long time and had nothing but casual clothes, most of which were out of date. I was very touched by this and annoyed at my own insensitivity. Also I was a little concerned that I had created an image that one had to dress for me. Society has somehow placed such unreal values on clothes that people are foregoing some of the great pleasures of life because they think they do not have suitable attire. When you go to a party these days you often find a mixture of people who act with deliberate snobbery in the way they dress. They are either trying to establish strong identification with the class above them or the class below. Some endeavor to display their radicalism, arriving with paint on their jeans or to practice one-upmanship by appearing in designer originals. Nonetheless, it can all work if the hostess accepts the situation and does not allow anything as superficial as dress to polarize her party. If the hostess knows her business, she has chosen people who, in the deepest sense, have something that will interest one another—and clothes be damned. The lady in the stunning Halston and Elsa Perretti jewels sitting next to the person in denim overalls will find that there are a lot of simple forces that will bring them together: sex, political positions, problems, taxes, kids.

Always keep in mind that style is individual. Fashion's importance lies in what you do with it to make it yours alone. If everyone is coming on as a Bowery newsboy, or a desperate Carmen Miranda, you may be the real winner in simple basic black. If there are forty pairs of boots marching across the cocktail party, your spectator pumps will be a thing of beauty and may lead to joy forever. Make your clothes work for you. They should emphasize your assets and disguise your flaws. Be brutal to yourself with a full-length three-way mirror. If what you see there is either embarrassing or discouraging, don't take to your bed with a bottle. Do something constructive with diet and exercise. Diet doesn't mean starvation, and exercise is not decathlon training. Cut out the fattening goodies (you all know what *they* are) and walk and stand instead of riding and sitting.

Clothes will spell out your message loud and clear. Decide if you want to arrive at the party as dirndl Daisy, sew-it-yourself-gingham, or Sensuous Sara in panné velvet. Let your common sense and social antennae alert you to whether your coat should be girls'-school chesterfield or exotic black-and-white monkey fur. Don't wear far-out clothes if you can't be relaxed and easy with the clothes themselves. A (Norma Kamali) parachute-silk astronaut suit, helmet, and goggles, will be a dismal failure if you aren't getting a kick out of the outfit, and instead start apologizing for what you are wearing as you enter the party and continue making amends until you leave.

Fashion in your life should be part of the entertainment of living. Today's fashion options are many, and which option you elect to pick up is your decision. Whether you are giving it or going to the party, what you wear is not going to be dictated by unquestioned rules of acceptability. You set your own standards and get dressed to enjoy the party. There are as many different kinds of clothes to wear to parties as there are different kinds of parties. Here are some clothes concepts for both men and women that work when they are ready to play.

Clothes that are overdecorated with sequins, metals, or hidden stays can be a great mistake, if you are bruised every time you are hugged, danced with, or breathe. There is a kind of Hollywood glamour to dresses trimmed with feathers and it is easy to be tempted. However, remember this—feathers molting is like dandruff falling: both are enough to spoil a moment or an evening.

If the outfit doesn't fit, correct it. Clothes too small wrinkle at the seams and that is a disaster. Clothes too large are laughable and that is tragic. Don't try to break in new shoes at the same time that you are trying to have a good time. Wear the shoes privately until you are sure there will be no public pain. And matching all your accessories is the biggest fashion flaw of all; it is in contemporary American fashion terms an "original sin."

Never buy party clothes because they are very fashionable. No one should allow himself to be a fashion victim or slave. A current color or shade that doesn't suit you can destroy you. It is essential to be aware of fashion changes but to extract from fashion only what is good *for you*. Don't blindly copy fashion, but adapt it to your needs.

You must be realistic about what you decide to purchase. Does it make any sense at all to blow your budget on a gala evening dress for one occasion, no matter how important he or the party seem at the moment, if years may separate the date from the next time you will be asked to another ball?

Your style doesn't have to cost a lot . . . a pair of basic silk-jersey dirndl pants can be accented with a thrift-shop 1920s diamenté belt and a wrap top of a long rectangle of fine cotton or chiffon.

Here is how to make an instant but sophisticated top: Put the rectangle around your neck, pulling the ends out equally at arm's length in front. Cross one over the other to tie in back. If the piece is long enough you may be able to bring the end back around to tie in front.

Don't get trapped in the double vice of conformity and good taste. You can free yourself by developing a personal style. Here are some ways to march your outfits right out of the ordinary:

1. Add some glamour to your wardrobe by traveling to the far-off places in your city: Chinatown, the ethnic shops that represent Czechoslovakia, Ireland, India, Japan, Mexico and Russia. Shop at the museums that have reproduced authentic copies of scarves and jewelry from all over the world:

a. A Chinese silk brocade jacket is a perfect light evening coat or an exotic top over jeans.

b. A heavily embroidered Czechoslovakian sweater worn on top of a full-length gray flannel skirt is winter-warm for any country-club date or comforting for an energy-saving hostess.

c. A small Irish-lace tablecloth tossed correctly over your shoulders creates the fashion illusion of a treasured heirloom shawl.

d. A nylon georgette Sari from an Indonesian import shop can be cut into scarves of sari length, and still leave you enough cloth to knot and tuck a turban or to wrap a Balinese skirt. Add any of these to your leotard and you will look like a washed-up (not out) native at the tropics beach party.

e. An embroidered Mexican white jacket with big patch pockets over black satin trousers, topped with a sheer gray cotton blouse, will let your friends know that you are both looking good and forward to the evening.

f. A black Japanese hopi coat with a colored silk embroidered dragon or good-luck symbol on the back of it will revive your most exhausted slacks, jeans, and skirts. If you have been playing "Come Back, Little Sheba" every morning as you shuffle around the kitchen, clutching desperately at your mutilated bathrobe, why not put it out of its misery and replace it with a Japanese kimono? Warning: it does take time and a little practice to keep the kimono sleeves from catching on doorknobs as you enter or leave rooms, from diving into your food or going up in flames if there is a lit candle in the house. However, once the kimono is mastered your grace of movement will astonish.

g. A couple of ordinary Russian-peasant flowered wool challis scarves wrapped around your head and twisted over each other will give you a very personal blend of contrasting colors and patterns. Learn how to blend in some exotic garment, out of its usual context with your regularly worn and well-loved wardrobe.

2. The most practical thing you can own is the basic shirtdress or any of the classics. The trick is to take a classical form and punctuate it with invention . . . so that you come up with something new without betraying the validity of the old. That is the secret of layering your clothes. You can wear two classic colored silk or cotton shirts over one another and layer the collars like the petals of a flower.

3. A classic-cut black or green blazer will get you through any dinner party. You can harden it with a turtleneck or soften it with a wisp of silk at the neck. Wear the blazer on top of whatever bottom would be congenial at the party. The bottom range will include satin, velvet, and flannel slacks with a pump, tight jeans with boots, a full peasant skirt with Capezios, traditional tweed skirt with loafers, and: the ubiquitous full-length jersey skirt and stiletto-heeled shoes. Wear one real flower boutonnière on your blazer or make your own cluster of satin flowers . . . the kind to be found on lingerie in the 'twenties.

4. A well-fitted riding jacket will support many different looks. You can dress it down or up with sweater and jeans, with an expensive silk shirt and a velvet skirt. For a surprise, add a lovely antique jeweled pin to the lapel.

5. Try functional work clothes for informal evenings and brunches . . . an oatmeal linen jeweler's smock is an easy and stunning look, white house-painter's pants are inexpensive and very stylish, particularly when combined with an oversized very full cowl-necked sweater. Your friendly neighborhood army-surplus store has supplies of checked wool lumberjack shirts. Try the combination of a riding jacket, the lumberjack bold plaid shirt, gray flannel slacks or straight-legged jeans and butch

boots. You'll hear more than "timber" from the men in your life.

6. Buy yourself a package of royal purple dye and a high-school-style warm-up suit in that gray, fuzzy-lined sweatshirt material with a slashed pocket front. Bring the dye and the suit together, and the richness of the color and the purity of the design will give you a fast-on-your-feet look even when you are lounging around with one friend and one deliciously messy late-night pizza.

7. Diamonds may be your best friend, but if you are a bit nervous to be out late with your "friends" on city streets, or if you are tired of your Kenneth Jay Lane "false friends," then get into nonjewelry jewelry. Wear a colored cord for a ring. Explore trimming shops and department-store notion counters, for these are hidden treasures to be found with which to make your own "jewelry."

8. If you are flat broke and can't afford to play with clothes, you can always have fun dressing up your face.

Be merciless in front of both your mirror and your closet.

Mirror: before you wear a put-together outfit, check it out in front of the mirror privately. What do you look like? Are you out of balance, too much on the bottom or too much on the top? Would you honestly describe yourself as dumpy, pear-shaped, chopped into clumps, or too long or too thin? Don't eliminate the outfit if there are problems, manipulate it. Try changing your jacket length, put your hair up or let it down, try a solid-colored blouse or change to a patterned one, try a smaller or larger purse or tote. Play fashion editor and edit yourself. Take away or add jewelry, shorten or lengthen a hem and so on . . . experiment until you are satisfied with the total look.

Closet: Prune any wardrobe mistakes—i.e., the fad that got away. If you haven't worn it for a year, send it to the cleaner's and then turn it over to a charity and take your tax credit.

Select your wardrobe with an open mind. Fashion stubbornness can deny you the pleasure of the new. Fashion prejudices such as "I hate orange" or "No lady wears a loud print" are old-hat. Personal style requires constant experimentation. It may well be time for you to arrive at the party wearing something new, a becoming outfit, things you were convinced you would *never* wear. More people will pay attention to you, for you will look different from your familiar taken-for-granted image. It is the unusual in you that you must bring out, for it is that which distinguishes you from everyone else. Once again, the charm of the unexpected.

Men dress in various ways to send various messages. In today's world of almost completely casual entertaining, how you appear at the party is essentially your own decision, and in most cases you will discover that whatever you wear is acceptable to your hosts, if it is you they really want at the party, not a fashion statement. I've broken down what I found to be the general direction men take in the clothes they wear to parties. Frye boots, skin-tight jeans, cowboy shirts with mother-of-pearl buttons and western embroidery, and a ten gallon Stetson will support your Marlboro man image. Don't run down to the tattoo parlor unless you are really sure. A variation on this look is the "rich wrangler"—the honcho who owns the ranch but doesn't work on it. The pants will be of heavy gabardine, the shirts are made of silk, and the boots will be custom-made. The furthest West either may have been may be Riverside Drive, but it doesn't matter. You are wearing clothes that allow you to play the part.

Don't generalize about fabric or colors. If being sophisticated and worldly is really what you are—or fancy you are—then indulge in silks, velvets, cashmeres, lush flannels, buttery suedes. These are textures that are important to both men and women. For a glamorous evening, a silk shirt, a velvet blazer, pleated flannel slacks are marvelously flattering. Select the colors that go with your natural coloring. If your eyes are blue, wear light blue shirts to enhance their color. If your complexion is sallow, stay away from washed-out browns and indulge in strong gray Donegal tweeds instead. Don't invest in too-startling or too-special colors, like shocking pink or anemic apricot unless you have a lot of clothes. Aggressive plaids are a mistake as a first jacket, but terrific in third place. Make the first choice a blue blazer, the second a quiet tweed jacket, and *then* let yourself go. The more frequently you plan to wear something, the easier it should be for you to change its look by switching accessories. Multipurpose is the password for a limited wardrobe. You don't have to re-equip yourself from head to toe each fashion season. Take a look at the party clothes you have and add to them garments that offer excitement: a new color in a shirt, a belt that is crisply slimmed down in width or thickened to hold a reproduction swashbuckler buckle, a hat that either will be fun (a groom's hat), or a dramatic extra (velour hat), a witty, easy, old vest, a pocket watch, a collar style that you have never worn before, a shirt and tie worn with an overshirt, an unexpected bow tie, a double-knotted scarf, or go further to achieve a baroque swagger to the scarf knotted around your neck; an oversized sweater for contemporary fullness. For a casual evening by the fire, create your own compatible sweater set with an alpaca cardigan and a coordinating turtleneck. A do-it-yourself alternative to the belt is a piece of rawhide, a narrow wool scarf, or an interesting piece of intertwined fabric. And at the bottom of the list, new sheepskin boots for an urbane statement or classical brown leather moccasins with tassel ties for appropriate country or city weekend party wear.

If all the ski sweaters purchased annually were on the ski slopes, the traffic would be unbearable. Most of the "skiing" is done at the supermarket or to après ski parties. This satisfies the jock in a lot of people. Mountain climbers wear their entire gear to climb the subway stairs. Riding clothes and English hacking jackets find their way around a quarter-acre suburban plot while the landowner tours his "garden" of two terminal azaleas and an arthritic ivy.

Yachting outfits of navy blazer, white flannels, and turtlenecks sail out of the closet and cruise at Sunday brunch at the next-door apartment. Jocks like to avoid fitted clothes of any kind and love the looseness of exercise clothes. Whether the guy actually made the team or not, he may yearn for the relaxed atmosphere of the gymnasium. There is great comfort in varsity sweaters, baggy slacks, worn, old and frayed shirts. The exercise suit you wore for late-night cram-and-bull sessions are a comforting memory for a casual evening with close friends. These are clothes that invite touching. Try any of these relaxed looks and you can come off softly stylish and avoid the sweaty and sloppy, if you do it intelligently.

Some of you may have gone to the Ivy League schools and even have comfortable trust funds and prefer to continue the preppy, Ivy-League look for cocktail parties, much as though you were a perennial sophomore. Or perhaps you never did smell the ivy, and it's only in God you trust, but you still want to appear as a pedigreed Wasp. You will dress in a soft, understated style and wear real tweeds, oxford shirts, windbreakers, chinos, sportshirts, Shetland sweaters, loafers, a battered but unstained hat.

Not a lot of people are investing in major jewelry today. I think the "investment" for your party wardrobe is better made in quality accessories—terrific shoes, imaginative scarves, appropriately tailored shirts, elegant ties. Your hose or stockings will make a difference. And pay attention to your glasses; if you need them to see that dark stranger across a crowded room, wear them but let them be simple, contemporary, and flattering to your face.

It's the total look that counts. Don't hold desperately to an earlier image. What looked chic in the 1930s is a joke today. The pie shape which was in proportion to your mane of hair in college may be ill-fitted to your bald head now. The distinguished look of the straight-laced 'fifties is boring in the 'seventies. The sterile perfection of "correct" clothes is replaced by you doing it your own way. You should be an independent man or woman who is perfectly capable of deciding for yourself what subtle updating you want to bring to your party wardrobe. By all means unbutton your casual shirt if it makes you look sexier but not if you look as if you were going to bed.

There is a line between studied carelessness and sloppiness.

A word about a man's height. If you are under 5'7" you have no desire to be shorter. Your posture will determine how tall people see you. Stand up straight, believe in your own authority, and you will command the belief that you *are* tall. If you slouch, apologize, or think small, you will come off even shorter than you are. Keep the lines of your suit simple, your lapels away from extremes (not too wide, not too narrow), some suppression at your waist and either a straight-back jacket or a single-vented one. Make your silhouette appear taller by wearing straight drop pants. What you want to achieve is a fluid, unbroken vertical line that will give you a taller silhouette. To put flared or tapered pants and bell-bottoms on a short man makes him look as if he has borrowed a grown-up's clothes. Assuming that you are small but perfectly formed, avoid the too-bold patterns—they can be overwhelming. Enjoy patterns, but be sure they are small; also small checks, small plaids, and the narrower pinstripes. Because your goal is the unbroken line, you will look taller in closely related colors; subtle shades of gray, blue, or brown will work very well for you. Sharp color contrasts will cut your height. All this fashion advice is useful if you are hung up about your height. If you feel tall, wear what pleases you.

If you are between 5'7" and 5'10", then you take a regular size in your suits. Many of the above cautions still apply, with the exception that you can get away with flared trousers and there is no need to confine yourself to the monotone look. Violently mixed patterns should be avoided, however. It takes a tall man to carry off too-strong multimixed patterns. Keep the shirts solid, the ties in contrasting colors, or it they are patterned be sure it is subtle or neatly dotted or striped.

If you are over 5'10" you are considered tall and there are far more options in choice of suits. You can stand up to a strong design, a wider lapel, but not too strong a color. The accessory of pink is a delight in a man of medium height. An endless pink suit on a six-footer may be too much. Your height does, however, make you a likely candidate for bolder and less restricted styles than the men you can look down on.

If they are arriving together, people should check with one another about what they are going to wear. The days of depending on arriving in a dark suit are over. I don't mean that you should look as though you have been costumed as a dance team, but you shouldn't look as though you met by accident. And once you do put yourself together for the party, forget about it. I believe in a great deal of fashion freedom but I still have a few rigid fashion rules for both men and women:

1. White for tennis and sneakers.
2. Grip rubber-bottom sole shoes for yachting. Leather soles scratch the teak deck and at the very least leave black marks. Think through how cold it may get before the party is over. Your host might be thrilled to see you in your bikini or thonged at noon but not be amused if you turn blue because you don't have a jacket when the sun goes down.
3. Follow established clothing protocol for riding and the hunt.

THE ART OF INTRODUCTION: Introducing people is a minor art. As a host you have to open up your guests' reserve, make them feel thrilled but not threatened and fascinated but not overawed. Here are some ways to introduce people from media stars to housewives, intellectuals to dress designers, boutique owners to criminal lawyers.

First consider the mini-bio. Among the rich and famous there are two schools of thought about introducing people with their credits. Some do it because it provides an instant frame of reference. Sample: "John Gielgud, I think you should meet Ethel Merman who was so wonderful in *Gypsy*." They don't want their friends to fumble about murmuring, "Ah, my dear, you look so familiar." Others don't because they think credits are pretentious.

Celeste Holm says credits are the height of bad taste. "They embarrass people. If someone has written a book that has been wonderfully reviewed in the media, I would be sure that the other guests knew it—but privately." However you introduce people, remember that as host you are the producer—your guests are the stars.

Thrill your best friends by introducing them in the most personal way you can, by revealing a marvelous thing they did for you. You might open with, "This is my best friend who: (a) saved me from drowning in Cancun, (b) introduced me and my husband, (c) found me my fabulous job as (what-ever-you-are), (d) made me dye my hair blond." The person who is introduced to your best friend will probably respond spontaneously, particularly if he is also a good friend, and say, "Oh, you have changed her life so much, she is much happier on dry land." "She is really the marrying kind and aren't they a fabulous couple." "She is so much happier in her new job." "Isn't she fabulous as a blond—better than as a mouse." They will chatter about you and, via you, reveal themselves to each other.

Another multiple-choice intro excludes you altogether and finds a common bond between two guests. Again, the same opening, "This is my best friend who (a) cut himself shaving when he heard you on the "Today Show," (b) just finished a cooking class with Craig Claiborne, just like you. He likes Mexican peppers so much he sniffs them like cocaine, (c) teaches hang gliding and weren't you trying to convince yourself that it isn't a new form of hara-kiri? (d) is looking for a bitch in heat, isn't your shih-tzu awfully horny these days? (e) just discovered the wonders of kreplach and should probably try your brand of delicatessen on the upper West Side. You can trade him kreplach for his own Chinese wonton."

Normally friendly, curious people react spontaneously to any nonlibelous mutual interest pointed out to them. People like sharing passions. But if they don't, skip it. Sometimes it is very hard to enjoy a stranger before you know his title and status. We often disguise real conversation with banal chit-chat. Kenneth J. Lane was once in London seated next to a woman whose place card said *Lady Margaret Walker*. It took me the entire first course to find out that her husband was Jimmy Walker, the Director of the National Gallery. She was very perceptive when he finally warmed up to her: "Ah, Mr. Lane, you like me better now that you know who I am."

Occasionally no introduction other than names works better. I found myself at a luncheon seated next to a gentleman to whom I had never been introduced. We had a perfectly lovely chat and it wasn't until he said, "My partner has a place in Bucks County," that I realized I was sitting next to Ed McCabe of the advertising agency, Scali, McCabe and Sloves. It may not have been the correct thing to do, but I rather admired my host Andy Warhol for not having made the introductions. If I had known I was sitting next to a major advertising executive I probably would have tried to sell him something.

And expect the unexpected. I was once asked by a friend to allow a young lady, who was mystically referred to as his "client," to sing before some of my influential guests. I had never, in fact, heard her sing, but I had respect for the person who asked me. "I suspect the first time Michelangelo walked into the Borgias, somebody had to say, 'Take a look at his painting,'" I announced grandly and sincerely, and told my guests that the thought of being part of the beginning of a new career was something that pleased me very much. Then, she sang. It was one of the few times in a lifetime of entertaining that I wished myself somewhere else. It was obvious that my friend's interest in the young lady derived from other than her talent as a singer.

Don't feel that the way to move a party is to move people around. There is nothing so irritating as having your hostess come over to you when you are enjoying a perfectly lovely conversation and drag you away to meet someone you could care less about. A considerate hostess will say, "When you have a moment I would like you to meet someone." That way a guest will not feel he is being torn away or imposed on. It's all a matter of proper phrasing, so that your guest is given an option as to when, if at all, the move is made. Be on the alert, however, to the fact that at most parties men gravitate toward men and women toward women. If you don't constantly mix the sexes, your party will resemble a teenage prom—boys on one side, girls on the other. In any normal mix usually one guest stands out. If you don't want a heavily unbalanced party, where a single star holds court, begin introducing people of opposite sexes not by mutual interests but by personality.

Special concern should always be shown to the star's wife or husband so that she or he will not feel the lesser part of the couple. It used to be that the man was always the luminary and the wife just part of his orbit. More and more these days, however, the situation is likely to be reversed. As the star finds his circle of admirers, introduce the other half of the couple separately to your other guests.

Always have some irrepressibly friendly and gracious people on hand. They are the ones who will talk to anybody, who can make anyone from your grandmother to a neurotic genius feel comfortable. They are the masters of small talk whose main asset is a sincere feeling for others. These friends will help set the tone of your party far more effectively than all the candies, stuffed pheasant, and fresh figs put together. Your warm, trusted, "old faithfuls" are the first people to be introduced to the shy person, the insecure, the stranger. Mix the shy with the friendly, the center-stage performers with the listeners, the blind with the sighted. Consider a dinner party a cassoulet, a pot au feu, a Mongolian hot pot. As host you are the Tabasco.

SEATING: For small parties never purposely alternate the sexes at the table. The use of place cards implies that you have established yourself as some sort of social guru. Trust in unprogrammed seating and, because your guests will have taken the predinner drink period to find their own dinner partners, they will flow naturally from drinks to dinner with that favorite person in tow. Once they get to the table, however, they will, out of politeness, ask you, "Where would you like us to sit?" You may now apply "Green's law of Natural Seating" and tell them to sit with whomever they please. It usually works, the natural flow of energy you have generated among your guests will always remain high. Breaking up a new attachment or an old one will destroy the ongoing rhythm.

You can, however, always manipulate a guest to the side of someone special, if it is necessary, without being blatant. If one of your guests is an unwieldy left-hander consider self-sacrifice by sitting next to him yourself. If you are serving Chinese or Japanese food with chopsticks and do not want to put on a public demonstration of how to eat with them, consider seating chopstick pros next to the neophytes. Place yourself in the role of director and do whatever you think will make your guests most comfortable, amused, and amusing. Dinner parties should ring with laughter and exude amiability.

As a rule husbands and wives are broken up at a dinner party. But, who knows, they may just like each other. Nowadays many married couples are separated a lot because of career commitments and your party may be one of the few occasions they have to be together. Newlyweds might consider mingling an intrusion because they are still enjoying each other. On the other hand some married couples eat with each other all the time and may find a dinner party a great opportunity to flirt with someone else.

If you are fortunate enough to know beforehand which guests are recent ex-lovers and which are ex-spouses, you are safer in putting the ex-spouses together than the former lovers. An ex-lover may still be smarting from jealousy or rejection; an ex-spouse is usually a more cordial person. If they worked out a marriage and then a divorce and still wind up at the same dinner party, you can assume they have mastered at least a pretty serious pretense of amiability.

If you have any choice in the matter of "ex's," a safe way to handle the problem is to invite them separately. If the wife is a greater asset socially than her ex-husband, I am more likely to invite her to the public events and ask him to a private supper. The last thing I want ever to do is play Solomon, or get involved in their competitiveness, their insecurities or their jealousies. What I do is to examine the occasion and make my decision on the basis of who would enjoy it more, or add more, and invite my guests accordingly. If they complain, they will see less of me.

For larger parties of twenty-four or over I have found that alternating men and women smooths out the seating process. With four tables of six you will require place cards or face a traffic jam. Plan your seating so that at each table you have someone you can trust to assume the host role. If you are having more than twenty-four at a separate table sit-down dinner, keep a seating diagram on the table near the coat closet for guests to check when they arrive and, of course, place cards at the table.

DINNER PARTY PERPLEXITIES

Lateness:

You can be late for your wedding or funeral, but never for dinner. Except for big open-house parties, lateness is inexcusable. Your thoughtlessness may result in the mousse drying up, the soufflé shriveling, or the duck going soggy. The 1960s was a decade when everyone was stoned, so everyone was late; the excuse was usually an accepted, if illiterate, "I got hung up." Nowadays no one is that inarticulate. Most hosts, when they suggest 8:00 P.M. for dinner, usually serve drinks for up to an hour and a half. This will tease the palate, and allow everyone time to get there. Dinner will be served by 9:30, but 8:30 is the very latest you can graciously arrive.

In New York and other big cities, even getting caught in a cab in cross-town or rush-hour traffic is really no excuse for being late. Smart New Yorkers sacrifice the status of arriving by cab for promptness. So if you're stuck in traffic, leave a cab at the nearest subway stop, put a token in the turnstile, and get to the party on time. Nobody needs to know you took the subway. And if you want to announce it, your host will appreciate your resourcefulness and punctuality.

As a guest, rather than be late, I would prefer to be early and tuck myself into a nearby bar and read a newspaper. Lateness is rudeness, and reveals one's lack of organization as well as insecurity. Remember Marilyn Monroe? People just stopped waiting for her. Nobody's *that* exciting.

Illness:

If you are the sickly type, chances are you won't be invited out very often. As a host, when you call a guest by telephone with an invitation, listen to his voice. Attempt to detect a slurring of speech, congested nasal passages, or the sniffles. If your worst suspicions are confirmed, don't invite him. Some people with colds or flus can't resist a party. Even though they feel rotten they have an irresistible urge to eat, laugh, drink, and play Typhoid Mary.

If, as host, you develop a last-minute illness, there is no alternative but to fake it. Polly Bergen developed a brilliant ploy for the sick hostess who discovered she had Asian flu a few minutes after the first two of fifty expected guests arrived: "I was hot, feverish, and nauseous, so I excused myself and held onto the walls as I wended my way to the bedroom. I took my temperature and found it was 102. I sat down on the bathroom floor to calm my nausea, and then lay down on my bed to rest for twenty minutes. Then I went back to the party, sliding along the walls, straightening myself out just as I got to my guests. I drifted through each room, said 'Hello' to everybody, because it was shorter than saying 'How do you do?' I got through all the rooms in five minutes. Then I disappeared back to my room and lay down again for another twenty minutes. Nobody suspected I was sick except for my two closest friends. They made sure the other guests were adequately supplied with drinks and food. Fortunately it wasn't a sit-down dinner."

Allergies:

It may not be considered chic to tell your guests what the dinner menu will be, but as Celeste Holm says, "At least I find out if

I'm serving anything my guests *can't* eat." I learned this the hard way one evening when I served a rack of lamb filled with kasha to a visiting Russian couple. Just as the platter was being placed on the table, the guest, with typical Eastern European candor said, "My vive does not eat lamb—it makes her womit."

Bringing in Baby:

If you're entertaining in a SoHo loft or on a deserted island, and a guest calls whimpering that she can't get a babysitter, invite her to bring the baby. Reassure her that she may breast-feed him in private. As for a child, a really informal affair cannot be spoiled by the presence of a well-behaved one.

On the other hand, if you have arranged a formal, orchestrated in-town party, there is only one course of action, be frank: Indicate that the baby or child is not invited, and don't make an exception. It may seem excessively cruel, but if you consider that the other guests have made all sorts of adjustments not to bring their children, it becomes an insult to them to allow someone else's child to attend.

Tender Care for the Teetotaller

I don't drink; in fact, I am a diet soft-drink freak. If a hostess can't provide my "fix" I don't want her to feel that she has failed in her responsibility. When I say, "Oh, I'd just adore some ice water," she shouldn't feel she has failed me. I do not mean to victimize her for her lack of foresight, but neither do I feel obliged to drink alcohol just to make her feel better. You might remember this the next time you entertain, however, and make sure your nondrinking guests have available to them a variety of their favorites, including diet sodas, club soda, Perrier water, iced tea, and ginger ale. Ideally, they should be permitted to serve themselves. By allowing them to pour their own drinks discreetly, you are sparing them embarrassment—particularly from people who consider all nondrinkers members of A.A.

Vittling the Vegetarian:

Vegetarians, God bless them, are definitely on the rise and

pose some intriguing challenges for the host. Assuming you are interested enough to want to cook for them you must first determine whether they are orthodox or reformed. An orthodox vegetarian does not eat meat, fowl, or seafood. The reformed type simply refuses to eat meat. Obviously those who can down poached salmon, chicken kiev, or lobster with clam sauce pose no real threat to a host and may even be invited in conjuction with your carnivorous guests. Handle your stricter vegetarian friends in one or two ways. First, if there are enough of them have them all over together or if you have a mixed affair be certain that there are sufficient number of meat and nonmeat dishes for all.

THE PARTY'S OVER: What does one do when the party goes on too long? I am very direct. As far as I am concerned, my home is my turf, and I feel no compunction about asking people to leave. Of course, I don't walk up to them and say "Scram." There are a number of other techniques that work quite well. For instance, if I have asked people in just for cocktails, I often have tickets for a concert or the theater. Letting the fact be known (whether it's true or not) automatically puts a time limit on the affair. But I do it positively. I say, "It's been wonderful seeing all of you, but I have a curtain to make." Nothing else is necessary.

Sometimes I plan a party weeks in advance, and then find myself booked heavily for the next day. I was in exactly that position once when I got a call to appear on the "Today Show." It was important professionally, and it meant that I had to be up at 4:30 A.M. the following morning and be reasonably coherent. I leveled with my guests. When they arrived, I explained I would have to disappear at a certain hour like Cinderella, but that they were welcome to stay on. With that I appointed a surrogate host, and it all worked beautifully. Though my guests didn't stay as long as they might have if I had been there, they didn't leave when I went to bed. It is the absence of panic on the part of a host or hostess that makes anything work. If your cast is well selected, you're going to end up with a reasonably decent play of the evening.

I believe it's terribly dishonest to say to someone on parting, "Sorry, we haven't had a chance to talk." The fact is that if you

—61—

really wanted to talk to that person, you would have. We must accept the fact that we can't eat everything at the smorgasbord, go to bed with everyone we'd like to, or be in two places at once—or talk to everyone at the party.

THANK-YOU NOTES: I believe in never using store-bought greeting cards, when sending someone a thank you note. Compose your own gracious, cheerful note—if not on stationery, then on hand-tinted antique postcards. An Art Nouveau card, opaque beige Tibetan papers printed with a tiny mandala, Japanese rice paper tucked into a Chinese red envelope are both effective and attractive. The more unique the note, the more memorable you become. John Weitz always sends his favorite books as a thank-you gift for dinner. "Flowers are financially wasteful and presuppose people can't read," he says. "I like to think my friends are literate. I've given Mary Hemingway's *How It Was,* Alex Haley's *Roots,* and James Clavell's *Shogun.* In hard cover, of course."

When you want to express your appreciation after a dinner hosted by an unmarried couple, send a gift to the hostess and mention the other partner in your thank-you note. They may not want to announce their lifestyle to the corner book seller or the neighborhood wine merchant. A thank-you note that I particularly enjoyed was sent to me by Marciarose, host of an NBC Sunday talk show. "My dear," she wrote, "clearly the touchstone of our relationship is that in our case love means never having to write a thank-you note."

Never write a bread-and-butter note after just a brief conversation. It's unnecessary and reveals you to be insecure and pushy. If you would, first ask yourself what you are thanking that person for. Six words of wit in an otherwise dreary life? Instead, if you think you would like to cultivate someone you have just met, use the telephone. I would always rather receive a call with some juicy gossip, or an invitation to lunch, than a dutiful, dull bread-and-butter note.

Are you disposed to entertain with generous kindness? Thats the way my grandmother described hospitality. The golden rule was quoted as a host-guest guide: "Just do as you would be done by—and have a happy time." It is clear that whether you are an experienced great hostess or a spirited, determined beginner, a party plan has to be carefully followed. Your warm, gracious welcome, your skilled preparation, your stimulating group of guests mean more than a Lucullan dinner and the rarest of wines. Your poise and your skill as a loving hostess gives each guest the joy of being pampered, being comfortable, and feeling very special. The brightest approach to etiquette is knowing when to honor traditional social rules and when to ignore them. Because there is no unquestioned code, you must judge each situation on its merits and decide what would be the kindest thing to do. Etiquette can't be the rigid code it once was. It has to evolve year after year both in society and for you—the private you and the public you.

FIVE: Small Dinners for Six to Twelve

Some call it "joy" of cooking and others think that to peel and chop and slice, to baste and to turn, to beat and to stir is therapy. I find it marvelously creative. Cooking, contrary to rumor and the mystique surrounding professional cooks, doesn't require a very high degree of expertise, but it does demand enthusiasm and imagination. Preparing an interesting dish, baking an unusual cake, creating an unexpected placesetting or centerpiece should be as much a part of your personal style as what you wear or drive, whom you marry or live with. Small dinner parties are the perfect time to share your style with others. I find a very special warmth about dinner served at a table, a party planned to allow old friends to become better acquainted with someone new in your life. Or a dinner for from six to twelve to gracefully bring together people who know each other well but have not gotten together in a while, is also very effective. Small dinners can include everything from formal situations to the spur-of-the-moment get-togethers, dinners for special occasions, or menus planned for the congenial gathering of neighbors who are in touch all the time. Here I always include some new faces to avoid the danger of the party floundering on the familiar.

There is no kind of entertaining that demands a more careful choice of menu, advance preparation of food, and intelligent planning of service than a sit-down dinner. The host's absence from the table is so much more conspicuous in a small group. Small dinners must have an attractive mood of ease and serenity, a relaxed hospitality should be the dominant note. It is not difficult, of course, to handle a sit-down dinner if there is a cook and serving maid for the dinner and a butler for coats and drinks. I sometimes do dinners in town with a full staff (hired for the occasion), but I most often do small dinners in which I serve without outside help. I bought a teacart about fifteen years ago, and it hasn't left my side for sit-downs without staff.

Main dishes on big platters can be served directly from the teacart. After dinner I may ask guests to pass their empty plates. These are stored on the lower shelf of the teacart, dessert and serving plates are lifted to the table to serve with coffee at a side table just a step away. It is easy to stay with your guests for the entire meal. If you are going to clear the table yourself, just remember that you are not a servant, so you do not follow the rule that calls for removing one plate at a time from the right. Just clear the plates two by two but *never stack at the table.*

Both in town and in the country I often do exactly the opposite and ask my guests to join me in the kitchen so they can help themselves to the dinner directly from the pots and pans and platters. There is something about a "chow line" that breaks down the most staid group; plunging into cooking pots is an unexpected and somewhat intimate experience to be shared together. The production line of food moves rapidly, and guests can select the amounts and kinds of food that please them most. I stay in the kitchen to direct the line, identify a casserole or reassure dieters. Then everyone goes to the table and is seated.

At small dinners it is the hostess who gives the signal to start by starting herself. If there are ten to twelve guests, the hostess frequently says, "Please start now." To guests served first, no hostess wants to sound like a nagging mother, so when she makes the request, guests should do exactly that, start! The hostess also gives the sign to leave the table. All it takes is laying the napkin beside her plate and starting to rise. I just ask the non-question "Shall we leave the table?" as I am halfway gone. Don't linger too long at table, you may be denying guests that relief of getting up from their chairs, freshening up in the john, or escaping from their dinner partners. People will return to coffee or liqueurs in the next room or in front of the screen that hides the dinner remains if your apartment has what is not-so-accurately identified as a "dining area."

I loved it when Eleanor and Franklin Delano Roosevelt

served frankfurters and rolls to the visiting King and Queen of England. I made a note that for visiting international guests an American dinner might be just the right touch. When you go abroad are you amused if your host serves you your native dishes? What you really want is the cuisine of the country you are visiting.

Don't let menus throw you, the only way to learn to cook is to cook. As you succeed, you will frequently repeat your triumphs. Suddenly you have a cooking repertoire and are infinitely more secure. It is then that you grow experimental and adventurous. Remember my own axiom: *Do not have any small economies in the kitchen, and always give your cuisine style.*

Here are a group of seven small dinners, ranging from casual to elegant, that I have given that were as enjoyable to me as to my guests.

A Vegetarian Dinner Party

Actually, an all-vegetarian meal can be a real challenge to an enterprising host and an interesting change for the meat eaters. For buffets, it's easy to serve a lovely variety of vegetable casseroles. For sit-down dinners, an all-vegetarian dinner is trickier. For a French dinner, consider crêpes filled with ratatouille, followed by a green salad, and ending with fresh raspberries and cream.

BATTER FOR BASIC CRÊPES
(30 to 40 pancakes)

3 eggs	1½ cups milk
dash of salt	1 cup flour
⅛ cup of sugar	2 tablespoons butter
½ teaspoon vanilla extract	

Place the eggs, salt, sugar, and vanilla extract in blender; cover and blend on low speed for 5 seconds. Add the milk slowly while running on low speed. Funnel in the flour, using wax paper and continue to run at low speed. Melt the butter in a crêpe pan and add slowly to the mixture while running at low speed. After baking each crêpe, wipe pan with lightly buttered cheesecloth. Tip the pan and slowly pour in crêpe batter, just to coat the pan. Tilt the pan immediately so that the batter will spread over the entire bottom of the pan. Cook quickly on medium heat until both sides are brown. Stack crêpes carefully on platter with second browned side up. If the crêpes are to be sauced later, cover with saran wrap and refrigerate.

RATATOUILLE NEGRESCO
Serves 6

1	onion, chopped fine	1	crushed garlic clove
4	tablespoons olive oil	1	tablespoon chopped
1	eggplant, peeled and		parsley
	cubed	½	bay leaf
1	zucchini, peeled and		dash thyme
	cubed		salt and pepper to taste
6	tomatoes, peeled and	½	cup Swiss cheese, grated
	cubed		

Sauté onion in oil until it is brown. Add the vegetables, garlic and parsley. Then add remaining seasonings. Cook for approximately 20 minutes or until vegetables are tender. Place in a shallow baking dish, sprinkle with Swiss cheese, and brown under the broiler.

There is a kind of Oriental stir-fry nonmeat creative cooking that does not depend on specific recipe quantities. You add whatever you have on hand, season as you wish, in whatever quantities you need. The Italians do it by inventing on the spot—anything goes into the combination of vegetables, fish, and poultry sauces to toss over different forms of pasta.

An Italian menu might be green salad, pasta with a fresh vegetable sauce of zucchini, tomato, mushrooms, peas, string beans, and garlic bread and zabaglione. The Chinese cuisine offers noodles with pea pods, mushrooms, leafy chard, bamboo shoots, and water chestnuts. This dish is usually cooked with chicken, but if you add enough vegetables, all crisply sautéed and gleaming with their brown, white, and green colors, nobody will miss the chicken. You can serve thinly sliced cucumbers dressed with rice wine vinegar and a touch of sugar on the side. And bean sprouts are the new passion of the Beautiful People.

For the adventurous cook, Chinese cookbooks also include all-vegetarian Buddhist recipes.

A Burmese casserole calls for cubed eggplant, sliced fresh mushrooms sautéed in garlic and oil, which are then gently blended with a touch of anchovy paste (and baked for 45 minutes in a 350° oven). You may also serve a Japanese meal, either an all-vegetable tempura (which is kin to the Italian *fritta mista*) of mushrooms, watercress, sweet potato, broccoli and onion, or an all-vegetable sukiyaki which includes spinach, mushrooms, onions, and vermicelli, with side dishes of rice, and a salad of lettuce, cucumber, and carrots.

TEMPURA
Prepare vegetables this way:
cauliflower, break into buds
carrots, peeled and cut into ½-inch strips
green pepper, sliced in strips
onion rings, ½-inch wide
yams (or sweet potatoes), peeled and cut into ½-inch thick slices
zucchini, cut into ½-inch slices

Put into blender and blend or whip briskly for 3 minutes.

2 *eggs*	¼ *cup soy sauce*
¼ *cup water*	¾ *cup white flour*

(*Whole-wheat flour can be used for more interesting texture. If used, add a little more water.*)

Heat oil in skillet to 375 Fry vegetables one kind at a time. Put enough for one frying into the batter and coat well, then drop into hot oil. Fry until brown. Zucchini and green peppers take the least amount of time, eggplant, carrots, and sweet potatoes take the longest. Cook the vegetables to taste. Drain and keep warm. Serve quickly to retain crispness. Serve with buttered rice or other cereal.

ZABAGLIONE

4 *egg yolks*	2 *tablespoons Marsala*
2 *tablespoons powdered*	*wine*
sugar	

(This famous Italian dessert should be made with Marsala wine but you can use other dessert wines (port or Tokay) or sherry.)

Beat the egg yolks with the sugar until thick and lemon-colored. Put in a heavy, round-bottomed bowl and set over hot (not boiling) water. Beat constantly with beater (electric or hand), adding the wine little by little until the mixture starts to hold its shape but is still smooth. If you cook too long, crust will form on the bowl. If this happens, pour out without scraping the bowl. Remove from heat and immediately place in thick cups or sherbet glasses, heated. Serve either warm or cold with a simple wafer. This dessert is not too rich or too sweet.

Most carnivores will sit down happily to an all-vegetarian dinner, as long as it fills them up. Your vegetarian guest, while he may be in a minority, will be ecstatic at the table. And you, as host and cook, will have enlarged your repertoire and aided your digestive system by getting just a bit more roughage into your body. Some current research indicates that vegetarians are healthier and have more stamina than meat eaters, but, as a steak lover, I prefer to doubt it.

A Formal Dinner for 6

PIGEONS ET CHOUCROUTE
POMMES PARISIENNES
BROILED ONIONS
GREEN PEAS
CHOCOLATE SOUFFLÉ

PIGEONS ET CHOUCROUTE

6 squabs	6 chopped shallots
olive oil	1 quart of sauerkraut
1 garlic clove	1 pint of champagne

Heat oven to 375°. Sauté squabs in butter with a small amount of olive oil added, along with slivers of garlic and chopped shallots. Place the squabs in a casserole, and heat drained sauerkraut in the pan, stirring to coat it with the butter and seasonings. This is put on top of the squabs, and a pint of champagne poured over all. Place in oven for 1 hour.

POMMES PARISIENNES

2 pounds of small potatoes
Butter   Parsley

Precook the potatoes in boiling water, then sauté them in the butter until well browned. Sprinkle with chopped parsley.

BROILED ONIONS

3 large Spanish onions	1 teaspoon each: salt,
½ cup melted butter	pepper, oregano

Peel and slice the onions ½-inch thick. Set on a well-greased flat broiling pan, paint generously with melted butter, sprinkle with seasonings, and broil on one side for 6 minutes until browned and tender.

GREEN PEAS

Just drop them into boiling water. Turn heat off. Give it a few minutes. Drain—add a little grated lemon rind.

CHOCOLATE SOUFFLÉ

3	tablespoons butter		chocolate, coarsely
3	tablespoons flour		grated
1	cup milk	5	egg yolks
¼	teaspoon salt	7	egg whites
½	cup sugar	½	pint heavy cream for
1½	squares unsweetened		whipping

Now do just as I say and the soufflé is guaranteed. It is a simple dessert and the mystique about its formidable quality is unearned.

Melt the butter in the top of a double-boiler over boiling water. Stir in the flour and cook for a couple of minutes. Keep stirring, add the milk, and with patience it will become a thick and smooth mixture. Stir in the salt and sugar, then add the chocolate and continue to stir. The chocolate will melt and combine with the sauce.

Now remove the top of the double boiler from the heat and let it cool. Beat in the egg yolks. Let the sauce cool completely. Make this sauce early in the morning and leave it at room temperature. Preheat the oven to 350°. Butter a 2-quart soufflé dish well and sprinkle it with sugar. Beat the egg whites until they are stiff but not dry. Fold a large spoonful of the egg whites into the chocolate sauce, then fold in the remaining egg whites.

Pour the batter into the soufflé dish and bake it for 30 minutes. You want your soufflé to be moist in the center but not runny.

Now leave the soufflé in the oven until you are ready to serve it.

My rule is to let the guests wait for the soufflé rather than the soufflé wait for the guests.

You will have to judge when you want to put it into the oven. I either do it after the main course is served or I separate coffee and dessert into another time period after dinner to be served away from the table.

Add a large glob of whipped cream on each portion. I prefer unsweetened cream so the chocolate flavor can be relished.

BRAISED HAM
HOME BAKED BEANS
HOT ROLLS
SPICED PEACHES
ASSORTED RAW VEGETABLES
BROWN BETTY

BRAISED HAM
Couldn't be simpler to do.

Cut in chunks:
2   *carrots*
2   *stalks of celery*
2   *onions peeled*
3   *bay leaves*
6   *peppercorns*

2   *cups of dry, white wine*
2   *cans chicken broth (about*
    3 cups)
½   *smoked ham, 8 pounds or*
    a 6-pound boned, canned
    ham

In a large pot place the chunky vegetables, seasonings, wine, and broth. Add the ham, bring the liquid to a boil. Now cover the pot tightly and simmer for about 2½ hours.

Remove the ham from the pot. Slice it and arrange on a platter. Freeze the strained stock in the pot for later use. Makes the best lentil and pea soup ever.

HOME BAKED BEANS

2 cups (1 pound) dried peas   1 medium onion, peeled
   or navy beans   6 slices lean bacon

Mix together:
   1 cup strong coffee   1 tablespoon mustard
   ½ cup molasses   1 teaspoon salt
   4 tablespoons tomato paste   freshly ground pepper

Soak the beans in water overnight, adding more water if necessary. Cook the beans briskly, uncovered, for one hour, or until they are tender.

Preheat the oven to 275°.

Put the onion and about a third of the beans into a 2-quart casserole and add 2 slices of bacon. Make two more layers, ending with bacon. Pour the coffee mixture over the beans, and add water, if necessary, so that the liquid just covers the beans.

Cover and bake for at least 6 hours, checking occasionally, adding hot water if needed to keep the beans just barely covered and skim off any fat that has risen to the surface. Remove the cover for the last hour of cooking.

BROWN BETTY

3 cups pared, chopped   ¾ cup sugar
   apples   ¼ teaspoon cinnamon
3 tablespoons butter   ¼ teaspoon nutmeg
2 cups soft bread crumbs   ¼ cup water

Pare and chop the apples. Melt the butter in a saucepan. Add the crumbs. Remove from the fire. Mix the sugar and the spices together. Butter the baking dish.

Put a layer of crumbs in the bottom of the baking dish. Add a layer of apples. Sprinkle with sugar and spice. Repeat, adding alternate layers. Reserve a layer of crumbs for the top of the pudding. Add the water.

Heat oven to 350°.

Cover. Bake for 40 minutes. Uncover. Raise the temperature to 400° to brown the top.

Serve with plain cream, sweetened and flavored with vanilla.

BAKED CHICKEN PARMESAN
RISOTTO MILANESE
GREEN BEAN PUREE
ORANGE SUNDAES

BAKED CHICKEN PARMESAN
Bake at 425° for about 50 minutes.

⅓ *cup salad oil*
2 *broiler-fryers, cut in serving-size pieces*
1 *teaspoon oregano*
1 *teaspoon salt*

paprika
¾ *pound fresh mushrooms*
6 *tablespoons grated Parmesan cheese*

1. Line a shallow baking pan with aluminum foil. Pour salad oil into pan. Place in hot oven about 10 minutes. Remove pan from oven.
2. Place chicken pieces, skin side down, in hot oil. Sprinkle with half the oregano and salt. Sprinkle lightly with paprika. Return to oven and bake 30 minutes.
3. Turn chicken pieces; sprinkle with remaining oregano and salt and lightly with paprika. Bake 15 minutes longer, remove from oven.
4. Spoon fat and drippings in pan over chicken. Pour mushrooms over chicken; sprinkle with Parmesan cheese; bake 5 minutes longer.

RISOTTO MILANESE

½ cup minced onion
½ cup butter
2 cups short-grained Italian
   rice
1 cup dry white wine

6 cups chicken broth
¼ cup freshly grated
   Parmesan cheese
¼ teaspoon of saffron

In a large, heavy saucepan sauté ½ cup minced onion in ¼ cup of the butter. Add 2 cups Italian rice, stirring the rice until it is well coated with butter. Add 1 cup dry white wine and simmer the rice for 5 minutes, or until the wine has evaporated. Add 1 cup chicken broth, heated, and simmer the mixture until the stock is almost absorbed, add the other 5 cups of chicken broth, heated, one cup at a time, letting the rice absorb each cup before adding more. Cook the rice for a total of about 15 minutes until it is tender.

In a small dish dissolve ¼ teaspoon of saffron and 1 tablespoon hot broth and add them to the rice. Add ¼ cup freshly grated Parmesan cheese blending them into the rice with a fork.

GREEN BEAN PUREE

3 pounds green beans
   butter

salt and freshly ground
   pepper

Cover the bottom of a pot with 2 inches of water and bring the water to a rapid boil. Add the beans and cover. Steam them until they are tender but not overcooked and soggy. Let the beans cool until you can handle them. Use the liquid and a little milk to purée the beans quickly in your Cuisinart. The puree should be thick but don't be concerned if it is not completely smooth. Heat the purée in the top of a double-boiler with a lump of butter, salt, and pepper.

ORANGE SUNDAES

2 6-ounce cans frozen
   orange concentrate
2 11-ounce cans mandarin

oranges, drained
2 quarts orange sherbet
   Cointreau

Partially thaw the orange juice concentrate. Chop the mandarin oranges coarsely and mix with the concentrate. Spoon over individual portions of the sherbet. Dribble some Cointreau on top of each sundae.

Dinner for 8

STUFFED CUCUMBER WITH GREEN MAYONNAISE
SHRIMP MARENGO
EPINARDS LISETTE
HOT ITALIAN WHEAT BREAD
COLD APRICOT SOUFFLÉ

STUFFED CUCUMBER WITH GREEN MAYONNAISE

4 *firm cucumbers*	2 *cups of peas*
2 *cups of string beans*	*chives*

Cut the unpeeled cucumbers in half lengthwise. Boil for 2 minutes. Remove from the heat. Put under the cold-water faucet, drain, and dry thoroughly. When cold, with a sharp knife hollow out within ¼ inch of the skin and fill with previously cooked, chilled, and diced string beans and green peas. Chill thoroughly and cover with green mayonnaise. Sprinkle with chives.

GREEN MAYONNAISE:

2 *egg yolks*	1 *lemon*
1 *teaspoon salt*	*watercress*
½ *teaspoon pepper*	*spinach*
¾ *cup olive oil*	*tarragon*

Put the 2 egg yolks in a bowl with salt, pepper. Stir well. Add the olive oil drop by drop, constantly stirring. When it begins to firm up add a few drops of lemon juice and pour the oil more quickly. This mayonnaise must be truly firm.

Now you are ready to add the purée. You'll need about ½ cup. Take equal parts of the herbs and boil them in unsalted water for 2 minutes, drain, put under the cold-water faucet and press out the water. Run them through your food processor. Add this to the mayonnaise, which will take on both the color and flavor of the herbs.

SHRIMP MARENGO

½	pound bacon	1	bay leaf
2	cloves garlic, finely minced	1	teaspoon salt
		¼	teaspoon pepper
1	cup chopped onion	1	tablespoon sugar
1	cup chopped celery	4	drops of Tabasco sauce
1	pound mushrooms, washed and sliced	3	pounds frozen shrimp, follow directions on package
1	2-pound 3-ounce can Italian plum tomatoes	2	green peppers, seeded and diced
1	6-ounce can tomato paste		
1½	teaspoon dry Rosemary		
1¼	teaspoon dry crushed basil		

Sauté the bacon in a Dutch oven. Remove the bacon and dry it on a paper towel. When all the bacon is draining, add the garlic and onion and cook until it is softened. Don't pour off the bacon fat; you will need all of it. Add the celery and mushrooms and cook only for 5 minutes. Crumble the dry bacon and return it to the pot. Now add everything from the plum tomatoes to the Tabasco sauce and cook it all for 30 minutes over a low flame. This can all be done the day before or the morning of the dinner party. All you do is reheat, adding the shrimp and green peppers about 10 minutes before serving. Don't overcook the shrimp; they should just be heated through and the green pepper should be crisp.

EPINARDS LISETTE

3 10-ounce packages frozen spinach
1½ pints of sour cream
1 envelope dried onion-soup mix
¼ teaspoon instant garlic
1 teaspoon dried dill
¾ cup Italian seasoned dry bread crumbs
¾ cup grated Parmesan cheese
butter

Preheat oven to 350°. Defrost and drain spinach but do not cook it. Add the sour cream, onion-soup mix, garlic, and dill. Place the mixture into a 1½-quart baking dish. Mix together the bread crumbs and the cheese and top the spinach mixture. Dot with butter. Plan to heat this about 25 minutes.

COLD APRICOT SOUFFLÉ

4 eggs
3 egg yolks
½ cup sugar
1 cup stewed dried apricots
1 tablespoon brandy
2 tablespoons gelatin
dissolved in 2 tablespoons lemon juice
½ cup heavy cream, whipped
Whipped cream for garnishing

Beat the sugar, eggs, and egg yolks until the mixture is very thick and pale in color. Puree the apricots—use your blender or food processor. Add the pureed apricots to the egg mixture with the brandy. Melt the dissolved gelatin over hot water and then pour into the apricot mixture, stirring while you pour. Fold in the whipped cream. Pour into a buttered soufflé dish and place in the refrigerator for 4 hours. Add garnishing whip cream when cooled.

BOULA AU GRATIN
VEAL LOAF
MUSHROOM SAUCE
ASPARAGUS CHINOIS
POTATOES MOUSSELINES
TOLLGATE ICED APPLES

BOULA AU GRATIN

2	pounds split peas	2	grated garlic cloves
10	cups of cold water	1	cup of cream
4	cans green-turtle consommé	1	cup of sherry
¼	teaspoon cayenne pepper hearty pinch of mace	1	salt cup of grated Parmesan cheese

Wash 2 pounds split peas and soak 1 hour in 10 cups of cold water. Cover and gently cook until peas are mushy. You must stir frequently. I also suggest that you place the pan on an asbestos mat to prevent sticking. Pass the peas through a sieve to make a thick puree. Add the 4 cans green-turtle consommé, the pepper, mace, garlic, and cream. Thin the soup with the sherry. Salt to taste.

Whip a small amount of the cream so that you can add 2 tablespoons to each cup of soup.

Just before serving, put the soup in ovenproof bowls. Place a generous spoonful of whipped cream and cheese on top, sprinkle with paprika, and place under the broiler until golden brown. The soup can be made the day before the party. All you then do is brown it before serving.

VEAL LOAF AND MUSHROOM SAUCE

3	cups bread crumbs	3	whole eggs
1½	cups evaporated milk	1	pound chicken livers
3	chopped onions	3	pounds ground veal
	salt and pepper	¾	pound ground pork
	a pinch of savory		several strips of salt pork

Heat oven to 350°. The bread crumbs are soaked in the evaporated milk; the onions chopped and sautéed in the butter, salt, pepper and savory with the eggs; and finally the raw chicken livers, dipped in bread cubes, put through the food processor. Mix all this into the ground veal and pork. Do it with your hands to be sure that it is well blended and then pack it very thoroughly into a well-greased bread pan. Very thin strips of salt pork are placed on top, and bake for 1 hour.

MUSHROOM SAUCE:

Put ¾ pound of mushrooms into the food processor, use the coarse blade, then sauté them in ½ cup butter over a hot flame. Add 2 tablespoons of flour, stir well, and add 1 cup of chicken stock and 1 cup of light cream; then a sprinkle of nutmeg and cover until slightly thickened.

ASPARAGUS CHINOIS

4	packages frozen asparagus tips, partially thawed	½	cup oil
		4	teaspoons Worcestershire sauce

Slice the asparagus on the bias, about ¼-inch thick. Heat the oil and the Worcestershire, and sauté asparagus over high heat, stirring briskly for about 8 minutes until tender but still crisp.

POTATOES MOUSSELINES

4	pounds potatoes	1½	cups soft butter
2	teaspoons salt	8	yolks of eggs
½	teaspoon pepper	1	cup of whipped cream
	a pinch of nutmeg		

Bake the potatoes in the oven. Cook them about ¾ hour in a hot oven. Take out and remove the skins, wash, add salt, pepper, nutmeg, butter, and egg yolks. Mix thoroughly. Add 1 cup whipped cream. Cover with melted butter and put in a very hot (450°) oven, preheated for 5 minutes.

TOLLGATE ICED APPLES

2   *pounds very good apples*
3   *cups sugar*
1   *cup water*
    The rind of 2 lemons

Prepare a syrup with the sugar and the water and the lemon rind. Peel and cut in very thick slices 2 pounds of very good apples. Put them in the syrup and let them cook for 2½ hours. Pour into a round mold. Chill overnight. When removed from the mold, surround with vanilla ice cream coated with cinnamon.

A Celebration Dinner for 12

TOLLGATE LAMB EN CROUTE
MUSTARD CARROTS
TURNIP PUREE
GREEN SALAD
ORANGE-FLAVORED CHOCOLATE MOUSSE

TOLLGATE LAMB EN CROUTE

1	boned lamb leg, 5–6 pounds net weight	2	teaspoons each rosemary thyme tarragon
4	lamb kidneys		
2	tablespoons of butter	3	yellow onions
½	cup minced mushrooms	3	carrots
⅓	cup madeira	3	celery stalks with leaves
¼	cup soft butter		plain pastry
1	teaspoon pepper		

Mince the kidneys, sauté in 2 tablespoons of butter with mushrooms over medium high heat, turn lightly for 7 minutes. Add madeira, cover and reduce to minimum heat. Simmer 10 minutes. Rub the lamb leg inside and out with soft butter and all the herbs. Make a vegetable bed of onions, carrots, and raw celery in a roasting pan. Stuff the lamb leg with the kidney mixture. Reserve any extra liquid. Roll up and tie about 2 inches apart with string. Set on the vegetables, roast 10 minutes at 450°. Reduce heat to 375° for 25 minutes. Remove from oven and cool.

Make the pastry:

1	teaspoon sugar	2½	cups flour
¾	cup of lard	1	teaspoon salt
¼	cup of butter	4–5	tablespoons of ice water

Cut lard and butter into flour mixed with salt and sugar. When grainy, mix with ice water. Form a ball and chill for 20 minutes. Roll between lightly floured sheets of waxed paper to ⅛-inch thick on a pastry board. Trim to a rectangle to cover the lamb, which you set in the middle. Fold the pastry around it, sealing the ends. Transfer seam side down to a roasting pan, paint with 1 beaten egg yolk and roast 30 minutes at 375°.

Pour off the vegetable juices and discard the vegetable bed. Combine the juice with any excess kidney cooking juice. If necessary add water to make 1½ cups, and thicken with 2 teaspoons cornstarch stirred in 1 tablespoon of madeira. Add salt and pepper.

MUSTARD CARROTS

2 pounds carrots
3 teaspoons prepared
  mustard

A marinade mixed together in a saucepan:

1 cup white wine
1 cup wine vinegar
1 cup water
1 cup olive oil
2 cloves garlic, minced

2 teaspoons salt
2 teaspoons sugar
2 bay leaves
1 teaspoon dried thyme

Bring the marinade to a boil and add the carrots scraped and cut in half crosswise and lengthwise. Boil the carrots, uncovered, in the marinade until they are just tender. Pierce them with a tip of a knife. The cooking time depends on the size and age of the carrots.

Remove the carrots to a shallow serving dish. Add the mustard to the marinade and blend it well. Strain the marinade over the carrots and allow them to cool in it. Serve at room temperature.

TURNIP PUREE

4–6 pounds, small white
    turnips
6 medium potatoes
2 cups chicken broth

8 tablespoons butter
  salt and freshly ground
    pepper
6 egg whites

Peel and slice the turnips and potatoes. Add to chicken broth in a large skillet or Dutch oven. Cover, bring to a boil, lower the heat to moderate and cook the vegetables until they are tender and most of the liquid has been absorbed, about 20–25 minutes. Mash the vegetables with a potato masher, if you like a chunky mixture, or use your Cuisinart or a food mill for a fine puree. Add salt and pepper to taste.

About 30 minutes before serving, beat the egg whites until stiff but not dry and fold them into the cooled turnip puree and bake it at 350° for about 30 minutes until the puree is puffed and slightly browned.

ORANGE-FLAVORED CHOCOLATE MOUSSE

In a small bowl combine ¾ cup orange-flavored liqueur, ¼ cup orange juice, and the grated rind of 1 orange. Let the mixture stand, covered, for at least 12 hours. In the top of a double boiler set over simmering water, combine 8 squares (8 ounces) semisweet chocolate, 1 stick of butter all cut into bits, and 1 cup sifted cocoa, and stir the mixture until it is smooth. Blend in thoroughly 1 cup fine granulated sugar and ¼ cup very strong coffee. Pour the orange mixture in a stream, stirring constantly until the sugar is dissolved. Whisk in 4 egg yolks one at a time and transfer the mixture to a large bowl. In a bowl beat 4 egg whites with a pinch of salt until they hold stiff peaks. Stir half the egg whites into the chocolate mixture. Pile the remaining whites on top and gently, but thoroughly, fold them in. Pour the mousse into twelve pots de crème or ½ cup ramekins and chill them overnight. Top the mousses with sweetened whipped cream.

SIX: The Big Party
or
The Whole Story of a Buffet
for 100 or More

The big party is not a difficult prospect if you adjust your head to thinking of it as a super-theatrical "food collection" rather than a meal. You are at once the designer and the manufacturer. Your goal is to produce an innovative and creative assembly of dishes to satisfy the endless variety of tastes of your friends.

For ten years at Tollgate Farm on the last Sunday of June I have presented my "collection."

Here's the way it works:

The date and season were chosen so that I could hold this party outside at the farm—sixty-five acres of Bucks County heaven. The decor is done by the best in the business—Mother Nature. The season sets the general direction of what can be served successfully—for example, less hot foods, more cold ones. The rest I have to choreograph.

Design your food and total party as a generous gift to friends. Avoid the completely familiar on your table as well as in the group. Add raw dishes that look and taste exciting and invite some new people. The same old food served to the same old people adds up to one word: boring. People need to be stimulated enough to "turn on" because there are new faces. The delight of the unexpected place and imaginative display on the buffet keeps interest high. So make a guest list with some old, some new. Remember the master-strategy—balance the talkers and the listeners—never evenly though, or you end up with it all sounding like the Tower of Babel. One good talker can handle five listeners. Invite young and old—and no artificial ghettos. A guest list made up entirely of fashion people is as dull as one made up exclusively of magazine types or any other group that supposedly has a lot in common. If you insist on tight career groups, your party usually ends up with all the wit and flair of a business meeting. Besides, that kind of narrowing down is terribly unfair to any other guest who is not interested or part of the majority group. Two drinks, and career groups begin to suffer from office-party hilarity. There is always an unconscious pecking order that begins to creep to the surface, bringing all the hidden insecurities and hostilities of people who are bound together by too-common goals, envies, and ambitions.

People really are on their best behavior when they are in "company" rather than being at the company. Don't be compulsive about balancing males and females. How much happier for an unmarried lady guest to just get there her own way rather than feeling that a social-service assignment has been given to some man who may be less interested than she. This is not to frustrate the professional matchmakers who can use a large party to bring a couple together—just don't make a big issue out of it.

Your job as a host is not to play God but just to ask people you like to come to your party.

Remember, the big party should be a big celebration—for guests *and* host. I approach all parties with the same attitude. Don't give a party as a dread duty or bitter burden. Give a party as a generous gift to your guests. A gift of people with whom they will have fun, a gift of food they will enjoy, and a gift to yourself of having everything ready to run smoothly.

The next thing to do when preparing for the big party, is to *check the utensils you will need.* My experience has been that paper plates and paper napkins are the only answer. For one hundred guests you need two hundred plates and napkins. People will go back for seconds and to try something they missed.

You will need 150 knives, forks, and spoons. Buy these at a restaurant-supply place. They need not be expensive, just functional. Guests will leave their plates and utensils and move back to the buffet. By having 1½ times the number of settings as guests you avoid the lost guest looking blank as to how he is going to eat a mousse with his fingers. Obviously, if you haven't the budget to buy the equipment—and wish more permanency than paper and plastic—you can borrow or rent it. I do feel that unless the party for a hundred is a community or charity affair you waste too much energy picking up and returning borrowed things. It also requires a CPA to keep straight the lists of who owns what.

The next thing to do is to *invite the guests.* I selected an annual date so that close friends would expect to be invited and therefore save the date. New friends wait to see whether they will be included—and with everyone else you take your chances. I invite people thirty days in advance by telephone first. This gives you an immediate yes or no. Keep a list with yes, no or maybe next to the name. I get a note out to them ten days before the party. I do it as a form note with only the name in the salutation left blank. These can be photocopied at someone's office. The information in the note clearly states date, time, and place of the party and, if necessary, the route to get there. Over the years I realized people wanted to know the level of dress. Country casual was my advice and a reminder that Tollgate is a working farm and walking shoes are appropriate. Assuming that you are not giving a black-tie Glyndebourne picnic, you will call your party casual, informal, sweater and skirts, festive, or dress up. Often guests will take their direction from you, so you decide on your outfit and prepare to tell them what it is as a help to the clothing-confused guests. If your party has a costume theme, then be specific about what it is. Even the most anticostume guests will make some effort, even if only a token gesture. Some indication is helpful of when the party usually breaks, so people can plan babysitter commitments, evening plans when your party is a lunch, and so on.

You will discover that even your nearest and dearest may have to cancel at the last minute. I always overinvite and overcook. Thus, telephone calls, letters, and wires that change the number are not serious. The other direction is also inevitable—people will add people—ranging from their own unexpected guests, a new lover they can't bear to be separated from, someone involving a public-relations manipulation, and so on ad infinitum.

Very large buffets often depend on outdoor action. Your aching shoulder, the almanac, or your cat's intense jungle behavior all may fail you as reliable weather forecasters. If so, you may find you have to cancel. Do it as soon as you decide and telephone your guests. If you can't reach any of them and they show up, enjoy it. Treat them as co-hosts sharing the experience of the weather disaster and cancelled party. No matter how disappointing, keep a proper perspective; it's only a cancelled party, so don't turn it into a wake. If you want to set up a rain-check date, do it right away. It is essential, however, to confirm the new date with a follow-up note and include your ardent wish for better weather.

For a party this size you have to be prepared for and not frightened by *WASTE*. In the fashion world, everything made to create the right ambiance for the collection is not always sold. The difference between running out of food and drink or having plenty for everyone is never more than $100. Just think of it as $1.00 a person. Do it and then forget it.

Plan the total menu. I do 40 molds and mousses, 100 pounds of meat loaf mixture, 30 pounds of ham, 25 chickens for salad, 20 cold ducks (carved in eighths), 48 breads (8 of 6 different varieties), and 60 loaf cakes of 6 varieties.

Be sure you have enough platters to handle the food with proper display and decoration. I encouraged friends who did not know what to give me over the years to give me serving platters and copper molds. The range in price of both items is from bargain-basement budget to carefree Cartier—all have been useful and enjoyed. Again, if you come up lacking, every city has restaurant-supply houses where such platters can be purchased, or you can arrange to borrow some from a restaurant where your patronage over the years justifies asking such a favor.

When you have assembled your platters it is a good idea to *plan your layout*—to think through which food you want to be served on which platter, bowl, casserole, or copper pots. I use every conceivable thing—including two aluminum laundry tubs filled with ice and crudités, or fresh vegetables in rough slices. My serving pieces range from a priceless eighteenth-century Lowestoft platter to the least expensive plastic bowl that takes on new meaning because of the richness of what is in it.

Just a quick glance will tell you that my buffet cannot be accomplished without six weeks of pre-preparation and two large freezers. The message "freeze until wanted" is what makes this buffet possible. Everything but the mousses and molds and aspics, chicken salad, rice salad, ham en croute, Goodwill bean-and-sausage mix are frozen beforehand. To simplify: all cakes, breads, meat mixtures, ducks, and chickens go into the freezer long before the party. I do everything in marathons. All breads are done over one long baking weekend. Cakes over two long baking weekends, meat mixtures over one, ducks on another and chickens on still another. The mousses, aspics, and molds are done the Saturday before the Sunday party. So is the potato salad, chicken salad, and cole slaw.

The morning of the party I am up with my chickens at 5:30 A.M. to do the ham, Tollgate meatballs and sauerkraut; to take out the butter beans and pears that have baked all night at a temperature under 200 degrees; to heat up the various bean-and-meat combinations; to make the rice—let it cool—so it can be mixed just a few hours before the party.

You will need a lot of pots and pans—so be careful. Don't schedule too many hot things that have to hit the top of the stove or the oven or you will never get the food out on time. (I do mine with four stoves and an eight-burner top.)

The best investment to make your kitchen more effective is a food processor. I use the Cuisinart because it is a superbly engineered machine that enables me to slice, chop, grind, puree, blend, and mix with ease. Gone is the strain and struggle of the meat grinder for pâtés or quenelles. And the chore of grinding nuts, hard cheese, and stale bread. If words like béchamel or velouté daunt you—or your own homemade mayonnaise seems too haute for your cuisine—a food processor will make you famous for your satin-smooth sauces. The speed with which you can do foolproof pastry dough or julienne vegetables is a significant timesaver. For all your mousses and molds the machine blends the gelatin mixture and ingredients in one operation. Turning it on is like rubbing Aladdin's Lamp; this single, revolutionary kitchen appliance plays the genie and does for your menus what a corps of chef's apprentices, vegetable boys, pastry makers, and devoted sauciers would do. I have discovered the value of purchasing two extra Lexan plastic bowls for my Cuisinart. This allows me to produce a larger quantity of a single dish or to whip up different combinations of ingredients for basic dips. With the extra containers I don't have to stop to wash out the single container (that comes with the processor) each time. NOTE: What this kitchen miracle *doesn't* do very well is whip cream or egg whites.

Check your spice cabinet and look over your recipes for any special ingredient you may need. I don't know many kitchen shelves that have fresh ginger or smoked oysters as part of the staples. *Buy extra eggs and extra cream.* You may want to do another mousse at the last moment and feel blocked if your creative-cooking urges cannot be fulfilled because of no cream or not enough egg yolks.

I never worry about religious dietary laws or special patterns. Making masses of food ensures that there is always something for everyone. As long as there's homemade bread, no one is going to be unhappy no matter what the problem.

The menu is simple to break down in your own thinking. You will have dishes with meat and without. You will have fish dishes—what would we do without tuna?—you will have vegetable dishes and fruit dishes. You will have cheese.

You are now discovering the role of the producer—to get it all together so that your other talents can go to work.

I *write out the menu as though it were a project assignment*—broken down by time, date and equipment needed. I list the ingredients for cooking and the preparation. Make an exact time schedule. For example, Friday morning mix first batch of bread dough at 9:30—let rise two hours. Bake one now. Repeat after lunch. Repeat at 4:00 P.M. Repeat Saturday as well. All breads done—cooled—wrapped in foil—date and describe on masking tape with a marker pen. Put into freezer. Give yourself a reward.

Make an exact marketing list. Your list is divided into what can be ordered six weeks ahead of time—including flour, sugar, canned goods, frozen vegetables, packaged goods such as bread crumbs, pie-crust mix, rice, etc., and what can be ordered to be delivered two days before and what can be delivered the morning of your party.

Now I *order everything in the canned goods and packaged goods area by the case.* Do it with your supermarket manager and *ask for the bulk discount*—usually ten percent, and it is worth it. Arrange with your local grocer (open on Sunday) to be available to you if you have a last-minute crisis.

I invite my guests for lunch at 1:00 P.M. I allow a one-hour period for arrivals, drinks, and walking around the farm. I allow a 45-minute period in which I present an entertainer. It is during this period that your friends proceed into service—decorate platters, unmold molds, aspics, and mousses, and transport the same dishes to the eight tables I put up in my garden.

In your planning *allow at least one hour to get all the food out to the tables.* I stage it by having young, strong friends parade from my kitchen to the enclosed garden area as though Henry VIII had invited himself to lunch. This has become a show in itself.

Over the years certain dishes have won extravagant praise. They are always repeated. Others are variations on the mousse and mold theme. And I firmly believe that both for my guests and myself I always add some new things to stir my own interests.

I keep all this in one file because it helps make next year's planning easier—the same is true of your marketing list. Here are recipes for a number of the perennial stars. They have glittered at Tollgate Farm; they can just as well shine on your country or city buffet table.

This Tollgate entertainment scenario can be expanded to two hundred and fifty guests or contracted to fifty. The plan works for private entertaining or club and organization functions. Whether you do fifteen molds or mousses, ten salads and hot dishes, or reduce the numbers to five mousses or molds, two salads or two hot dishes, still check your equipment, balance your menu, time your preparation, and plan your service. The style or beauty of your party can be as innovative and attractive as you care to make it. Whether you are entertaining in your backyard, living room, or patio or on your high-rise terrace, at the fire house or church basement, the master plan works. Whether the party is downtown, or out-of-town, inner-city or outer-suburb, air conditioned or outside—*the plan works.* You can work with friends and prepare a mile of mousses or do a mini-assortment by yourself. Either way your guests will be happy if each one gets a piece of aspic.

The largest array of foods served at the Big Buffet consists of the gelatin molds and mousses.

Before you plunge into this special realm of cuisine you should familiarize yourself with the do's and don'ts of gelatin.

—One tablespoon of gelatin can turn about two cups of liquid into a solid. Gelatin put out by Knox comes in granules that are individually packaged to the equivalent of one tablespoon.

If you are doing a clear aspic you normally need only two hours of chilling in the refrigerator. But it takes a minimum of four hours of chilling if you are combining your liquid with fruit, fish, meat, vegetables, or nuts.

My experience has taught me to do my molds the day before my party. I have always gotten the best results just by doing the following:

1. Sprinkle one tablespoon of gelatin granules over the surface of ¼ cup cold water and let it soak for about 3 minutes until it has absorbed the moisture and is translucent. Have ready at the boiling point 1½ to 2 cups fish or meat stock (don't panic— canned bouillon or chicken broth works just as well), fruit juice, milk, wine, or water. Combine it with the soaked gelatin and stir until dissolved.

2. There are endless recipes that tell you to wait until the aspic thickens before adding your solids. I never bother about this because my molds are going to be in the refrigerator overnight and they always end up doing their thing. I just mix it all together and pour it into the molds.

3. Allow about 1¼ cups of solids for each cup of aspic. I do rinse each mold in cold water before filling it. I have never suffered a defeat in unmolding a gelatin salad.

4. Here is the inside story of the layered molds I make using fruits, nuts, and vegetables. The trick is to learn which things have different weights and porosity. Put them in a slightly gelled mixture—one hour in the refrigerator and let them find their own levels:

a. The *floaters* are: apple chunks, banana slices, fresh grapefruit sections, pear slices, fresh strawberry halves, broken nut meats, and marshmallows.

b. The *sinkers* are: cooked prunes, orange slices, fresh grapes. Right to the bottom will go canned cherries, peas, pineapple, plums, raspberries.

5. The other layered molds are just done in separate se-

quences. Fill ⅓ of a mold with a given aspic—refrigerate until solid. I do all of these first and put them on the bottom shelves of my refrigerator. Check three hours later and usually a mold is firm enough to add your next layer and three hours later the final layer. The color and food varieties are as varied as your own imagination can make them.

6. One of the things I do that may help you to avoid unmolding disaster is to run a knife through your aspic mixture to release any air bubbles that might create weak points and crack the mold later on.

7. The only food I know of that resists gelatin's advances is fresh or frozen pineapple. Tinned pineapple, which has been cooked, presents no problem.

8. Obviously, gelatin has to be kept very cold but it really should never be frozen.

9. One of the tricks I learned years ago was to use a damp cloth to lightly moisten the dish or platter I was going to place the mold on. This allows you to move the mold around for correct placement and garnishing. The slightly wet surface allows the mold to slide rather than stick.

I use a very thin knife inserted into the edge of the mold. In there are found places that will release the vacuum. For small parties, I keep a bowl of hot water nearby and dip a hand towel into it. Then you put the warm towel over your mold that is placed on your platter—voilà!—it comes out easily. For the Big Party I fill a large sink with hot water and lower the mold into it for just a second. You should practice this, for if the water is too hot or you hold the mold too long, it will start to melt. If it does, you just unmold it and cover the runny edge with some colorful garnish.

10. If you are multiplying a recipe two to five times (I usually do mine four times the original recipe), I have learned that if the original recipe called for 2 cups of liquid and you are doubling it, use only 3¾ cups of liquid in the expanded version.

11. The most tasty gelatin molds are the ones in which you do not use too much gelatin. Overuse results in a rubbery concoction that is not pleasant. The final mold should be slightly quivery, not rigid, when shaken.

12. Avoid keeping your trays and platters where excessive heat

(from stoves or direct sunlight) is present. Ideally, they should be chilled, but the more practical way is just to keep them cool. I keep mine in the basement of the farm and bring them up when they are ready to be used.

13. Gelatin is very bland, so don't guess at seasoning. I advise strongly that you test and adjust seasoning before pouring into your mold.

14. If the mold is going to be in the refrigerator for 24 hours (mine are for the Big Buffet), then be sure to under-salt it.

15. One of the reasons for the success of the aspics at Tollgate is that I often add a wine or liqueur to the aspics. I caution you not to add too much—one or two tablespoons of either to a cup of liquid in the mold recipe will give it a taste lift that is important.

Obviously, all molds have to be balanced properly between the gelatin and the liquid content if they are to become firm. It is essential that you include the wine or liqueur as a substitute for an equivalent part of the liquid called for in the recipe. You add it when the gelatin is dissolved and starting to cool.

My rule is very simple—a dry white wine for seafood, veal, and chicken molds. Use the sweeter wines, such as sauterne, cognac, or any of the fruited liqueurs for the molded fruit salads.

All one needs to create endless magic with molded salads is the basic recipe plus the many other "added ingredients" that make the selection varied.

THE BASIC GELATIN SALAD FORMULA

I have found that this will produce a molded salad that will serve five people.

Soak one tablespoon gelatin in ¼ cup cold water. Dissolve this gummy, swollen mixture in ¼ cup boiling stock (chicken bouillon or beef bouillon both work as well as stock). Add this to 1½ cups cold stock or 1¼ cups cold stock plus ¼ cup tomato juice.

Two tablespoons vinegar or 1½ tablespoons lemon juice (I use the reconstituted lemon juice in the bottle).

Salt and paprika   1 tablespoon chopped onions
Celery salt

. . . Add to this mixture 1½ to 2 cups of solid ingredients.

When preparing for one hundred or more, you set up an assembly line. I set up 6 bowls. I chop onions, cucumbers, celery, green peppers, stuffed ripe or green olives and fill each bowl with one of the ingredients. Line up your condiments—celery, garlic, and onion salt, tarragon, parsley, dill, chives—so that you can reach them easily and add them to your basic aspic when appropriate.

I make four times the basic aspic recipe each time and then add two cups of the tunafish, salmon, or crabmeat, with different vegetables and condiments for four molds. The next time I do another "four times the basic" recipe and add two cups of cooked chicken, turkey, or ham.

You see, just by changing the balance of the flavors we have already done four molds in six different combinations.

As you play this mass-production cooking game you will develop courage in the kitchen and not require direct recipe guidance.

However, for the hostess and cook delegating responsibility here are some of my recipes:

BASIC ASPIC AND ANY OF THE SEAFOOD MOLDS

I use ½ bouillon and ½ chicken stock. Remember —your guide is two cups of solid ingredients to your original recipe.

To make up the 2 cups you have the fish and then diced celery, cucumbers, or green peppers. Vary it by adding chopped hard-boiled eggs or sliced green olives.

Pour it all into your wet molds and chill until firm.

The next group of molds will be the mousses. Usually your mousse is based either on mayonnaise or whipped cream. Here are two recipes that will work for either, no matter which seafood you decide to use.

SEA FOOD MOUSSE

Soak two tablespoons gelatin in ¼ cup cold water. Dissolve it in ¼ cup boiling water. Add it to ¾ cup mayonnaise.
Combine it with:

1 cup flaked crabmeat or flaked tunafish	½ cup chopped cucumber
½ cup chopped celery or carrots	2 tablespoons chopped, stuffed olives
2 tablespoons chopped parsley	2 tablespoons lemon juice salt and pepper

Don't be afraid to season strongly, otherwise by the time the mousse is served it may be bland.

LOBSTER MOUSSE

Soak one tablespoon gelatin in ¼ cup water. Dissolve it over boiling water. Combine:

¾ cup minced celery	1½ cups canned or cooked lobster meat
⅔ cup minced apple	

Season these ingredients with salt and pepper. Set aside.
Now take your gelatin mixture and stir into it:

¾ cup mayonnaise	Tabasco (just a few drops)
2 tablespoons lemon juice	
1 teaspoon dry mustard	whip ½ cup cream and fold in
½ clove pressed garlic	

Now fold this mixture into the other fish ingredients. Place the mousse in a wet mold. I like to do this in a ring mold, so that the center can be filled with watercress. I surround this mold on a platter generously loaded with drained marinated sliced cucumbers.

The next direction is for the
MOLDED VEGETABLE GELATIN SALAD

Dissolve the contents of one package of lime- or lemon-flavored gelatin in 2 cups of hot water. Add to this 1½ cups finely diced vegetables. You can (and I do) combine the Veg-All tinned vegetables with diced, fresh unpeeled radishes, cucumber, olives, and pimentos. And

½ diced green pepper	¾ teaspoon salt
2 teaspoons grated onion	¼ teaspoon paprika

My experience has been that for vegetable molds it is a good idea to *wet* the mold.

The fruit gelatin molds are the easiest to do and can be very exciting as color accents on your buffet—they are very popular.

Once again I use an assembly-line system. I make 8 packages of Jell-O in the following flavors and colors in separate pots. I treat them as paints to be used to create variations in color and design—

Lemon—yellow
Lime—green
Orange—orange
Raspberry, strawberry, etc.—red
Black cherry—dark red

This means 5 pots full of 8 packages of Jell-O mixed with the two cups of water as directed.

Then I have an array of tinned fruits and nuts to use as fillers:

Pineapple—yellow
Apricots—orange
Peaches—gold
Plums—dark red
Cherries—pink and dark red

There are many other possibilities and some are to combine and make a black cherry and almond aspic. The rule I use for Jell-O molds is for each single package I allow 1½ cups of prepared drained fruit alone. If I wish to combine it with nuts I just make sure that the total volume of the fruit and the nuts per package is equivalent to 1½ cups. Never fails.

Now to do layers of three molds is easy—just wait for each layer to firm up before adding the next. I use a four-hour automatic check on this and it always works.

Another variation is to substitute ½ cup of mayonnaise for

each one cup of water in the directions. This gives you a rich, creamy mousse layer to play with from both a flavor and design standpoint.

Another trick is to create mint gelatin for these fruit salads. Add ¼ cup of crushed mint leaves in the cup of boiling water before pouring it over the Jell-O. Let it steep for 5 minutes and then strain the leaves out and proceed as directed. It's a lovely flavor and you can heighten the aura of mint by adding a few drops of green food color.

The last of the basic molds recipes is the tomato aspic. The canned varieties work very well and if you pep them up with lemon, Tabasco, and Worcestershire sauce you then move on to add other ingredients that give you a whole new series of molds.

For the purist who is uncomfortable unless everything is made from scratch, here is my

BASIC TOMATO ASPIC

½	cup tomatoes	3	tablespoons chopped
1	teaspoon salt		onion
½	teaspoon paprika	1	bay leaf
1½	teaspoons sugar	4	ribs of celery with leaves
2	tablespoons lemon juice	1	teaspoon dried basil

Combine and simmer all this in one pot for about 45 minutes and then strain. Put the pot back on the stove under a low flame. Soak 2 tablespoons of gelatin in ½ cup cold water. Dissolve the massed gelatin in the strained hot juice. Add water to make 4 cups of liquid. Chill the aspic and add 2 cups of solid ingredients.

Once again you can do individual items or combinations. Use your assembly line of olive slices, chopped celery, chopped green peppers, chopped or grated carrots. Here I have found that a little extravagance goes a long way—I use caviar (red or black), smoked oysters, sliced avocado wrapped in anchovies, etc. You may want to keep the aspic plain and do it in a ring mold—then fill the center with caviar (red) mixed with sour cream or shrimp salad or chicken salad or cottage cheese mixed with nuts and chives.

Another direction is to do a tomato aspic either in individual molds or a large fish mold that you will slice with a center of a taste-treat surprise.

Just fill your mold up to ⅓ of its capacity. Then after it has properly set, combine:

> 1 *3-ounce package cream*
> *cheese*
> 1 *tablespoon anchovy paste*
> 2 *drops Worcestershire*
> *sauce*

. . . And then roll this blended cheese into balls. Drop a ball into each individual mold or ice-cube mold and cover with aspic. If you use a larger mold then just place the balls around so that a usual slice will include one or more. The cream cheese will combine with many different things to create a surprise—add enough herbs, including basil and tarragon, to the cheese and make the balls; add caviar; add onion mix.

SEVEN: Do Let Them Brunch Up On You

You will do well if you wish to impress the bunch with brunch.

Brunches are mostly weekend or holiday events, for that is when most people enjoy sleeping late and are happy to combine breakfast and lunch in one big meal. Brunch keeps gaining in popularity because it reflects our currently casual approach to entertaining. It can be set up for any budget or in any space. The accent is on relaxation and fun. Forget the cloth if the table is a glass, iron, or wicker wonder and just use a plant as centerpiece.

Brunch is usually served from ten to two o'clock. The later the starting time, the more dishes suitable for lunch are included. An invitation for a brunch that mentions a specific time implies a small group, and it is expected that guests will arrive on time. An invitation such as "Come to brunch after noon" signals a lot more latitude. This means that more people are expected and guests can arrive anytime within the next hour.

As host, forget any ceremonies such as waiting for all the guests to arrive. Feed them promptly, as late-rising guests are usually ready to eat. I will seat eight for brunch, but any larger number is served with food in covered dishes kept warm over hot plates on warming trays or by chafing-dish flames. If you can seat all your guests, you may want a juice starter course at the table. However, don't leave the glasses of juice standing by themselves. Why not serve it directly from tall glass pitchers resting in an iced champagne bucket.

If everything from the stairs to the floors are to be used as seats, make it a one-plate brunch.

If you're bored with the same old people, the same old things, the same old way, then try an imaginative brunch. There are winter brunches before a blazing log fire, spring brunches for christening the new cabin cruiser, summer after-tennis brunches held at courtside and fall private brunches given at a private restaurant. A bon-voyage brunch may be scheduled for the morning or afternoon of a dear friend's departure by boat, plane, bus, or train. Give a brunch built around a new sport such as kiting, or a revived pleasure like croquet. You don't have to live in New England to throw a good old-fashioned clambake. Fresh clams and live lobsters can be flown to the most land-locked area in a matter of a few jet hours. They pack them in their own native sea water in containers that convert to cookers.

Try the New York brunch. Deck the tables with lox, cream cheese, and bagels. Extend it from there with assorted white, smoked, and marinated fish. Chopped liver smothered in raw onions, assorted Dutch cheeses, and Danish pastries make a version of a Scandinavian smorgasbord, or you can do a traditional smorgasbord, and if you do, be sure to add a selection of rich fruit jams.

As a dedicated brunchman, I do the cold-country buffet often, for after you set out the assorted foods on the platters you can simply join your guests in the waiting line. Then there is the TV event (football, tennis, golf) brunch, on individual trays to be eaten with the fingers (fried chicken, spareribs, eggrolls). The outdoor brunch (estate, garden, patio, terrace, fire escape) with food ranging from fondue to barbeque; the international pancake brunch with a wide selection of toppings such as Swedish ligonberries, English currants, Vermont whole maple syrup, Russian caviar and sour cream, fresh fruits and berries, Grand Marnier sauce and beehive honey.

Consider the open-sandwich kitchen brunch. Make it yourself with all the fixings of various breads, seafoods, delicatessen, cheese, salads, and dressings. Or the ski brunch—*après* everything or nothing. Thick peasant breads and fresh creamery butter and two thick soups. Try scallop chowder or country minestrone.

A wet brunch (hot tub, pool, pond, stream, lake, or ocean) could include exotic fruits, poultry, and meat salads, and a fiesta brunch involves a chic chili surrounded by tacos, enchiladas, and safe, bottled water.

If you are doing a small al fresco brunch, a hibachi or a portable broiler with a smoker top is perfect for appeasing early-afternoon appetites with any number of mixed grills, ham steaks, lamb chops, sausages, bacon, kidneys, onions, tomatoes, mushrooms.

Be sure you have a large bread basket piled high with warm, quick bread. Between the quality frozen foods and the best bakers, you should be able to find the silkiest of soft rolls or tender croissants that seem to melt as you bite into them. Italians adore panettone—a luscious mound of yeast cake with raisins and candied fruit. And for the American or those visiting foreigners blueberry muffins, corn muffins, bran muffins, and pecan buns.

Some of your brunch guests may need to be stimulated, others soothed at the start. You may want to skip the usual screwdrivers made with vodka and offer "Mimosas"—champagne and orange juice—or juice served with rum, sherry or pernod. For others you may want to start the night before by chilling the Bloody Marys. Here is my recipe:

HORSERADISH BLOODY MARY

Celery sticks are edible stirrers.

In large pitcher, combine one 46-ounce can (5¾ cups) tomato juice, 2 cups vodka, 2 tablespoons lemon juice, 1 tablespoon prepared horseradish, 1 teaspoon Worcestershire sauce, few drops bottled hot pepper sauce, and ¾ teaspoon salt. Chill several hours or overnight. At serving time, pour over ice. Use celery-stick stirrer in each glass. Makes 2 quarts.

Brunch is the most leisurely of all meals, so it is a good idea to have plenty of coffee served continually. The best coffee in the world will taste even better if you own an electric grinder and grind fresh beans just before brewing. Set up both tea service and Sanka on separate trays so they can be made available to people who prefer them.

And though brunch *looks* leisurely and effortless it, too, requires all the meticulous advance planning of the sit-down supper or informal buffet. Here are the simple rules that should be standard brunch procedure for you:

1. *Write everything out on a pad.* Leave nothing to chance or any last-minute decisions. Start with—
  a. the menu
  b. the equipment
  c. the service
  d. the timing
  e. the emergency alternative

Terrific tension can accumulate if there is no serving spoon available for one dish or no pad to protect the serving table. Just think it all through. Lay the equipment out as though you were plunging into surgery. It goes a long way toward making the operation a success.

I owe you an explanation for emergency alternatives. I learned years ago that you should always have a couple of possible dishes that can be prepared in a very few minutes if a culinary accident occurs. Temporary help are willing, and like amiable friends have been known to spill, drop, maim, and mutilate food between the kitchen and the table. Pets have been driven wild by your magical use of herbs and spices and jumped on a roast, a fish, etc. It is simple to cook up a box of minute rice and allow it to cool in advance. Extra mayonnaise, some canned fish and spices, and you have a substitute rice salad. I always hard-boil a dozen eggs and have extra fresh vegetables that can be cut up immediately. Combine these two with the simplest of dips and you have an "oeuf et crudité" platter that no one will suspect you didn't originally plan. None of this extra food will go to waste, but what delicious insurance just in case. The whole point about planning is that then you can talk to your guests without ¾ of your mind trying to outguess your stove. I have seen distracted hosts nod and murmur "how marvelous" to a guest who had just explained that she had terminal cancer. There is a kind of entertaining high some hosts experience out of insecurity, then proceed to communicate to the guest via the faraway look in the eye—a message that he wishes the guest were equally far away.

Get it all together and you and your guests can enjoy it together.

2. *Don't put off for later what you can do now.* After you've gotten your party plan on paper, do right away what can be done. Do the day before, or that morning or afternoon, whatever can be done in advance. The real secret is that if you are having a good time at your party so will your guests.

Brunch which combines both breakfast and luncheon foods is one of my favorite weekend ways to entertain. I do noon brunches, and I always allow enough time between the arrival of the guests and the meal itself so that each guest doesn't feel pressured about meeting a deadline. Food should be sufficiently varied and interesting so that it avoids either food clichés or the too exotic. Do remember that brunch is reasonably close to the time people get out of bed. Most stomachs don't want to drive miles to an amusing eggplant-and-kidney pie. Here are fourteen brunch menus that I have served happily to my guests.

Any of my menus can be broken down so that you can use the appealing recipe from the menu without necessarily following the whole menu.

Menu One

BLENDED ORANGE AND PINEAPPLE JUICE
BAKED EGGS IN TOMATO SHELLS
MIXED SAUSAGES AND SALAMIS
TOASTED SCONES AND ENGLISH MUFFINS
ASSORTED PRESERVES AND HONEY BUTTER

Fill eight juice glasses half full of crushed ice. If you don't have a mechanical crusher just take ice cubes rolled in a bath towel and hit them with a hammer. Place glasses in your freezer. Blend frozen orange and pineapple juice and just before serving pour into your glasses from the freezer.

BAKED EGGS in TOMATO SHELLS

8	medium-size tomatoes	8	eggs
2	dashes salt	8	teaspoons grated
2	dashes pepper		Parmesan cheese
2	dashes basil		

Cut off the tops of the tomatoes. Scoop out the pulp and drain the tomatoes. Combine the salt, pepper, and basil and mix it all up. Then sprinkle the inside of each tomato shell with the mixture. Break the eggs, one at a time, into a small dish and gently slide one into each tomato. Bake in a moderate oven (350°) for 20 to 25 minutes, or until the eggs are almost set to the degree of doneness you prefer. Sprinkle each with one teaspoon grated Parmesan cheese and place under the broiler until cheese is just bubbly. Garnish with a dab of parsley.

MIXED SAUSAGES AND SALAMIS

Pan-fry sausages until brown. Then add assorted thin slices of salamis to the hot grease. Drain both sausages and salami and surround your baked tomatoes with a circle of the meats.

TOASTED SCONES AND ENGLISH MUFFINS

You do know that you can't cut them with a knife but must separate them with a fork. Toast the scones and muffins when you broil the cheese topping on the eggs.

Let your jams be reasonably familiar but always have at least two fresh combinations: lemon-and-lime marmalade—fresh strawberry- and- rhubarb jam— gooseberry preserve.

I always have both coffee and tea. Always India tea, not China, for brunch.

Iced milk flavored just a little with chocolate and cinnamon along with plain cold milk is an easy extra beverage.

Menu Two
(serves 6)

DICED PAPAYA WITH LEMON JUICE
HAM AND BANANA ROLLERS
RICE AND PEAS PILAF
A GREEN SALAD
HOT BISCUITS AND BUTTER

DICED PAPAYA WITH LEMON JUICE

Peel two firm, ripe papayas. Dice and spoon into sherbet glasses or small fruit bowls. Cover each serving with about one tablespoon of lemon juice.

HAM AND BANANA ROLLERS

Just wrap thinly sliced smoked ham, spread with a mixture of Dijon mustard and white horseradish, around firm, whole, peeled bananas. You secure the ham to the bananas with toothpicks that have been cut in half. Place them in a shallow baking pan, coat generously with melted butter, and season actively with freshly ground black pepper. Bake in a medium oven (350°) for about 20 minutes.

RICE AND PEAS PILAF

This is a combination of equal parts of freshly boiled rice and fresh peas, buttered and united together.

GREEN SALAD

I reached this point and realized how many depressing green salads I have seen just because the term is like a large wastepaper basket—too often there is too much thrown into it, so that you have less salad and more litter.

Let's examine the salad greens and see if we can't end up with the sure-fire winners. Any child could describe the principal ingredient for a green salad as lettuce. But it takes some maturity to develop awareness of the endless differences:

Head Lettuce (Iceberg)—Certainly the most common market variety. It is tightly packed and if fresh is a crisp-leafed variety. Its color can be very dark green to almost white. Always cut it at the core and then pull it apart. Then you hand-break it apart into bits for salad or pull it apart if you use it to cover the bottom of a platter or as a garnish.

Boston Lettuce (Bibb Lettuce)—This is a medium green, loosely headed but delightfully tender and truly delicious green. "Handle with care" should be the watchword. Boston lettuce bruises easily and turns brown quickly. Perfect for a green salad, but requires *careful* washing and patting dry leaf by leaf.

Leaf Lettuce—This is not a head of but a bunch of lettuce. It is somewhat coarser in texture and it can be used by itself only when it is very young. However, it combines very well with other greens and the texture difference is interesting to the tongue.

Romaine or Cos Lettuce—The royalty of the lettuce family. Long, aristocratic leaves and very crisp, although the head is rather loosely packed. Romaine has excellent staying power and retains its texture and character better than any of the other lettuces. I use a lot of it for green salads.

Curly Chicory—Use this carefully. The leaves are tender but they have a slightly bitter taste. So use this frizzy green sparingly, to complement the other greens in the salad bowl.

Endive or Belgian Endive—This green is grown indoors and is carefully blanched until ready for the market. The stalks are long and tightly headed. For salad the head is usually quartered or halved or sometimes cut into ½-inch circular slices. It has a clearly defined flavor and I prefer it by itself as a salad. (Endive is superb cooked as well. Just braise it as you do celery.)

Escarole—A broader-leafed member of the chicory family. The leaves are sturdy and lightly curled. I find it slightly bitter and always think of it as a bit of seasoning in the salad.

Lamb's Lettuce or Field Salad—The soft, almost tongue-shaped leaves of sage green are a real delicacy. It comes in very small

—110—

heads and I just wash it and place it whole in a mixed salad without breaking or cutting.

Spinach—Just wash the leaves very carefully a number of times. I remove the coarse stems and just break the leaves into rough pieces.

Watercress—This green has a very peppy tang. I love it by itself. It is also one of the great garnishes.

I do have a vegetable and flower garden so I find I often can add a touch of other greens for variety. At various seasons I have added turnip tips, bean sprouts, bits of fern and nasturtium leaves.

A green salad should always be given a fresh facial in ice-cold water. Then the greens should be either dried on a clean towel or air spun and then placed in your refrigerator. It is important that practically all the water be absorbed before the mixing of your salad. Too-early tossing and mixing is exhausting for a salad—and what you end up with is a salad ranging from lazy and limp to sad and soggy.

There are acceptable salad herbs. You add them both to punctuate the salad as well as to stimulate the taste buds.

Menu Three
(serves 6)

CHILLED CHICKEN CREAM
CHINATOWN'S CHICKEN SALAD
HOT BISCUITS AND HONEY

CHILLED CHICKEN CREAM

1 can condensed cream of chicken soup	½ cup milk
	1 teaspoon lemon juice
1 cup light cream	½ teaspoon celery seeds

Combine all ingredients in an electric blender; cover. Blend one minute, or until creamy and smooth. Chill. Pour into mugs. Garnish each with a firm piece of celery as a stirrer and serve with tiny croutons covered with a veil of paprika.

NOTE: Start a small collection of individual mugs and cups and saucers. The break from the ritual of the matched set is in itself a welcome relief from the usual. It also solves the problem of broken sets. If something is broken, just replace it with something visually compatible but forget the desperate search for the perfect match.

CHINATOWN'S CHICKEN SALAD

1	3-pound whole broiler	6	cups broken salad greens
2	cups of water	1	cup chopped celery
	handful of celery tops	2	green onions, sliced
1	teaspoon salt	5	large radishes, sliced
6	peppercorns	1	can (3-ounce) Chinese
1½	cups soy dressing		fried noodles
1	bunch fresh broccoli	1	hard-boiled egg

1. Simmer chicken with water, celery tops, salt, and peppercorns in kettle 1 hour (or more) until tender. Remove chicken from broth and let drain in shallow pan just until cool enough to handle. (Strain the broth and save for soup.)
2. Remove the skin from the chicken, then pull the meat from the frame in large pieces. If the bird is still warm you will see that the meat pulls away easily. Cut it into bite-size pieces, place in a shallow pan; pour over ¼ cup soy dressing. Cover and chill at least 2 hours to blend flavors.
3. Trim and discard outer leaves from broccoli. Cut off ends to make about 4-inch-long stalks. Split the large ones lengthwise. Cook covered in about 1-inch depth boiling salted water in large frying pan 15 minutes, or until crispy tender; drain well.
4. Place in shallow pan; pour ½ cup soy dressing over. Chill at least 1 hour.
5. When ready to serve, pile salad greens, celery, green onions, and radishes into a large salad bowl. Pour remaining ¾ cup soy dressing over; toss lightly to mix.

Arrange marinated broccoli with stems toward center in a ring on top. Fill ring with marinated chicken, spoon noodles around the broccoli.

6. Make eight slices of radishes. Press white of egg, then yolk through sieve onto separate sheets of waxed paper. Spoon white of eggs on top of chicken; Top with radish slices, overlapping slightly. Garnish with sieved egg yolk.

SOY DRESSING:
Combine ½ cup soy sauce, ½ cup salad oil (or peanut oil), and ½ cup wine vinegar with 1 teaspoon salt and ½ teaspoon ground ginger in a jar with a tight-fitting cover. Shake to mix well. Makes 1½ cups.

Menu Four

HONEYDEW MELON WITH LIME WEDGES
ZUCCHINI LAMB BAKE
PEANUT POTATO SALAD
LEMON SHERBET

ZUCCHINI LAMB BAKE
(serves 6 to 8)

2	*pounds ground lamb*	2	*cups (1 pint) sour cream*
1	*teaspoon garlic salt*	12	*zucchini, each about 5*
¼	*cup fine, dry bread*		*inches long*
	crumbs		*salt and pepper*
6	*tablespoons grated*	12	*ounces sliced mozzarella*
	Parmesan cheese		

In a frying pan over medium heat cook the lamb, stirring until the meat has lost all its redness. Drain the fat, then stir in the garlic salt, bread crumbs, 4 tablespoons of the Parmesan cheese, and sour cream. Set aside.

Cut zucchini in thin, lengthwise slices; sprinkle lightly with salt and pepper. In a greased, shallow baking pan arrange about ⅓ of the zucchini slices; spoon lamb mixture over top, then make another layer of zucchini and spoon another layer of lamb mixture and cover with the remaining zucchini slices. I always make this ahead of time and so you just cover it and chill.

Allow about one hour before serving. Bake, covered, in a 350° oven for 45 minutes.

Uncover it and then arrange the mozzarella slices over the top, and sprinkle evenly with the remaining Parmesan cheese. Bake uncovered for about 10 minutes longer or until the cheese is golden.

PEANUT POTATO SALAD

(NOTE: I have had an enormous success with this unexpected summer salad. The unique flavor and crunchiness is a good taste contrast to the zucchini and lamb.)

2	*pounds red new potatoes*	6	*slices bacon, crisply fried*
	boiling salted water	½	*cup mayonnaise*
½	*cup chopped green celery*	2	*tablespoons cider vinegar*
½	*cup green pepper*	1	*tablespoon chunk-style*
¾	*cup thinly sliced green*		*peanut butter*
	onion	1	*teaspoon curry powder*
¼	*cup chopped parsley*		*(leave it out if you hate*
¼	*cup diced cucumber*		*curry)*
¾	*cup salted Spanish*		*salt and pepper*
	peanuts		

Cook the potatoes in boiling water until just tender when pierced, about 30 minutes. Drain. When cool, I don't peel but you can if you can't stand the skin. Cut the potatoes into ½-inch chunks. Combine potatoes with green pepper, celery, green onion, parsley, cucumber and ½ cup of the nuts. Crumble bacon and mix into the salad. In a small bowl stir together the mayonnaise, vinegar, peanut butter, and curry powder (if used). Pour over potato mixture and mix well. Season to taste with salt and pepper. Cover and chill. I do it the night before because you need an absolute minimum of 4 hours if it is going to be interflavored and cold enough.

Just before serving, stir it actively and garnish with the remaining salted nuts.

Menu Five
(serves 6)

MUGGED FRUIT SALAD
GUACAMOLE—CORN TORTILLAS
OLÉ BRUNCH EGGS

MUGGED FRUIT SALAD

Cut up fresh fruit and mix with tinned fruits for salad. Marinate fruit mixture in an undiluted can of pineapple juice. Serve very cold in mugs topped with a sprig of mint.

GUACAMOLE—CORN TORTILLAS

Prepare about one cup Guacamole from your favorite recipe or take the easy way out and thaw an 8-ounce can of frozen Guacamole dip; Use as a spread for tortillas. You buy the tortillas ready to go. Wrap the corn tortillas in foil, then heat in a 350° oven for about 20 minutes.

While the tortillas are in the oven prepare the eggs—

OLÉ BRUNCH EGGS

4	slices bacon, diced	oregano leaves
1	onion, chopped	6 eggs
2	cloves garlic, minced or mashed	6 ounces jack cheese cut in ⅓-inch cubes. It'll make about 1½ cups
1	large can (1 pound, 12 ounces) Italian-style pear-shaped tomatoes	¼ cup lightly packed chopped fresh coriander—and if that's a
3	tablespoons chopped green chives	problem to find, don't panic—parsley will do
½	teaspoon each salt and	

Use a 10-inch frying pan—if you have a good-looking frying pan use it as a serving utensil; if you have an old, beat-up frying pan, use *it* as a serving utensil. These eggs are delicious and no one will care about the utensil. Another thing to realize about serving directly from the stove or oven—you can get away with any utensil if you approach the whole meal as "Country Kitchen" rather than high-luster "In Town" sophistication.

In the frying pan cook the bacon over medium heat until crisp. With a slotted spoon, remove the bacon and set aside. Add the onions and the garlic to the drippings in the pan and cook, stirring until the onion is soft. Stir in tomatoes, chives, salt, and oregano. Bring to a boil, stirring. Boil until sauce is mushy (about 15 minutes). Stir regularly.

Reduce heat to low and carefully slip in eggs, one at a time. Do this by cracking your eggs into a plate and letting the eggs slip from the plate into the tomato sauce. Sprinkle cheese and bacon over top.

Cover the pan and cook until the eggs are set—about 6 to 8 minutes. Remove from heat and sprinkle with fresh coriander—serve from the pan.

Menu Six
(serves 6)

PEACHES WITH AN ORANGE GLOW
CHIVE OVEN OMELET
BROILED BACON AND MUSHROOMS
SWEET ROLLS

PEACHES WITH AN ORANGE GLOW

Take two packages of frozen peaches—dump into a bowl. Cover with a large can of undiluted orange juice and 2 tablespoons of Cointreau—let thaw. Later, spoon into 6 sherbet glasses.

CHIVE OVEN OMELET
(Serves 6)

8 eggs, separated	½ teaspoon onion salt
2 tablespoons flour	¼ teaspoon Worcestershire
3 tablespoons milk	sauce
2 teaspoons chopped chives	dash pepper
½ teaspoon salt	butter

Beat egg yolks until creamy—you remember how we separated the eggs. Gradually beat in the flour, milk, chopped chives, salt, onion salt, Worcestershire sauce, and dash of pepper. Beat whites until stiff, but not dry; Fold thoroughly into the yolk mixture. Spoon into a well-buttered shallow 2 quart casserole; Bake in a hot oven (400°) for 13 to 15 minutes or until the top is golden brown. Serve immediately in a baking container.

BROILED BACON AND MUSHROOMS

The bacon and mushrooms should be broiled and drained on paper. Figure 2 slices of bacon and 3 mushrooms for each guest.
   A basket of assorted sweet rolls—tea—coffee.

Menu Seven
MY FATHER'S BRUNCH
(serves 6)

It is meat and potatoes and a marvelous one-dish meal. Serve it with your own homemade rye bread and lots of hot coffee.

¼ cup butter or margarine	6 eggs
2 cups cubed, uncooked	¾ teaspoon salt
potatoes	dash pepper
¼ cup finely chopped onion	2 tablespoons light cream
1 cup cubed ham	½ cup shredded jack cheese
¼ cup chopped parsley	

Melt butter in a 9- or 10-inch frying pan. Add potatoes and onion; cover and cook over medium high heat, stirring occasionally to brown evenly for about 20 minutes or until potatoes are tender and golden. Add ham and cook a few minutes longer until lightly browned. Sprinkle mixture with parsley and reduce heat.

Beat together eggs, salt, pepper, and light cream until well blended. Pour egg mixture over potatoes and ham. Cover and cook until eggs are almost set, slipping spatula around edge of the pan occasionally to allow egg mixture to run down, about 10 minutes. Sprinkle with cheese and cover again until cheese melts. Cut in wedges to serve.

Combine it with some broiled tomatoes. I top the tomatoes with a mixture of dill, lemon juice, and seasoned pepper before broiling.

Menu Eight
(serves 6)

BOWL OF COLD, FRESH FRUIT
TONGUE, RICE, AND EGGS
GARLIC BREAD

BOWL OF COLD, FRESH FRUIT

Chill your fruit and your bowl overnight. Garnish with leaves from bushes or trees available to you. Put 3 or 4 sharp fruit knives in the bowl. I stick the knives into the fruit to reassure the timid that one can cut a banana or apple if you don't want the whole piece. If you are serving grapes then be sure that there is a pair of fruit-flower scissors at hand. Without the scissors, after a couple of guests have had a go at the bowl it will look as though it has been attacked. If you are having more than six for brunch then have 2 fruit bowls. I use six as the number to multiply by. More than six, then I double the recipe and the serving platters and bowls. It just makes it all work faster and easier than the seemingly endless waiting around one bowl while a procrastinator tastes everything in his head before selecting his food.

BOILED BEEF TONGUE (SMALL)

The best-flavored tongue is beef tongue and a good rule to cook by is that the smaller-size tongues usually are better. Just under 3 pounds is tongue at its prime.

It is an easy food to prepare. One should realize that not everyone can handle eating tongue—the same applies to heart, brains, kidneys. I always have one alternative dish ready just in case. Tongue is perfect because it is so easy to separate the meat slices from the eggs and rice which can stand together as a delicious brunch course.

Here are some facts about preparing a tongue. I don't scrub it or blanch it. I have tried both and the difference was either not apparent or so unimportant that I did not feel that it was necessary. But in case you blanch at the thought of not doing it here is how it is done. The purpose of blanching a tongue is to remove the excess salt. You place the tongue in a large pot and cover it with cold water. Bring the water slowly to a boil, uncovered, and continue to simmer it for about 10 minutes After this you drain the tongue and plunge it into a cold-water bath. Just fill up one of your sink basins with cold water and your tongue can plunge comfortably. After you take it out of the bath you put it into seasoned boiling water to cover.

SEASONED WATER:
Before putting the tongue into the water, prepare the water. I add—

 1 *whole small onion stuck*
    with 3 cloves
 ½ *cup chopped celery with*
    leaves
 3 *bay leaves*
 4 *peppercorns*

Reduce the heat immediately and simmer uncovered for 2 to 3 hours.

To skin the tongue easily just take the pot from the heat, remove the tongue, and allow it to cool so that you can handle it. It skins very easily at this point. The colder it gets, the more difficult. Trim it and return it to the pot and let it cook completely in the cooking liquor. You want to cool this one because it will slice better. (NOTE: As you get to the tip of the tongue cut your slices on the diagonal.)

RICE AND TWO FRIENDS (EGGS AND TONGUE)

1½ cups of rice	½ teaspoon salt
3 tablespoons of butter	¼ teaspoon pepper
3 cups of beef bouillon	

Wash, drain, and dry (let the air do it) 1½ cups of rice. Put in a pot over medium heat and melt 3 tablespoons of butter or margarine. Add the rice and stir with a wooden fork until all the rice is covered with butter. Lower the heat and continue to stir for 10 minutes. Now—and I use canned beef broth—add 3 cups of beef broth, ½ teaspoon salt, and ¼ teaspoon pepper, and cover. The never-fail way to tell when your rice is done: the rice is cooked when the surface is dotted with small holes. Turn your oven on to just below 200°, and put the rice into the oven to dry.

SAUCE FOR TONGUE:

½ cup of almonds	3 tablespoons of flour
2 cups of water	¼ cup of ginger snaps
⅔ cup of seedless raisins	1 teaspoon grated lemon
6 tablespoons of butter	rind

Sliced almonds come in tins—so just take ½ cup out of the can. Simmer the almonds and ⅔ cup of seedless raisins in 2 cups of water. It takes about ½ hour. Drain the water and hold it.

Now melt 6 tablespoons of butter and then blend in 3 tablespoons of flour. Add the raisins and almond liquid to make

3 cups of liquid in all. Add the ¼ cup crushed ginger snaps. Add the raisins, almonds, and 1 teaspoon lemon rind (grated).

The second friend is the eggs. You scramble 8 eggs in a *saucepan* in which 2 tablespoons butter have been melted, add ¼ teaspoon salt and ½ cup heavy cream. *Don't overcook!!* The trick is to stir constantly. It takes longer but they are truly delicious.

Place the rice in a ring mold and, using a knife, tap the entire mold to eliminate air holes. Then remove the rice mold onto the serving dish. The center of the dish is filled with the scrambled eggs and the slices of tongue are placed around the rice. Because everyone does not like raisin sauce I serve the sauce in a separate bowl. I keep a bottle of madeira wine on the side and indicate to guests that it is a hearty addition to the tongue and sauce if so desired.

GARLIC BREAD

Be sure your knife is very sharp—then cut uniform slices ¾- to 1-inch thick from a crusty loaf of French or Vienna bread. Spread garlic butter generously on one side of each slice. Stand the slices upright, close together, in a bread-loaf pan. I line the bread pan with aluminum foil. Fifteen minutes before serving time, heat oven to 400°. Heat loaf until piping hot and crusty. It takes about 15 minutes. Transfer, still in loaf shape, to oblong bread tray and serve at once.

GARLIC BUTTER
Cream butter in a bowl rubbed with a cut clove of garlic. Add ½ teaspoon of garlic salt and a few drops of garlic juice.

Menu Nine
(serves 6)

❦

CAPE COD CONSOMMÉ
GREEN NOODLES WITH BASIL AND TOMATOES
BAKED SAUSAGE PATTIES
BISCUITS, HONEY AND BUTTER
POTS-DE-CREME

CAPE COD CONSOMMÉ IN CHAMPAGNE GLASSES

6 envelopes of MBT instant chicken-broth mix
1½ cups of cold water
3 cups clam juice
18 ice cubes

Set up a large pitcher near your blender. Then place the MBT powder, water, clam juice, and 2 ice cubes per envelope in the blender. Cover. Turn on high speed. Blend for 30 seconds or until the ice disappears. Pour into your waiting pitcher. When you have blended 6 envelopes, put one ice cube in each of six champagne glasses and pour the soup over. I often set everything up and perform before guests so that the drink can be served immediately.

GREEN NOODLES WITH BASIL
(FETTUCINE VERDE CON BASILICO)
(6 servings)

3 tablespoons olive oil (or salad oil)
1 large onion, sliced and separated into rings
½ pound mushrooms, sliced
2 cloves garlic, minced
4 large, ripe tomatoes, peeled and chunk chopped (about 6 cups)
¼ cup chopped parsley
⅛ teaspoon each marjoram leaves and pepper

1 teaspoon salt
½ teaspoon sugar
1 cup fresh basil leaves, gently diced
⅓ cup dry wine
1 package (8 ounces) spinach-flavored noodles
boiling salted water
2 tablespoons soft butter or margarine
freshly grated Parmesan cheese

In a large frying pan heat the olive oil over medium-high heat. Then add the onions, mushrooms, and garlic and cook. It is important that you keep stirring until the liquid has evaporated. Now add the tomatoes, parsley, marjoram, pepper, salt, sugar, about ½ of the basil, and the wine. Bring to the boil, then reduce the heat, cover, and simmer for about 30 minutes. Uncover and cook rapidly, stirring until sauce is reduced to about 3 cups—about 20 minutes—turn on warm.

Cook the green noodles according to package directions. Drain well. In a shallow serving bowl, mix noodles lightly with the butter, the remaining ½ cup basil, and about 1 cup of the sauce. Top with the remaining sauce. Accompany with the Parmesan cheese to sprinkle on top of each serving.

BAKED SAUSAGE PATTIES
(6 Servings)

Form 1½ pounds bulk pork sausage into 6 patties about 3½ inches wide. Place in a rack in a broiler pan. Bake at 425° for about 25 minutes. They are done when they are no longer pink in the center.

POTS-DE-CRÈME

If you don't have the antique lidded pots-de-crème, there are very respectable inexpensive reproductions available in any department store. I don't bake these because it is a lot easier to manage and control the consistency if you use a good double-boiler.

The reason for this is that too-high heat will toughen the albumen in the eggs and keep it from holding the liquid in suspension. Just cook it until the custard is thick enough to coat a spoon. It is important, however, when you take the pan from the heat, that you continue to stir it rapidly to release the steam. Watery custards are just the result of the steam condensing and becoming part of the custard instead of escaping into the air. Keep your custards in the refrigerator.

For chocolate pots-de-creme, combine and cook over very low heat:

8 ounces best-quality	2 cups of half and half
grated semisweet	2 tablespoons of sugar
chocolate	

Cook and stir these ingredients until they are blended and the milk is scalded. Scalding does shorten the cooking time. But you must cool the liquid enough to keep the eggs from curdling when you add them.

Beat into the cooled liquid:

| 6 lightly beaten egg yolks | the rind of one grated |
| 1 teaspoon vanilla | orange |

Strain the custard. Pour into your lidded cups. Chill very well and bring out directly from your refrigerator.

Menu Ten
(serves 12)

ORANGE JUICE
SCOTCH EGGS
DONGHIA GARDEN SALAD
BLACK BREAD AND BUTTER

SCOTCH EGGS

1 pound of lean, ground	2 eggs, raw
pork	bread crumbs
6 eggs, hard boiled	

Divide the pound of ground pork into 6 portions. Shell 6 hard-boiled eggs. Take each hard-boiled egg and put a coat of the ground pork around each egg. Beat 2 raw eggs, lightly dip each Scotch egg in the raw eggs, and roll in bread crumbs. Fry in 350° deep fat until the pork is cooked. Each of the eggs will be a lovely golden brown. If you place them on a bed of green parsley, the color contrast will be perfect.

DONGHIA GARDEN SALAD
(Serves 12)

1½ *pounds red potatoes in their skins*
1½ *pounds carrots*
1 *head of celery*
1½ *tablespoons vinegar*
4 *tablespoons olive oil*
1 *teaspoon salt*
½ *teaspoon pepper*
½ *teaspoon dry mustard*
½ *cup diced lean ham*

1 *cup mushrooms*
¼ *teaspoon salt*
a squeeze of lemon
2 *grated apples*
1 *cup stiff mayonnaise*
2 *tablespoons each of chopped parsley, tarragon, and finely cut chives*

Boil 1½ pounds of potatoes in their skins until tender—no further. Boil in salted water 1½ pounds of carrots. Shred the white stalks of 1 head of celery. When the potatoes are cool to handle, peel and cut in thin slices and the carrots likewise. Put aside 1 potato and 1 carrot. Mix the potato, carrot, and celery in a bowl. In a small bowl mix 1½ tablespoons vinegar, 4 tablespoons olive oil, 1 teaspoon salt, ½ teaspoon pepper, ½ teaspoon dry mustard. Pour this over the sliced vegetables and marinate for one hour. In another bowl place ½ cup diced lean ham, 1 cup mushrooms that have previously been boiled for about five minutes; cover with ¼ teaspoon salt, a squeeze of lemon, and 2 grated apples.

Mix the contents of the 2 bowls and one cup very stiff mayonnaise. Place salad in a mound. Sprinkle liberally with chopped parsley, tarragon, and finely cut chives.

Take the potatoes and carrots that you held out—slice them on the diagonal, and decorate the salad at the base of the mound.

Menu Eleven
(serves 8)

½ RIPE PAPAYA EACH
HAM AND EGGS AFLOAT
BUCKS COUNTY SALAD
BRANDIED CARAMEL FLAN

For the ripe papaya, check out the exotic vegetable stand in your area. Every town has one store that has its eye on what fruits and vegetables are available at the delicacy section of the wholesale market. There are mangoes, persimmons, and papayas available. They are a welcome change for people who are wedded daily to their classic vitamin-C orange juice before rushing for the 8:02.

HAM AND EGGS AFLOAT

1 pound sliced baked ham	salt
8 slices of white bread, toasted-buttered-halved	1 tablespoon dry mustard salt and pepper
10 eggs	

1. Lightly grease (or spray with PAM) a 14 × 9 × 2-inch baking dish. Arrange the slices of ham against the sides of the dish. Cover the bottom of the dish with the toast slices. Use the toast slices to anchor the ham slices.
2. Separate the eggs. Place the egg whites in a large mixing bowl and place each of the egg yolks on a separate small saucer. Use 8 yolks.
3. Beat the egg whites with ½ teaspoon of salt and the mustard until stiff. Pour the stiff egg whites into the dish, creating a full sea of white caps.
4. Make eight depressions with the back of a wooden mixing spoon in the stiff egg whites. Bake uncovered about two minutes or until slightly set.
5. Slide an egg yolk into each depression. Sprinkle each with a little salt and pepper. Bake uncovered about eight

or ten minutes, or until the whites are slightly golden and the yolks are set. Serve immediately.

BUCKS COUNTY SALAD

2 cups of boiled sliced
   potatoes
2 cups of shredded peeled
   apples
2 cups of steamed string
   beans

salt
pepper
½ cup of mayonnaise
2 small heads of lettuce,
   quartered

Take equal parts of boiled sliced potatoes, shredded peeled apples, and sliced steamed string beans. When the potatoes and string beans are cold, mix with apples, salt, pepper, and mayonnaise. Place in the salad bowl, cover with a small amount of mayonnaise, decorate with cubed string beans. Take the quartered head of lettuce and surround the mixture.

CARAMEL FLAN MOLD

¾ cup sugar

CUSTARD:
2 cups of milk
2 cups of light cream
6 eggs
½ cup sugar
½ teaspoon salt

2 teaspoons vanilla extract
⅓ cup brandy
   boiling water
1 tablespoon brandy

1. Place the ¾ cup of sugar in a large, heavy skillet. Cook over medium heat, until the sugar melts and forms a light brown syrup. Keep stirring so that there are no lumps.
2. Pour the syrup into an 8-inch round and shallow baking dish. Be sure it is preheated. When you rotate it to coat the bottom and the sides, be sure you have a cooking glove or pot holder to use. Just set the pan aside.
3. Set the stove to 325°.
4. Now for the custard. In a medium saucepan, heat the

milk and cream until bubbles form around the edge of the pan.

5. Using the large mixing bowl of your electric mixer, beat the eggs slightly. Add the sugar, salt, and vanilla. Gradually stir in hot mixture and ⅓ cup brandy. Pour into the caramelized baking dish.
6. Place the baking dish in a shallow pan; pour boiling water to ½-inch level around dish.
7. Bake for forty minutes or until a knife inserted in the middle comes out clean. The custard has to cool. I let mine cool overnight. You should count on an absolute minimum of 4 hours.
8. To unmold, run a small spatula around the edge of the dish to loosen the custard. Turn it out on a flat serving platter—you can shake it but do be gentle or you will crack the custard. The caramel acts as a sauce.
9. Take the tablespoon of brandy and warm it slightly. I use a ¼ cup metal mixing cup on the low heat of the stove. Ignite it and pour it over the flan.
10. I serve the custard in odd peasant and native dishes that I have collected around the world. If you can't make the trips—a visit to an international bazaar or a department store will produce a similar catch. If you poke around flea markets and antique stores, you can find odds and ends of dishes that will offer a visual variety to your table or buffet service.

Menu Twelve
(serves 6)

CHILLED PINEAPPLE AND ORANGE JUICE
TOLLGATE SCRAMBLE
SEASONED BAKED TOMATOES
TOASTED ENGLISH MUFFINS
LIME SHERBET

TOLLGATE SCRAMBLE

8 strips of lean bacon	10 eggs
8 medium-size mushrooms	salt and pepper (season to
4 young green onions	taste)
16 ounces canned crabmeat	

Quarter the bacon strips. Pan-fry over medium heat. At the same time wash the mushrooms. Trim the root ends of the stems and slice. Cut the roots and all but 2 inches of green tips from the onions. Slice on the diagonal—but slice them very thin. Add mushroom and onion slices to the bacon. Stir and cook over medium-high heat for about 2 minutes.

Meanwhile beat the eggs in a bowl. Add the crabmeat to the skillet. Cool another 3 minutes. Pour the egg over the crabmeat mixture. Sprinkle with salt and pepper. Stir over medium heat until the eggs are set but not dry. Be sure everything is ready because this dish has to be served piping hot.

SEASONED BAKED TOMATOES

To peel tomatoes, first wash them and then you can find which one of these techniques you prefer:
1. You can stroke the skin with the dull edge of a knifeblade until the skin wrinkles and can be lifted off.
2. You can dip the tomato into boiling water for one minute and then plunge immediately into cold water and peel.
3. You can "toast" the tomato on the end of a fork over a flame until the skin is tight and shiny. Then plunge it into cold water and peel.

6 ripe, peeled tomatoes	2 teaspoons curry
1 cup tomato sauce	½ cup grated sharp cheddar
2 tablespoons red currant	cheese
jelly	dry bread crumbs

Butter a baking dish with 3 tablespoons of butter and arrange tomatoes. In a separate pot combine the tomato sauce, curry, and jelly over low heat and stir without boiling for 5 minutes. Pour the mixture over the tomatoes. Sprinkle with cheese and crumbs. Set the stove at 425° and bake for 15 minutes. Baked tomatoes should be served hot from the oven.

Menu Thirteen
(serves 6)

CHILLED PINEAPPLE AND MINT
EGG CROQUETTES
CREAMED CHIPPED BEEF
LENTIL SALAD
LEMON SHERBET

EGG CROQUETTES

2 *tablespoons butter*	7 *hard-boiled eggs*
2 *tablespoons flour*	1 *cup flour*
¾ *cup milk*	1 *egg mixed with 1 cup*
½ *teaspoon minced onion*	*milk*
1½ *teaspoons parsley,*	1 *cup cracker crumbs*
chopped, pinch of celery	*deep fat for frying*
salt and pepper to adjust	
seasoning	

Melt the 2 tablespoons of butter in a frying pan—blend in the 2 tablespoons of flour. Cook over low heat, then add ¾ cup milk, the onion, parsley, celery salt, salt and pepper. Bring to the edge of the boil (a light boil) and cool. Chop hard-boiled eggs in a mixing bowl. Pour the cooled sauce over them and mix well. Chill in the refrigerator for about 2 hours.

Take out and form into 8 croquettes—roll in the flour, dip in the 1-egg-and-1-cup-of-milk mixture, and finally roll in cracker crumbs. These croquettes can be made the day before—just bring them to room temperature before starting to cook.

Fry them in deep fat for 5 minutes at 350°—or you can pan-fry them. Just keep them about 1½-inches thick and pan-fry them in 1 inch of cooking oil. I fry them about 3 minutes on each side.

CREAMED CHIPPED BEEF

1	pound chipped beef	4	cups of milk
6	tablespoons of butter	2	tablespoons chopped
6	tablespoons of minced		chives
	onion	½	teaspoon paprika
6	tablespoons of minced	4	tablespoons dry sherry
	green pepper	4	tablespoons of capers
6	tablespoons flour		

Chipped beef is packed very solidly in pressed sheets. First you pull apart the 16 ounces of the chipped beef. Then you melt the 6 tablespoons of butter—sauté in the melted butter, 6 tablespoons of minced onion, 6 tablespoons of minced green pepper. Sprinkle all this with 6 tablespoons flour. Now take your quart of milk and, stirring constantly, add it very slowly. Then add the beef. Simmer these all together until it starts to thicken. Then take it away from the heat and add your seasoning:

2	tablespoons chopped	4	tablespoons capers
	chives	½	teaspoon paprika
4	tablespoons dry sherry		

Serve your egg croquettes topped with the creamed chipped beef.

LENTIL SALAD

1	pound lentils	1	cup chopped parsley
	water	1	cup olive (or salad) oil
1	tablespoon salt		juice of 2 large lemons
1	medium onion, quartered		salt and freshly ground
1	medium red onion, sliced		pepper
	and separated into rings		

I use processed lentils so that I don't have to soak them for 30 minutes. Either way you then cover the lentils with fresh water to 2 inches above the lentils. Add 1 tablespoon of salt and the quartered onion. Bring to a boil; cover and simmer until the lentils are tender but not soft. It takes about 25 minutes. Drain and discard the onion. Chill in the refrigerator. I do this the night before. In the morning I put the chilled lentils in a salad bowl, mix with the onion rings, parsley, olive oil, lemon juice, and season to taste with salt and pepper.

Menu Fourteen
(serves 6)

SPIRITED TOMATO JUICE
SEA FOOD QUICHE
SAUTÉED MUSHROOMS
MOUSSE DE FRUITS

SEAFOOD QUICHE

2	unbaked chilled pastry-lined 9″ pie pans		pepper, nutmeg
1	pound Swiss cheese	¼	teaspoon cayenne
4	tablespoons cooled melted butter	2	tablespoons each: flour and dry sherry
8	eggs	2	cups crabmeat
4	cups light cream	2	cups raw, cleaned shrimp
1	teaspoon each: salt,	20	tiny bay scallops

The easiest thing in the world is to use any one of the established pie-crust mixes. I have found that when I don't want to do pie crust from scratch I use Flak-O. It takes me about 5 minutes to remove the box from the shelf to lining my pie pans.

Slice the Swiss cheese tissue thin and line the bottom of the chilled pastry. You can chill pastry very effectively in your freezer. Do the pastry first—put it in the freezer and then organize the rest of your ingredients. When you are ready to start, the pastry will be chilled.

Melt the butter, remove it from the heat and let it cool.

Beat the eggs very lightly. Add the cream and all the seasonings plus the flour. Beat it until the mixture is very smooth. Add the cooled butter and the sherry and beat it again until the consistency is very smooth. Strain this over the cheese and top it with the crabmeat and shrimp and dot the top with the bay scallops. Sprinkle a delicate coat of grated Swiss cheese and paprika over the pie. Preset your oven to 350° and bake it for 40 minutes. They should be allowed to cool for about 15 minutes before you cut into them and serve.

SAUTÉED MUSHROOMS

Try to get fresh mushrooms and then you will not have to wash and peel them. Just slice them and sauté them in a frying pan. My rule is that for every cup of mushrooms I use 2 tablespoons of butter and 1 clove of crushed garlic. Sprinkle with lemon juice and a little salt and pepper. I figure a cup and a half of mushrooms per person.

MOUSSE DE FRUITS

This is a dish that I make first thing in the morning of the brunch day. It is incredibly simple but marvelously effective.

Take 1 pound of mixed fruits in season—I always add fresh pineapple and bananas whenever available. Peel the assorted fruits and remove any stems. Cut bananas for a split and then cut in half. Any pineapple should be thinly sliced but not chopped or diced. Apricots, peaches, plums should be halved—apples and pears quartered—grapes separated. Set the fruit attractively in a serving dish and place in the refrigerator for at least 3 hours before serving.

Separate 8 eggs. Put the 8 yolks in your blender—add 1 cup of kirsch and 1 cup of sugar. Let it whip up to a lovely froth and pour it over the fruit. Beat the egg whites and cover the bowl with the meringue. Serve in small bowls accompanied by iced tea.

EIGHT: The Country Weekend

I was once the weekend guest of a deliciously decadent French countess whose royal lineage may have been dubious but whose money was impeccable. Her chateau, located on the Lac Du Bourget, was a triumph of sinful pleasures: stained glass windows, brocaded curtains, and inlaid tables provided a feast for the eyes; a 24-hour staff gratified our every whim; horses stood ready for command; swans glided near the boathouse, and Gregorian chants wafted on the breeze from the twelfth-century monastery nearby. For companionship, there were beautiful people with whom one could drowse in the sun, float on the lake waters, row in tandem, swim, or wash one another's backs.

Breakfast was served in the dining room at nine. For those who preferred a more *petit* déjeuner, coffee, bread, fruit, and cheese were available at eleven. Luncheon, taken on the terrace overlooking the formal gardens, was an orgy of flowers and gourmet delicacies. Two round tables, covered with linen cloths, were shaded by red umbrellas which cast a pink reflection on the white porcelain service. Calves liver, quenelles of pike, lamb chops, poached salmon with aspic were followed by salad, bread, cheese, and wine. Dinner at nine included champagne cocktails, individual quiches for appetizers, trout, lamb, and fresh raspberries in cream for dessert. After dinner, brandy, liqueurs, and coffee were served in the living room. Believe me, a weekend at my farm is nothing like that.

At Tollgate Farm, my Bucks County retreat, there is no organization beyond what time dinner is served, no staff, no social activity, no dress code, and no truly formal gardens.

My feeling is, why have a place in the country if you are going to bring the values of the city along with you? In the city we are all programmed from morning until night with business and social activity. Cocktail parties, duty parties, and testimonials are the norm for people who lead interesting, busy lives. Before you know it, your calendar is booked solid, and you are completely locked in. So a weekend at my house is an escape to clean air, informality, and convivial guests.

It is amusing, though, how people pay lip service to the notion that there is something good and wholesome about country life. Mother Nature, they avow, is the goddess to whom they owe allegiance, because our society espouses the goodness of ecology, nutrition, nature, and health foods. (It is chic to think that way now, just as it was terribly smart during the 'twenties to reject nature. The prevailing philosophy then was that one should live in the cellar.) So, you mention the country and everyone says, "I love the country." But *take* them to the country, and you will be hard put to remove the city from their psyches. You can dress them in country clothes, you can play country music for them, and all they really want to know is "What time are cocktails?" And they want the cocktails inside, the closer to the bar, the better.

At a country luncheon in England given by Angus McGill, a wonderfully funny writer on the *Evening Standard* in London, his guests arrived and immediately plunged into the alcohol (double martinis in enormous glasses). When lunch was served, I had the feeling I was attending one of the few luncheons in the world where both the food and the guests were completely boiled.

Preparing a Guest List

As far as I am concerned, creative people who are doing interesting things make the best country guests. Theater folk, and motion-picture people are fascinating because just their talk about their daily activities is a constant source of wonder to others. As I begin to plan my guest list, the common denominator I am looking for is some degree of mutual interest, even if it is apparent to no one but me. Many of my friends relate to each other quite differently from the way one might suppose, because they are much the opposite of their public image. The most difficult guests—and I don't ask them back—are people who have made their own lives too elegant. Also, I don't want guests who come on like reigning stars or celebrities. I find that the best way to deal with prominent people is to entertain them with other very prominent people. That way nobody is a celebrity. It's pretty hard for them to name-drop when everyone knows all these people as friends and neighbors.

It can be dangerous to entertain a plethora of people whom you don't know intimately, particularly people's wives, lovers, and friends. One or two outsiders may be acceptable, but if there are too many of them, it is as if you are entertaining in a waiting room. Your energy is taken up with seeing that they are comfortable, or trying to determine whether they are going to turn out to be friends. Sometimes a weekend can become a disaster even if you think you know someone well. I invited an acquaintance whom I had known for a long time, but whom I had never asked before. He arrived at Tollgate with all the trappings—a limousine and chauffeur. As his driver finished unloading his Vuitton luggage, I asked whether he was planning to leave for Europe on Sunday. "Will you have one of your staff take my luggage to my room?" he asked. I simply replied that he was looking at the staff, and that all the clothing he really required for the weekend would be a couple of clean shirts and a pair of trousers. The local movie house, I explained, aptly called the Barn Cinema, which specializes in oversaturated popcorn, was the only external activity of which he could possibly partake. When he asked what accommodations I had prepared for "his man," I suggested the Holiday Inn on Route 202. I must admit there was a certain edge to my voice, but it also contained humor. What amazed me was that I had never been aware of this man's pretensions before. I offered him a perfectly lovely eighteenth-century bedroom; he went upstairs, and it was no more than ten minutes later when he came down and said, "Robert L., you will forgive me, but I cannot stay, I can't stand the bloody noise." To me the country has always been a a place of glorious silence, and I couldn't understand what he was talking about. "Everything creaks," he announced, "and the birds are relentless." Of course, he left. The irony of it all is that he has spent endless time at parties telling everyone what an absolutely sensational place the farm is. No doubt he had envisioned Windsor Castle with the guests numbering the crowned heads of Europe.

Favorite Guests

Vivien Leigh really loved to garden. She was my first guest at the farm. It was June, the time of year when the wild strawberries were in season, and Vivien pointed them out to me, because I wouldn't know a wild strawberry from a tame one. I remember leaving her alone in the garden and returning to the house. After awhile, I looked out to see what had become of her. There was Vivien, on her hands and knees, looking as if she might have lost her contact lenses. When she finally returned to the house, she proudly presented me with a little bowl of *fraises du bois,* told me the history of this type of berry, and how it came to be called by its name. We sat there in my bare rooms, just the two of us, eating these tiny, delicious little berries.

The Earl of Litchfield is a delightful man, but his royal background gives him a rather different perspective from the rest of us. Patrick tells you that he is terribly interested in gardening, but gardening to him is something quite apart from kneeling on the ground to weed or divide some bulbs. Gardening, as far as he is concerned, implies a morning conference with the gardeners on his estate, and getting a report on the condition of the azaleas, or discussing opening his grounds for a flower show. The late David Webb, the jewelry designer, adored gardening as well, but could spend the entire afternoon without saying a word, deriving enormous satisfaction from simply puttering and absorbing the sun. Kenny J. Lane professes a great appreciation of flowers, but I suspect that he would be wearied by the first weed.

When Rex Reed feels comfortable in a situation, he absolutely loves to be "on." He is one of the great raconteurs of all time, and if you've never seen his imitation of Ruth Gordon, you have never appreciated either of them fully. The walk, the talk, the mannerisms, can keep a house party enthralled for hours. His description of his experience during the filming of *Myra Breck-*

inridge is the howl of the century. Rex cooks brilliantly, and his specialties are country dishes. He makes superlative gravy and southern biscuits, and that may be his great contribution to mankind. I love having him as a guest because he is so contrapuntal. He goes against the beat of the farm; he sleeps later than most people, and absolutely hates the sun.

I have a deep affection and admiration for Bill Blass, and yet, we are most successful when we deal with each other privately. He, publicly, affects the image of a rather quizzical, slightly snobbish person when in reality he is a very kind, warm, generous human being. Bill is someone who has an active interest in many things. We share a mutuality of interests—professionally, personally, and psychologically. Never have I had an evening when I have been bored by Bill Blass.

Celeste Holm and her husband Wesley Addy are wonderful guests because of her great vitality and his endless interest. He is an actor, a distinguished white-haired man whom one would probably remember best from the film *Network*. His forte is that he is a superb listener, and provides excellent balance when there are too many prominent egos around.

Marcia Rose, the NBC hostess and her husband, Jerry Shestack, the well-known lawyer, are favorites too. She is like a little girl in the kitchen, watching everything and wanting to learn how to do all the things she sees me do. Angelo Donghia is also a joy in the kitchen, and is very generous about cooking both for the freezer as well as for the guests. Joyce and David Susskind, and Vidal and Beverly Sassoon are so easy and comfortable to be with. The Susskinds, along with Wayland Flowers and Jack Hoffsis, are among my most witty and entertaining guests. Anne Baxter and Leonard Bernstein are superb intellects and can keep a group endlessly intrigued. June Weir, Julia Meade, and Donald Brooks are truly appreciative of my efforts as a host, while Marlene Dietrich and Tom Crater never let me do anything for them. They are compulsive cleaners and more than earn their keep.

Battle Plan

A typical weekend at Tollgate involves six to ten guests, which means that all five bedrooms will be occupied. Preparations are made by a wonderful couple who live on the farm, and when I arrive the house is spotless. They do not function in the house during the weekend, but do assist in providing transportation from the bus and the train depots.

Generally, dyed-in-the-wool New Yorkers become tense the moment they cross the Hudson River. It has something to do with their fear of the unknown, plus the fact that they lead very predictable (though sometimes hectic) lives which are conducted within a few miles of real estate. Once you have convinced one of these big-city stalwarts to leave his surroundings, be prepared for some peculiar behavior. Tucked into his fashionable, overloaded luggage, and readily available, is a well-worn timetable which, by the time he has arrived, he has memorized in its entirety—at least the part concerning return schedules. (If you make the mistake of inviting two or more such people, they will spend the entire weekend quizzing each other on New York–bound schedules.

Certain insights and preparations are essential if your guests are to be comfortable and enjoy their visit. As a rule, assume that all your guests will arrive hungry. The chances are they were too excited to eat an adequate breakfast and couldn't agree on which lousy diner to stop at for lunch. The moment they arrive, offer them something substantial to eat. Nothing is more distressing to a traveler than to arrive hungry at three in the afternoon and discover that dinner is scheduled for eight. I always announce that everyone is free to raid the refrigerator or the freezer; if you run a more formal establishment, make sure that you have set out snack food and fruit for the starving. Spare your guests the anguish of spending the afternoon concerning themselves with the delicacy of asking for something to eat.

For God's sake, make certain the rooms you select for your friends are spacious, adequately prepared, and private. There is nothing more deflating to a weary voyager than to discover, on being taken to his room, that he is sharing a closet with an over-dressed debutante who is now away at college. I once occupied someone's "spare" room and spent the better part of an hour trying to fit my belongings and luggage into a closet filled with spare parts from my host's Corvette. Clear out half the bedroom closet, if not the whole thing, and *make sure* there are sufficient hangers available. Also clear some dresser drawers, as well as the top of the dresser, and provide a portable tray for your guests' toilet articles. Not everyone travels with a complete toilet kit, and it can be an exercise in both frustration and balance for a person to carry all those personal items from the bedroom to the bathroom, particularly if he is also trying to carry a towel and a change of clothes.

I have a problem about sleeping in overheated rooms, and I have spent many a sleepless night in other people's homes trying to keep from being asphyxiated. If the bedrooms in your home have individual heating or air-conditioning controls, be sure that you make your guests aware of their location. Also, show them where the lights are, or leave a light in the hallway so they may find their way to the bathroom if necessary. (Many people experience some degree of "discomfort" when they use other people's bathrooms. One person I know has a radio connected to the bathroom light socket. As soon as the light is turned on, music is heard. "They can then grunt and flush with impunity," observed the considerate host.) Your guests should be afforded a high degree of privacy and be made to feel welcome by all family members. There is nothing more embarrassing to a visitor than to discover that he is displacing someone from his bedroom. The way to handle this situation is to have the "exiled" family member announce the fact before it is discovered, and in such a manner that the guest will not feel uncomfortable about it. ("The short change in location will be a welcome relief from the usual household routine.") Also, have him take the belongings he will need, so that he does not constantly have to return to his room for articles of clothing. If the visitor is sleeping in the den, which is the usual site for TV viewing, remove the set prior to his arrival so that he doesn't have to fight off a dozen Johnny Carson fans in order to get some sleep.

Special Touches

What I do for my guests is make it easy for them to be on their own. Each of the bedrooms has a small hotplate and a coffee maker. Also included is a little can of coffee, sugar, Sweet and Low, Cremora, and some teabags. While it is not a major breakfast, for the person who can't face the world without a cup of coffee, it's a godsend.

Another little touch which charms my friends is a convenience basket at bedside containing some things that they may have forgotten, or have need of: black thread, white thread, needle, comb, gum, Di-Gel, soft and hard candy. There is nothing so desperate to anybody's life as not being able to find one's comb. Few coiffures, either male or female, are presentable on awakening, and it can destroy an ego that took long years in the making, to go downstairs looking unkempt. My convenience basket also includes an extra toothbrush and a little sample of toothpaste.

The basket idea can be extended to contain little gifts that suit individual personalities. Vivien Leigh was terribly interested in gardening and cooking, so I found a cookbook that had been written by Marie-Elena Booner in 1810. The book contained recipes the author had found in her travels on tour. An early copy of *Theatre Arts* magazine, circa 1922, with a superb picture of Lynn Fontanne absolutely delighted Vivien.

Some people are "cologne freaks." I go to Caswell-Massey and buy some inexpensive, but remote, cologne and place it in the basket with a little note saying something such as: "Let me know if you like this." Anything that establishes the fact that people are special inevitably charms them. Flowers, of course, are always lovely, but you never know when someone may be allergic, or when they may have an unpleasant association. It is quite possible that you have placed a bouquet of daisies in the room of the very person whose mother was killed clutching a bouquet of same. The important thing is to have a sense of the appropriateness of what you are doing.

Other provisions for my guests' arrival include buying food in huge quantities, preferably by the case. Since I have large freezers, I can do this with meat as well. You can never go wrong with "classic" foods. My freezer never contains less than two or three standing rib roasts, legs of lamb, pot roasts, chuck, ground sirloin, and thick T-bone steaks. When I buy steaks, I get them cut in a form that can be served individually. I know, of course, that no one is going to finish one of these large cuts unless he is a glutton. So, after dinner, I put the name of the guest on a marker, and wrap the leftover meat and bone and place it in the refrigerator. The quests know there is always something to nibble if they get hungry later in the evening.

I always bake before my guests arrive, too, at least a cake, a pie, and some cookies. These are not meant as a dessert, because for that course I am more apt to do a soufflé or custard, but it is lovely to have a treat offering, such as a piece of cake, when someone is in the mood. On hand as well is ice cream—usually including some exotic flavors such as pumpkin, pralines and cream, coconut or red poppy, which is Bill Blass's favorite. I keep a list tacked up on the freezer so that everyone will know that they are stored. People are always nostalgic about the food of their childhood, and so I make sure that popsicles, fudgicles, and penny candy are stocked as well.

A variety of teas and coffees are provided too—it is so easy to do now that General Foods has made them so popular. Guests like the experience of investigating the different blends they might not ordinarily order when they are out.

Meals

Since I am not Jenny Grossinger and am not running an inn, and I want my weekends to be a vacation for me as well, I don't prepare breakfast for my guests. Of course, if somebody desperately can't cope with getting breakfast for himself, I will. I experienced it only once where someone said, "I have always remembered an omelet that you made for me. Would you fry me an omelet?" So, of course, I did.

Early morning is the best time of day for me. I arise very early

— 142 —

and prefer not to see anybody at that time. It makes me extraordinarily happy to go downstairs, when the house is quiet, and have a cup of tea and read. That is the time when I finish reading novels, read articles in magazines that I have marked for myself, and thoroughly enjoy being alone.

Of course, all my guests have been apprised of the location of the fixings for breakfast. Bacon, sausage, English muffins, lots of lovely jams and preserves, country butter are lardered for the weekend. There is something about country air that makes everyone wake up ravenous, no matter what their city breakfast habits might be. One thing I try to make clear to my guests is the difference between an omelet pan and a frying pan. There is nothing that infuriates me more than having someone fry his eggs in the omelet pan and then dump the pan in the kitchen sink. What makes my omelet a specialty is all that lovely milk grease that has accumulated over the years. And I don't want it washed away in a moment of ignorance.

Lunch is not a formal meal, either, but I do expect everyone to come to dinner. If, for some reason, my guests can't make dinner, I'd like to know it in advance. I don't want to bake thirty popovers when eight will suffice. Besides, I would like to spend some time with my guests.

Food, Glorious Food

Probably my greatest culinary invention, Tollgate Meatballs, was created during one of my country weekends. In retrospect, the weekend also stands out as being one that might be properly entitled, "A Host's Nightmare." One evening, two cars drove up to my house, and a group of people got out, including the new, second wife of an old, dear friend. My problem was that I had invited the group for the following weekend, but somehow we got our signals crossed. I welcomed them with a dazed stare, and made the split-second decision not to reveal the mistake, because I did not want this young girl's first social venture with her husband's friends to turn into a disaster. So, with one part of me giggling, wondering what I was going to do, I asked them into the house and served some drinks. I silently thanked God for such modern inventions as the microwave oven and the freezer. Taking mental inventory of my larder, which uncharacteristically I had permitted to become depleted, I came up with a meatloaf mixture, the crock of sauerkraut I had received as a gift from some of my Polish neighbors, a plentiful supply of apples and sour cream. The sour cream was on hand for the little omelet I had planned to make with caviar for my solitary dinner on Sunday evening.

Hurriedly, I made the meatballs and then proceeded to layer the available ingredients. I sauteed the meatballs first and then did a layer of sauerkraut, a layer of apples, and then a layer of meatballs, repeating the process several times until my supply ran out. Of course, it was purest invention, but I smiled bravely. The concoction was then placed on the stove, and I took more orders for drinks from my unexpected guests. During the next hour I conducted my visitors through the house, feeling rather like a tour guide at the Vatican (I have done it so frequently). All this time the aroma of the sauerkraut and apples began to permeate the place; the longer it cooked, the more wonderful and enticing it became. By the time we sat down, my guests' appetites had peaked. I added the sour cream at the last moment and served the dish in individual bowls with my homemade black bread. Of all the dishes I have ever cooked, I never remember evoking a stronger or more favorable reaction. Tollgate Meatballs, born in a moment of desperation, have continued to delight my guests ever since.

Social Activities

Since I believe that a country weekend should be a free, unstructured affair, my contribution to my guests is to explain what is available at the house, as well as to describe the highlights of the local area. For those who want a well-organized weekend, there are hosts who specialize in planned events. Phyllis Cerf Wagner, for instance, is known to her friends as "The General," because when she entertains she has everything plotted down to the last detail. Molly Parnis, the famous Seventh Avenue designer and hostess, does a similar kind of social programming.

Many of my weekenders haven't the vaguest idea that my farm in Bucks County is only a few miles from the great historic site where Washington crossed the Delaware; also, that there is a whole world of antique shops and an extraordinary museum. What I do not do is create culture trips or guilt responses by insisting my guests visit specific locations. But I do think it is a nice thing to make known that they are in a resort area where various things are accessible. I also have published material on the subject that they can look at.

Our town newspapers, the *Doylestown Intelligencer* and the *Bucks County Gazette*, report on what's playing at the movies and the playhouse, and what's happening at the local churches. There is even a discotheque for people who like that sort of thing. I don't go myself, but, of course, I don't like Regine's either. For those who prefer activity in a more naturalistic setting, there are fishing rods, garden tools, and loads of chores to do in the kitchen.

Every weekend I offer to include many of my guests in the cooking procedure. There is added incentive, of course, because it is generally understood that whoever cooks the meal does not do the dishes. Other people do the dishes.

Two of the chores that I pass on to others is setting the table and cutting flowers. I'd rather cook. Since I am such a "klutz" when it comes to flowers, I am really fortunate in having lots of friends who have a magical facility in this area. I let them cut flowers to their heart's content. Since Chris Zaima loves and appreciates gardens very much, he is one of my chief floral arrangers.

The most treasured part of the weekend for me is sitting with friends in front of the fireplace. My house is full of lovely antiques and I use everything. I don't want to live in a museum, and I don't want to deny either my guests or myself the pleasure of eating off very good eighteenth-century Delft pieces. My point is, why have these things if you aren't going to use them?

Guests have suggested that I get someone to take a lovely picture of the farm and have it reproduced as a postcard. It is a good idea, and sometime I must get around to it, because my companions are always asking for them. I do keep plenty of postcards around with pictures of other Bucks County landmarks, however, as well as stamps. There is also a basket that is marked "outgoing mail," because people tend to write postcards and not mail them.

Rainy Weekends

The supreme test of your ability to function as a host will occur when your best-laid weekend plans are dampened by an uninvited and unwelcome guest called rain. Considering that everyone is primed for a holiday in the sun, without some carefully planned alternatives your party can turn into an exercise in boredom, and result in many an early or unscheduled departure. Over the years, I have catalogued a series of events which I call my Rainy Day Emergency Kit. Some of the activities have turned out to be so much fun that I have been tempted to use them during nonrainy days.

The Betty Crocker Bread Bake-Off

Essentially, this is a bread-baking contest, but it is best conducted after your guests have consumed several mellowing drinks. Each guest draws one bread recipe from my files, at random, and is provided only with the ingredients specified on the card. Absolutely no help or assistance is offered concerning the manipulation of the materials. The resulting products can range from surprising, marvelous, to disgusting, disastrous. All participants are permitted to take their handiwork home as souvenirs. The booby prize will be awarded to the least inspired effort: the chore of cleaning up. (Beverly and Vidal Sassoon baked bread one afternoon. Her loaves looked more attractive, but his tasted better. I think it was Vidal's skill in sculpting hair that had something to do with his kneading technique.)

Paint Your Partner's Portrait

The group is divided into teams of twos, each team being provided with a set of watercolors, brushes, and a pad and paper. To make the event a bit more competitive, each participant contributes a few dollars to the winner's kitty. Each team submits an original watercolor of the other person, and the results are judged as team efforts. Usually, guests with real artistic talents serve as judges. The works are prominently displayed until it is time to leave; then they are wrapped carefully and distributed as memoirs of the weekend.

For Those Who Prefer Not to Move

A recording of a play may be just right for the mood of the afternoon. If you are fortunate in having video equipment, a taped cassette of a drama can be shown right on your television screen. Movies can be viewed as well if you have a projector, and you have had the foresight to prepare for just such a contingency. (I have one friend who is prominent in the television industry. His "rainy-day kit" consists of video cassettes containing some of the great cinema classics. He invites his guests to vote for the movie they wish to see.) If you have a piano, and are lucky enough to have a pianist among your guests, there is nothing more delightful than injecting music into a soggy afternoon. Old sheet music can lure everyone into singing and create a climate of great fun as well as nostalgia.

Scheherazade

Edward Molyneux, the famous British designer, invited me to a summer weekend party at his home in Surrey, England. Rather than the usual English mist, we were greeted with unexpected rainfall, which created heavier than normal problems for the host. We all were involved in the fashion world and were quite familiar with each other professionally, but the English do not establish personal relationships as quickly as Americans. Their idea of a rapid-growing friendship is a liaison of at least a year and a half.

After two days, I remember being taken aside by Edward and asked if I could help in some way to save the party from dying. By that time there were at least a dozen cases of accumulated bursitis, arthritis, and frost bite, since it was unpleasantly cold and none of us had brought the kind of proper clothes for an Arctic evening. I announced to the assembled group that we were going to play *Scheherazade*, which meant that we would all have to tell a story. I began with a rendition of an upper-class porno film, using veiled images of people in the fashion world. I talked about the excessive heterosexuality of a designer, who somehow had become defensive about his sexual proclivities. (In the fashion world, where being gay is not unexpected, one is more apt to be defensive about being heterosexual.) I regaled them with the sado-masochistic inclinations of another designer, and filled them in on an affair of a top model who disappeared into an elevator with Clark Gable. (She was not seen until three days later when she reappeared exhausted, but with a happy smile and clear skin.) I wove a tale of very much the same genre as a cheap but stimulating paperback, and the party came alive. The weekend was saved.

Clothes

Most of my guests know that they don't have to bring a lot of clothes with them. For a long time I didn't dress at all, though I have had guests who have changed on the hour. I was interviewed by a reporter for the *Adelaide Times* on the occasion of presenting a fashion show in all the major cities in Australia. Adelaide itself is like something in a time capsule, a completely Victorian town. It is so far down under that my dropping in had about the same impact as a visit from Oscar Wilde to Buffalo in the 1890s. The reporter, a stately, tweedily attired woman in her sixties, announced that she was the gardening editor. If you remember the early pictures of Queen Mary with turban, cane, and the regal posture of a reigning monarch, you have some idea of how she looked. Her earth-shattering question to me was, "Mr. Green, what type of wardrobe do you prefer when working in the garden?" With my penchant for headline making, I flippantly announced that I wore "dead clothes." "Clothes from dead people?" she asked in amazement. "No, my own," I replied. Then I explained that by "dead clothes," I meant attire that was no longer fashionable for a man in the fashion industry, even though the garments might be in excellent condition. "It seems a shame to throw out a pair of perfectly good but too-wide gray flannel slacks, or let them get eaten by moths, if you can still get some use out of them," I told her. The reporter's face had the look of "Oh, dear," so I asked her, "What does a gentleman wear in the garden in Adelaide?" "A gentleman in Adelaide wears appropriate shoes, socks, trousers, waistcoat, jacket, collar, tie, and, I might add, proper gloves," she announced firmly.

Holidays

Holidays on the farm, especially Thanksgiving, Christmas, and the Fourth of July, seem even more meaningful to me than they do in the city. Thanksgiving and Christmas at my country place are pure Dickens, with a roaring fire in the grate, surrounded by a family of friends that I have created over the years. My family is the authentic twentieth-century family, a group that has chosen each other because we share a true communion.

No doubt my bountiful celebrations stem from unfulfilled childhood fantasies, when visions of sugarplums had to sustain me rather than the reality. Of course, many of my friends have difficulty imagining that I was a child and are convinced that I, like the legendary Athena, came full size from the head of Zeus. Be assured that I, as a child, bumped from the mainstream of life, vowed that one day it would all be the way I had dreamed it. Having an eighteenth-century house has provided the total escape from unhappy memory.

Thanksgiving

Thanksgiving is a time of extraordinary, bountiful harvest. I like to explore old cookbooks and discover how the holiday was spent in the days when it first originated. One of my greatest vegetable finds was creamed, boiled radish. Let me tell you it is a taste sensation that can only be dreamed about. While others may prefer the turkey, I am devoted to vegetables that are not a cliché: zucchini strips with bacon, broccoli mold, sweet-potato

—149—

pudding with dates, eggplant, and oysters. Although I always have a turkey for the traditional folk, I also like to stuff a goose with prunes and apricots. If you've never tried goose, you really owe it to yourself to partake of one. Of course, it doesn't lend itself to sandwiches for a midnight snack the way turkey does, but it is exactly right for a holiday palate that has become jaded.

Stuffing for the turkey is generally the sausage and chestnut variety, but I prefer to make it separately instead of inserting it in the cavity of the turkey. For dessert, my favorites are pies: apple-raisin, pumpkin, and coconut pear. The pears have been soaked in brandy for twenty-four hours and are steeped heavily enough so that you can fall comfortably asleep in front of the fire after dinner. (See the next chapter for full dynamics of "The Fast Feast.")

Christmas

When I was ten, I lived in Boston with a middle-class family in an apartment house. The Donovans, a family who had befriended me, lived in their own house across the street. To this day, I remember them with glowing love because they took me into their lives.

It was the first opportunity I had had to observe a family with a father at firsthand. When he came home from work, beautifully dressed, his three boys ran up to him and kissed him with a lot of warmth and hugging. This was in sharp contrast to all the stern fathers of the Victorian novels and movies I was familiar with. This was a real father, alive with his children, and they were always touching. It was because of my hunger to be touched that this made such a profound impression. The Donovans also seemed to have special relationships with their priest and with a member of their family who was a cardinal. I was furious that I didn't have a priest in my life, and I think one of the funniest conversations I ever had with my mother on the phone related to this: "Why don't you marry a priest so we can have one also," I begged. Celibacy was something I thought you did if you were a good salesman.

The Donovans became very important to me, and little things have become part of my life as a result of knowing them. At Christmas they had a beautiful old-fashioned tree which they had cut down and carried home. They all shared in decorating it on Christmas Eve and Mrs. Donovan had the sensitivity to know that I wanted desperately to be invited. I never would have allowed myself to ask, but when she finally invited me, it was heaven. I quietly observed them stringing popcorn and cranberries, and to this day I do my own old-fashioned Xmas tree that way.

When the time came for opening gifts, Mrs. Donovan's face clouded over. Of course, nobody had remembered to buy me a Christmas present. I didn't expect one; I wanted one, but I didn't expect one. I remember her taking a little merchant-seaman knitted cap and giving it to me. It taught me a lesson that I draw upon every Christmas: I always have something in the house in the event that someone drops in unexpectedly. It doesn't have to be expensive, a paperweight from Azuma, or a fan will do. I keep the gift all wrapped up in a drawer for that person who never thought he would be receiving a present.

I remembered the Donovans one night as I was riding in a limousine to midnight Mass in Paris. Theirs was a homemade Christmas built on genuine family love. The Christmas I was going to celebrate in the great cathedral would be made up of strangers. I think that distinction is what I keep in mind in my Christmas celebrations, the feeling that ours is not just a party of the moment, but a renewal that goes on and on. It is a recognition that no matter how bad civilization has become, or how desperate all broken promises are, somehow we are given Christmas again and again.

Now I always have two trees, the large one done with ornaments sent by friends from all over the world, and the small one trimmed in a way that would have delighted the heart of Tiny Tim, or possibly even Scrooge. Candy of every variety is clustered on each bough: silver drops, popcorn, English toffee, chocolate, peppermint canes. All are suspended from the tree. At the base are the cookies that I have been preparing for weeks.

For Christmas dinner there is duck with a rich sauce made of cranberries, horseradish, and lemon juice—just tart enough to complement the sweet dark flesh of the fowl. Roast beef with madeira sauce is the other main dish. Because there are so many things available to eat, I like to keep the vegetables simple: turnips, white potatoes, and peas uncluttered by sauces are a perfect complement to the richness of the feast.

Mother's Day

My mother, who is now an octogenarian, lives in Florida— Miami Beach to be exact, so I don't see her too often. Our only family ritual occurs in May when the dear lady makes her annual pilgrimage up north for Mother's Day. We celebrate the occasion by holding a weekend reunion at the farm. Although I consider Mother's Day exclusively a commercial stroke of genius, my mother glories in all the saccharine emotion she can squeeze out of the day. What does make it rather charming is that it is the time of year when the azaleas, tulips, and daffodils are in full regalia. Mother would expect nothing less, having an imperiousness not seen since the last days of Queen Victoria— and that certainly makes mine pale by comparison.

Her indomitable manner is, perhaps, best illustrated by a telephone call I received one day when I was on a crucial conference call with Hugh Hefner in one city and Richard Avedon in another. I had told my secretary I was not to be disturbed unless it was a matter of life and death. In the middle of my conversation with these two titans of the world of glamour, my secretary poked her head around the door and announced, "It's your mother." My first reaction was, "Oh, my God, it's happened." So I had to say to both gentlemen, "Forgive me, but I must put you on hold. It's a very serious matter." Needless to say, Mr. Hefner was not amused. I pressed the other button to hear my mother ask, "How do you wash emeralds?" I was dumbfounded. "I told my secretary not to interrupt me unless it was a matter of life and death," I screamed. "To me," Mother calmly replied, "my emeralds *are* a matter of life and death."

When I was a young man, I went to a Broadway opening with my mother and stepfather. In the lobby we ran into my real father. He and I had agreed that if ever I bumped into him when he was with a date, I was not to call him "Dad." Those were the days when divorce was an embarrassment. Besides, I was born when he was only eighteen, and his ego made it difficult for him to explain to people that he had a fifteen-year-old son, when he was so young-looking himself. He acknowledged me with marvelous cool and I referred to him as, "sir." My father's date turned to admire my mother's dress, and my mother explained that it was a Valentina. The girl then introduced herself and her date, my father, Charles Lamont to my mother. My mother smiled sweetly and announced, "Oh, we've met. It was a long time ago, at a wedding."

My mother lives in a cooperative apartment house called Mimosa, strategically situated between the Fountainebleau and Doral Hotels. Within this exclusive enclave live many mothers of famous people. The three posh lobbies constitute their microcosm, and she and her lady friends sit around congratulating themselves on the accomplishments of their children. My mother is always vying with a lady named Etta—who just happens to be the mother of Don Rickles (whom she refers to as Donald). There is no question that "Donald" has a far bigger name than mine, but my mother absolutely refuses to recognize the fact.

One morning she opened the Miami *Herald* and there, on the front page, was a story in which I was mentioned as having criticized President Ford's wardrobe. I had described him as dressed in "dapper department store." Armed with her newspaper, mother sat steadfastly in the lobby for two and a half hours never wearying, until Etta finally made her appearance. "Etta," she said, waving the newspaper in her face, "We all know how Donald earns his living in Las Vegas insulting people. But you know the kind of people who go to Las Vegas. What you have to understand, Etta, is that when my son insults people, he insults the President of the United States." (Mother's request for next year's Mother's Day gift: "More clippings!")

The Fourth of July

What better day for a picnic than the Fourth of July? It is probably one of the best-observed American traditions, and the only one on which we as a population would be in total agreement. Since the perfect picnic setting for me is an area that is semiwooded with water nearby, my pond represents an ideal locale. One must know one's guests' tastes intimately before choosing to go ahead with this type of meal. Even when you can produce an event that is smoothly run, there are some people who are not thrilled by picnics. Sometimes my neighbor, Phil Bloom, and I host a joint affair when we feel that our guests are compatible. As often as not, however, our "compatibility quotient" misses the mark. On one such occasion James Thurber was asked by a classic Connecticut lady, "Mr. Thurber, I don't quite understand why you draw women so unattractively. What sort of men would be interested in those women?" Mr. Thurber turned and without missing a beat retorted, "Why *Thurber* men, of course." Another time, a rather insipid lady turned as she heard S. J. Perelman drop a Latin phrase. "I'm curious, Mr. Perelman, do you speak Latin?" Mr. Perelman turned his lean, marvelous face to the woman, stared directly into her eyes and replied, "Yes, madam, but only to the servants."

A picnic can be done in a variety of ways depending upon your group. You can treat the occasion as though it was an affair where Diamond Jim Brady was wooing Lillian Russell and behave accordingly: a cornucopia of cold lobster in mayonnaise, a cold bird such as duck, quail or pheasant; cold veal and pâté and peaches stuffed with ham mousse. Or, you can have a classic American picnic of fried chicken and wonderful salads or cold cuts and barbeque. But whatever you choose, there are ways to improve the style and quality of the occasion with imagination.

Instead of the usual fare, I have served a nice cold gazpacho from a punch bowl, with a platter of chopped vegetables and croutons nearby. This ideal summer treat also doubles as a refreshing cocktail for the teetotallers, or for those who prefer to drink wine later on. Cold chicken tarragon, wine, bread, fruit,

Opposite: Josephine Premice's tablesetting for Robert L. Green dinner. (*Andres Lander*)

Right: Tablesetting at Andy Warhol's "Factory" prior to luncheon for Robert L. Green. (*Andres Lander*)

Below: Thanksgiving dessert buffet at Tollgate Farm. (*Andres Lander*)

Opposite: Robert L. Green preparing meat-loaf in his country kitchen. (*Andres Lander*)

Right: Luncheon setting on screened porch at Tollgate Farm. (*House Beautiful*)

Left: Baskets of breads waiting to be set out for buffet lunch. (*Bill Bernardo*)

Below: Thanksgiving buffet at Tollgate Farm. (*Andres Lander*)

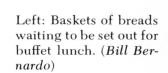

Decorated mousses and molds for party buffet. (*Horst*)

Opposite: Celeste Holm and husband Wesley Addy caught in a relaxed moment at Tollgate Farm. (*Andres Lander*)

One of the farm carts filled with fresh fruit for guests' nibbling pleasure. (*Bill Bernardo*)

Bill Blass, Steven Kaufmann, and Julia Meade at Sunday luncheon at Tollgate.

Below left: Julie Newmar came to lunch in her original "Daisy Mae" costume. (*Marji Kunz*). Right: Prince Egon von Furstenberg and Robert L. enjoying cocktails with other guests on the lawn at Tollgate. (*Marji Kunz*)

Above· Urbane David Susskind
engaging in some good country
talk.

Robert L. with his mother Eva L.
(*Marji Kunz*)

Left: A relaxed Ralph Lauren visiting me in the country. (*Andres Lander*)

Below: Angelo Donghia explaining his design plans for an eighteenth-century Chinese pavillion at Tollgate. (*Bill Bernardo*)

Bobby Short entertains picnic guests in the impromptu stage in the barn at Tollgate Farm. (*Andres Lander*)

David R. Taylor, Romney Tree and Robert L. Green at Big Sur, California. (*Brad Fuller*)

My own trinity: Cathleen Nesbitt, Noel Coward, and Lynn Fontanne. (*Arnold Weissberger*)

Dirk Bogarde and "best friend" relaxing on the lawn. (**Tom Murray**)

Above: Dear friend Vivien Leigh at Tickeridge Mill, her sixteenth-century house in Sussex. (*Arnold Weissberger*)

Left: Favorite friends Tom Tryon and Joan Fontaine. (*Arnold Weissberger*)

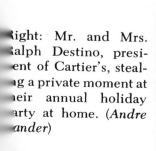

Right: Mr. and Mrs. Ralph Destino, president of Cartier's, stealing a private moment at their annual holiday party at home. (*Andre ander*)

Pierre Cardin as Robert L. Green's guest lecturer at the Fashion Institute of Technology, New York City. (*FIT Photo File*)

My New York Lunch Bunch: Van Johnson, Milton Goldman, Dolores del Rio, Arnold Weissberger. (*Arnold Weissberger*)

Brilliant Judy Holliday at stage door of "Born Yesterday." (*Arnold Weissberger*)

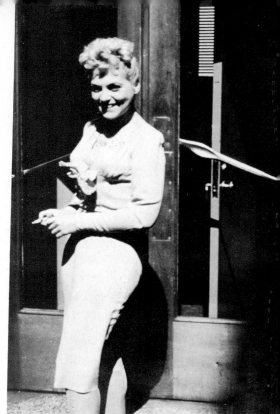

Polly Bergen, co-chairman of Goodwill Industries' Charity Auction, at Tollgate Farm with Robert L. Green. (*Andres Lander*)

Front view of Tollgate Farm. (*David R. Taylor*) Looking down the garden path through the roses to Chinese Viewing Pavilion, designed by Angelo Donghia, at Tollgate Farm. (*Bob Smith-Felver*)

and cheese complete the menu, and there is little work involved. My gazpacho recipe other than puréed tomatoes and the usual condiments, contains some real Spanish magic—roasted almonds and hard-boiled eggs. There never has been another cold soup like it.

But if you should decide that sandwiches are what you really want, there are some noncliché suggestions in the "Summer" section of Chapter Nine on the dynamics of the picnic.

The Weekend's Over—The Thank-You Note

Cole Porter's definitive thank-you note characterizes the quintessential disaster weekend. It is a "charming souvenir" that hopefully I will never receive.

Mrs. Lowsborough-Goodby
by Cole Porter

Mrs. Lowsborough-Goodby gives weekends
And her weekends are not a success
But she asks you so often, you finally soften
And end up by saying yes.

When I wrote Mrs. Lowsborough-Goodby
The letter I wrote was polite
But it would have been bliss
If I dared write her this
The letter I wanted to write.

Thank you so much Mrs. Lowsborough-Goodby
Thank you so much
Thank you so much for that infinite weekend with you.
Thank you a lot, Mrs. Lowsborough-Goodby
Thank you a lot
And don't be surprised if you should be quietly shot.

For the clinging perfume
Of that damned little room
For the cocktails so hot
And the bath that was not

For those guests so amusing
And mentally bracing
Who talked about racing and racing and racing
For the ptomaine I got from your
    famous tinned salmon
For the fortune I lost when you
Taught me backgammon.

For those mornings I spent with
Your dear but deaf mother
For those evenings I passed with
that bounder your brother

And for making me swear to myself
There and then
Never to go for a weekend again.
Thank you so much Mrs. Lowsborough-Goodby
Thank you, thank you so much.

A Bouquet of Souvenir Recipes from a Country Weekend

TOLLGATE FARM MEATBALLS AND SAUERKRAUT
(Serves 8 to 10)

2 pounds ground beef, chuck or round

¼ cup finely chopped onion

2 teaspoons chopped fresh tarragon

1 clove garlic, finely chopped

1 teaspoon salt

½ cup soft bread crumbs

2 eggs, lightly beaten

½ teaspoon Worcestershire sauce

¼ teaspoon freshly ground pepper

½ cup bacon drippings

¼ pound slab bacon simmered in water 10 minutes—drained and diced

2 one pound 13-ounce cans of sauerkraut, squeezed dry

1 bay leaf

1 cup dry white wine

2 cups of chicken broth additional salt and pepper

1 pint sour cream

1. Combine beef, onion, tarragon, garlic, salt, bread crumbs, eggs, pepper, Worcestershire sauce. Mix lightly with hands. Form into 18 to 24 balls and brown quickly in bacon drippings, which have been heated in a heavy skillet. Set aside. Do not cook through.

2. Combine diced bacon, sauerkraut, bay leaf, wine, and broth in a heavy Dutch oven or saucepan. Bring to a boil, cover and simmer until most of the liquid has been absorbed, 2 to 3 hours. Season to taste with salt and pepper.

3. In a heavy casserole or kettle place a layer of sauerkraut and a layer of meatballs and repeat until all are used. Cover and simmer 1 hour. Add broth if necessary. Just before serving, stir in the sour cream and reheat.

HAM AND CHEESE SOUFFLÉ
(Sunday Brunch)
(Serves 8)

3½	cups French bread (¾ loaf cubed)	1½	teaspoons dry mustard
4½	cups cubed ham	4½	tablespoons melted butter
¾	pound cheddar cheese (mild), cubed	6	eggs
4½	tablespoons flour	4½	cups milk
			red-pepper seasoning

Grease pan

1. Layer ⅓ of bread, ham, and cheese; 1½ tablespoons flour, mustard, and 1½ tablespoons butter.
2. Repeat step 1 time.
3. Separate bowl—beat eggs with milk and red pepper. Pour on top of mixture. Chill overnight. Bake uncovered 1 hour at 375°.

BLOODY MARY SOUP
(Sunday Night Supper)

2	quarts water	1	bay leaf
1	onion	1	teaspoon salt
2	pounds flanken		

Cook until meat is tender. Add water. Remove bay leaf, bones, and onion.

Add:

1	quart Bloody Mary laced well with vodka and Tabasco sauce		green pepper
		2	carrots
1	medium potato	½	cup corn
2	onions, chopped	½	cup beans
1	small turnip	½	cup peas
	a small parsnip	½	cup baby limas
2	stalks celery	1	tablespoon barley

Cook until vegetables are soft, about 2½ hours.

GAZPACHO (Serves 20)

4	cans (2 pounds, 3 ounces) whole peeled tomatoes	10	cloves garlic
1	can (15 ounces) whole peeled tomatoes	6	hard-boiled eggs
		18	tablespoons oil
6	slices moist white bread	18	tablespoons vinegar
24	roasted almonds		salt, parsley

Puree all the ingredients in the electric blender and then through a fine sieve. Add a few ice cubes and refrigerate. Chill. Before serving, thin out with cold water if necessary. Separately serve cubed onion, green peppers, cucumbers, tomatoes and croutons.

FRUIT ICE IN A FRUIT SHELL
STRAWBERRY-ORANGE ICE

Make 2 cups strawberry purée in your blender (about 3½ cups strawberries). Cut in half and strain the juice from 4 medium-size oranges (about 1½ cups). Add juice and ½ cup sugar to puree. Cover and freeze solid. Remove the pulp from the orange shells. Wrap the shells in appropriate material and freeze. When frozen, remove puree ice from freezer and let stand until you can break ice into pieces with a wooden spoon. Pour into a large mixing bowl and continue to smash ice. With an electric mixer beat slowly at first and then gradually at higher speed till mixture is slushy. Whip until mixture is smooth, like a thick cake batter. Spoon batter into frozen orange shells; refreeze. Garnish each with whole strawberry. This will make 8 half-cups of strawberry-orange fruit ice.

CHRISTMAS GOOSE WITH APPLES AND PRUNES
(Serves 8)

1	pound dried prunes	2	teaspoons cinnamon
8	medium-size cooking apples	4	cups freshly made bread crumbs
5	tablespoons butter	1	10-pound young goose
2	tablespoons brown sugar	1	teaspoon salt

Peel, core, and chop the apples. Heat the butter in a large skillet and saute the apples until lightly browned. Add the sugar, cinnamon, and bread crumbs and cook, stirring, for 2 minutes. Pour boiling water over prunes. Let stand for 5 minutes. Combine with the apples.

Dry the goose thoroughly inside and out and sprinkle the cavity with salt.

Stuff the goose with the apple mixture and truss. Pierce the skin of the goose all over with a fork to allow the fat to drain off while cooking.

Place the goose on a rack in a roasting pan and roast breast side up in a preheated 400° oven for 15 minutes. Reduce the heat to 350°, turn the bird on its side, and roast 1 hour. Turn the bird onto the other side and roast another 50 minutes. Turn breast side up for last 15 minutes roasting time. It will take 2¼ to 2½ hours' total time for the goose to cook.

Place the goose on a serving platter, remove trussing strings, and let stand 10 to 15 minutes before carving.

ROAST BEEF SALAD
(Serves 8–10)
4   *cups julienne roast beef*

CHUTNEY DRESSING:

1 *cup mayonnaise*	*chutney*
1 *cup chili sauce*	2 *teaspoons peeled grated*
½ *cup drained chopped*	*white onion*

Mix together ingredients for dressing until smooth. Line salad bowl with mixed greens. Arrange roast beef strips as spokes with the bottoms buried in the center of the bowl and the tops fanned out to line the sides of the bowl. Pile 6 hardboiled eggs, quartered, in the center of the bowl. Pour the chutney dressing over everything.

Ices

Ices are made of sweetened fruit juices usually diluted with water. They are sometimes called sherbets as well, but a milk or cream sherbet is made with milk or cream, not water.

Sherbets can be frozen and then made into balls stuffed into scooped-out fruit shells. Use the same ice with the same fruit or coordinated with a contrasting fruit.

The shortcut is to just buy some very fresh fruit and the best-quality sherbet and put them together and into your freezer wrapped in foil.

The long way around is to pick your own fruit and make your own ice. That is what I do. Here is my own ice recipe for a variety of flavors.

LEMON ICE

2 cups sugar	1 tablespoon grated lemon
4 cups boiling water	rind
¾ cup lemon juice	

Dissolve the sugar in the water. Be sure to cool it. Add the lemon juice and the rind. Pour into individual molds and freeze.

You can be wonderfully creative by making your own fruit-juice combinations. Here are some of mine. In each case you want to end up with a quart of liquid. You can always add water to your juices to reach the 4 cups.

ORANGE AND LEMON

3 cups of orange juice	grated rind of 2 oranges
¼ cup lemon juice	sugar syrup to taste

RASPBERRY AND CURRANT

⅔ cup raspberry juice	2 cups sugar syrup
1⅓ cups currant juice	

MÉLANGE DU FRUIT

1½ cups grapefruit juice	½ cup lemon juice
1½ cups orange juice	sugar syrup to taste

GRAPE, ORANGE, AND LEMON

2 cups grape juice	¼ cup lemon juice
⅔ cup orange juice	sugar syrup to taste

MINT AND LEMON

Use lemon-ice recipe and flavor with oil of peppermint and color gently with green vegetable coloring.

Let Them Eat Bread

I have had nonriding guests who were turned on by the sounds and scents of my stables. Some people loathe it. Newly mown grass, spring rain, and flower-scent drenched air may elicit either enthusiastic or desperate cries depending on your guests' allergies or their sinus condition. The permeating scent of fresh bread or cake baking has, however, produced nothing but sensual sighs and gluttonous groans. Guests who came from families where baking was a custom go numb with nostalgia right before your eyes. Not everyone is mad for the sounds of music, but there is unanimous approval for the smells of baking. My most urban guests are the ones most completely astonished that I can produce a miracle such as a loaf of bread, and are overwhelmed that anyone they know can bake a cake. So let's get on with the bread making—

The first thing you are going to notice is that I am not going to give you the exact amount of flour to use. The reason for this is that all flour contains a protein substance called gluten. When you wet gluten it has the unique property of stretching to become an elastic framework. The amount and strength of the gluten varies with the flour. The absorptive properties of flour vary with temperature and humidity. It is for these reasons that I am also not going to give exact times for beating and kneading. After a few tries you'll learn to recognize when the mixture "feels" right. To me it "feels" right when it is not sticky at all and has a smooth, almost satiny feeling when gently caressed.

A word of caution: I tried the new instant-type all-purpose flour (really good for gravy), and everything went wrong—my one big bread failure.

So far, the recipes out of my collection use regular all-purpose flour.

Next—for yeast-bread recipes one uses one of two liquids—milk or water. Milk gives bread a velvety grain and adds nutrients. If you make your bread with all water it will have a heavier and crispier crust. The most common example is French bread. I have found that water is the best medium for dissolving dry yeast, so whatever recipe you use, be sure at least ¼ cup of the liquid is water to dissolve the yeast.

There are two forms of yeast: the dry and the compressed.

They both work but the dry lasts longer. (If you want to check compressed yeast, crumble it between your fingers. If it crumbles easily it is still good.)

If your children start to ask questions, just explain that when yeast is put into action in the dough, fermentation begins and carbon dioxide is given off. This gets trapped in the glutenous framework of the dough and causes it to *rise*.

Flavor and tenderness are added when you add fat. I prefer to use salad oil—you just pour it. However, I know a lot of friends who use margarine and a few who are petrified of Mother Nature and use butter. (It's not nice to fool Mother Nature!) One thing you will want to do is to brush the crust of your bread with a fat to give it a softer, shinier crust.

All recipes have some sugar and salt. This is for flavor, too. There are endless variations including brown sugar, honey, molasses, syrup in place of granulated sugar. The one sure thing is that the more sugar you use, the browner the crust becomes.

If you want to add a golden color, beat up an egg, then let its volume replace an equal amount of liquid in the recipe.

My experience has been that I have been able to add raisins, nuts, spices, and herbs without adjusting other proportions.

Temperature is very important when working with yeast. The ideal is a kitchen spot of about 80 degrees. But don't panic if there isn't one. I always use a heavy pottery bowl. I warm it with hot water when I start to mix the dough, then repeat it again when I put the dough in the bowl to rise. I have filled my sink with hot water and set the bowl and the dough into it. Another sure-fire way is to put the dough and bowl into the oven with a roasting pan below it that is full of boiling water.

Here is my

BASIC WHITE BREAD RECIPE

You will need two bread pans. They can be either metal or glass and 5¼ x 9¼-inch size or 4½ x 8½ inches. Mix in a heavy pottery bowl. It should be about a 4-quart size.

Sift more than 6 cups of flour in a large bowl so that you can dip out your 6 cups as you need it without straining. I find taking the temperature of scalding milk doesn't amuse me, so I don't. If you must play bread nurse then the rule is heat the milk to just below the boiling point to scald it, then let it cool to about 105° if you are using dry yeast; or cool to 95° if you are using compressed yeast.

Why don't you just adopt my trick, which is to use one cup of very hot water with one cup of evaporated milk (which needs *no* scalding). I have always found that it works. Recently I had no evaporated milk and the country store was closed so I dissolved ¼ cup dry skim milk in two cups (less 2 tablespoons) of warm water and the bread was delicious.

HERE ARE THE INGREDIENTS:

¼ *cup warm water*
1 *package yeast, active dry or compressed*
2 *cups scalded milk* or 1 *cup evaporated milk with* 1 *cup* very *hot water*
2 *tablespoons melted butter, margarine, or*

salad oil
2 *teaspoons salt*
2 *tablespoons granulated sugar*
6 *to 6½ cups regular all-purpose flour (sift before measuring)*

HERE ARE THE STEPS:

1. Pour water into bowl; add yeast and stir until dissolved. Stir in the milk, then add the melted butter, salt, and sugar; stir until well blended.
2. Stir in 3 cups of flour—but do it one cup at a time. Add fourth cup of flour and beat until dough is smooth and elastic. This is tiring, so take breaks whenever you feel like it. Mix in the fifth cup of flour to make a stiff dough.
3. Take the sixth cup of flour—use half of it on your board. Turn the dough out on the floured board. Keep a coating of flour on the dough as you knead.
4. Flour your own hands; fold the dough toward you with your fingers, then push it firmly away from you with the heel of your hand. Add more flour to the board as it is kneaded in. At first it looks crude and messy and then suddenly it all comes together and the dough no longer sticks.
5. Kneading is finished when the dough is smooth and satiny.

Grease the bowl—put the dough in—grease the top of the mound lightly. Cover the bowl and set in a warm place to rise.

6. Let it rise for about 1½ hours. It usually doubles in size. The simplest test is to put your fingers into the dough—if the mark remains then you can shape the dough.
7. Punch the dough down with the heel of your hand. Squeeze out the air bubbles. Shape it into a smooth ball—then divide it into two equal parts for the two loaves.
8. Form each loaf into a smooth oval. Turn over in one hand; with your other hand pinch seam in center; turn the ends into the center like folding the flap of an envelope and just pinch it closed.
9. Put your loaves into greased pans with the seams down. Cover; let rise in warm place until loaves are almost doubled (45 minutes). Bake in 375° oven. Drop the temperature to 350° if your bread pans are glass.
10. It will take about 45 minutes until they are nicely browned and just starting to pull away from pan sides. Remove from oven; turn loaves out of pans to cool—this is important because if you don't the bread will "sweat" on the bottom and be mushy. Play it cool and let it cool before slicing or wrapping for freezing.

Once you have done this a few times you will be ready to play with some of the variations. Here are some that I use for my Big Party—

DARK RYE BREAD—You just follow the basic recipe but use 3 cups of rye and 3 cups regular all-purpose flour. In step one, leave out the sugar; and instead of all milk I use ½ cup dark molasses with 1½ cups of milk.

OATMEAL BREAD—Follow the basic recipe but use two cups of oats—I do this by whirling rolled oats in my blender until they are fine—and four cups of regular all-purpose flour.

PUMPERNICKEL BREAD—Follow basic white recipe. For flour use 1 cup whole bran cereal, 2 cups of rye flour, and 3 cups of whole-wheat flour. I mix them all together in my blender. In step one, I add 1½ tablespoons caraway seed. Just remember that the more dark flour in the all-purpose flour the longer it takes to rise—figure on 2 hours. The darker breads don't double in bulk.

ONION BREAD—Follow the basic white recipe but note these changes. In step one, use a regular can of onion soup—shake it well before pouring—add enough warm water to make two cups of liquid in place of all milk; omit the sugar; use only one teaspoon of salt; and add two tablespoons of minced onion. In steps eight and nine shape the loaf into a ball and place into a 1-quart round casserole—and just bake.

HERB BREAD—Follow basic white recipe. All you do then is just add, for each single loaf, the following amounts:

> 1 *tablespoon savory*
> 1½ *teaspoons basil*
> 1½ *teaspoons oregano*
> 1½ *teaspoons thyme*
> 2¼ *teaspoons marjoram*

FRENCH BREAD—It won't take the place of France but it isn't bad. Follow the basic white recipe with these changes. In step one, use water in place of milk; omit shortening. In steps eight through ten, shape into two long oblong loaves; let rise on a lightly greased baking sheet; brush with water and make diagonal slashes in top with a sharp knife before baking. Place in a hot oven (400°) and be sure there is a shallow pan of hot water in oven bottom—until it is crusty and brown—it takes about 45 minutes.

I did have some trouble for a while with the French loaves coming out too flat. But I discovered that after you have made the long oblong of the dough, if you will fold over one edge to the center, repeat the same for the second edge and taper the ends slightly, you will end up with better-shaped loaves.

Now Let 'em Eat Cake

There are infinite possibilities that cooking has to offer. The endless display of buffet food offers a lesson in combining great ease in cooking and great beauty.

For many people, no meal is complete without something "sweet." The trick here is to make a number of things that can be frozen and then defrosted easily the day of the party. I have found after experimenting with large cakes, pies, tortes, and tarts that the simplest is a finger bite-size dessert. Here are some ideas that have worked for me in large numbers. All of these things can be refrozen so I am never concerned about making too many. I turn my kitchen into an active bakery for one long weekend and produce enough "dessert" for the party and lots of snacks, teas, lunches, and picnics for months afterward.

CINNAMON-WALNUT STRIPS

⅔	cup butter	1½	teaspoons cinnamon
⅔	cup sugar	1½	cups finely chopped
3	egg yolks		walnuts
¾	cup farina	3	egg whites
¼	teaspoon salt		

THE SYRUP:

⅓	cup sugar	½	teaspoon vanilla
3	tablespoons water		

Cream butter and sugar together thoroughly. Beat in the egg yolks. Combine farina, salt, and cinnamon until well mixed, then add to the butter mixture. Add chopped walnuts and stir again. Beat egg whites until stiff but not dry and fold into the mixture. Grease a 9 x 14-inch pan and bake at 375° for 20 minutes. Use the baking time to prepare the syrup. Cook the ⅓ cup sugar, 3 tablespoons of water, and vanilla together until the boiling point is reached. Remove from the heat.

Lightly spoon the syrup over the strips which have baked for 20 minutes. Put the pan back at 375° for 15 minutes. Take out of the oven and let stand until completely cold. I then cut them into strips about ⅜-inch wide and fill a bag. You will get about 35 bite-size pieces out of this. I do ten pans of this.

CHOCOLATE BROWNIE BITES

You can get tiny muffin tins in any good gourmet-supply department store, specialty shop, or hardware store. I use ten of them.

This recipe will make about 70 bites:

5 ounces (squares) unsweetened chocolate	2 cups sugar
¾ cup butter	1½ teaspoons vanilla
4 eggs	1 cup sifted flour
¼ teaspoon salt	1½ cups chopped nuts

Melt chocolate and butter and cool slightly. Beat eggs, salt, and sugar together until light and fluffy. Add melted chocolate mixture. Add vanilla. Stir in the flour, then stir in the chopped nuts.

Grease actively (I use PAM) the tiny muffin tins. Spoon in the brownie mixture and bake at 350° for about 15 minutes. Cool. You can then use the following frosting:

TOLLGATE FROSTING:

2 ounces (squares) unsweetened chocolate	1 teaspoon vanilla
2 tablespoons butter	3 tablespoons fine orange peel
1 cup powdered sugar hot milk	large pecan halves

Melt butter and chocolate together. Stir in the powdered sugar and then add just enough hot milk to make frosting of spreading consistency. Stir in the vanilla. Add the orange peel. Spread each brownie bite with some of the frosting and decorate with a pecan half. Put in bags of 35 each and freeze.

APRICOT BARS WITH A NUTTY MERINGUE
I defy anyone to eat only one—

½ cup butter	⅛ teaspoon salt
¼ cup powdered sugar	1¼ cups sifted flour
2 egg yolks	1½ cups apricot jam

THE NUTTY MERINGUE:

5 egg whites	fine texture)
½ cup powdered sugar	½ cup finely chopped
½ teaspoon vanilla	almonds
1 cup walnuts (ground to a	

Cream butter and sugar together thoroughly. Beat in the egg yolks and salt. Stir in the sifted flour. Press the dough in a 9 x 14-inch pan and bake at 375° for about 15 minutes—just until lightly browned. Cool casually. Spread with the apricot jam. Take a deep breath and you'll start smiling no matter how tired. Someone should do a whole line of kitchen perfumes.

Plunge into the meringue. Beat egg whites until stiff. Gradually beat in the powdered sugar, beating constantly until very stiff and glossy. Fold in the vanilla and the ground walnuts. Spread this meringue on the apricot jam, sprinkle with shredded almonds, and bake at 425° for about 10 minutes or until meringue and almonds are brown. Take out, and when they are cold, cut into bars. This will make about 35 and I freeze them in that number. I do 20 of these pans because I give them away to the kids on Halloween as a treat and to weekend guests as part of a snack package when they leave.

WALNUT KISSES

1¼ cups powdered sugar	chopped fine
3 eggs, separated	⅓ teaspoon cream of tartar
1 cup walnut meats,	½ teaspoon vanilla

Sift the sugar. Measure it. Chop the nut meats finely. Add the sugar gradually to the egg yolks. Blend well. Add the nut meats.

Beat the egg whites until foamy. Add the cream of tartar and the vanilla. Beat until stiff, but not dry. Fold the egg whites into the mixture.

Drop from a teaspoon or a pastry tube onto a greased, lightly floured baking sheet ½ inch apart. Sprinkle with powdered sugar. Bake for 30 minutes in a cool oven (215°). Makes 35 kisses. Freeze. I do ten batches of these.

NINE: Celebrate the Four Seasons

Spring: Children's Parties

Children are little people but they are not short adults. Their imagination is infinite but their attention span is brief. If you can tap into the first without straining the second you will all have a happy time. When planning a party for children remember it is a party for them, not for you. The children may not find your plans as much fun as you imagined they would. Therefore, I would advise you to be flexible, unflappable, and have plenty of paper towels on hand.

When should you have a party for children? Anytime at all, except, I think, at conventional party times. Christmas is always a time for family celebrations and Halloween is a neighborhood event. As a child, I was delighted at the idea of a happy *un*birthday party. There was something really special about a party for no good reason except the pure joy of it. And never having forgotten that feeling of my boyhood, I bring that idea to the parties I now give as a grownup for my young friends. So the parties included here are all celebrations sans occasions. They take all seasons into account, but children inevitably make me think of spring.

Now, as far as decorations for children's parties go, they don't. In my experience children seem infinitely less involved with their surroundings than with the projects and events that have been planned for them. The one exception to that rule is the party table itself. That should be laid out with care and style. It is the one place children come to rest and so their wonderful powers of observation are captured when they sit down to eat.

A word about food for children. I sometimes think that they have only three taste buds. One for sweet, one for plastic and one for what they call "yukky." Remember, children will never eat what they don't recognize. And I might add, if they don't recognize it and they try it and they like it and you then tell them what it is, they won't like it. Just try giving a child a delicious zucchini dish and then telling him or her that it is zucchini. Not since that big dinner party at the House of Atreus has there been such a reaction. During childhood, children eat child food: fried chicken, frankfurters, hamburgers, french fries, macaroni, spaghetti, peanut butter, pizza, ice cream, cake. A simple list and absolutely foolproof. It is more than I can bear to prepare it. It seems too uncivilized somehow, but there it is.

The time of day for giving a party depends very much on the kind of party it is and the ages of your small guests. If it is an outdoor party, swimming or sledding, then by all means plan it for the warmest part of the day. If it is a wiener roast then nightfall is the most fun. If the children are still of napping age the party should be called for mid-afternoon or mid-morning and end immediately after lunch. For children under twelve all parties should be limited to two hours or less. Things are almost guaranteed to break down after two hours (mostly the adults in charge). The ages of the children determine the number to invite. Very young children (two and three years old) are usually accompanied throughout the party by their parents, which adds to the number of guests. A reasonable guide to follow is the age of the children plus one until the age of three, and plus two until the age of seven. By the time children are eight years old the number can safely expand to a dozen. But a dozen is, I think, the very limit for any party for young children.

Being invited to a party should be a very happy event. The invitation is part of the party too. The best way to convey this is to make the invitation an activity. There are several ways to do this. You can write an invitation and cut it up before placing it in the envelope; then the child has to put the jigsaw puzzle together to find out the who, where, when, and why. Or decorate balloons. I adore balloon invitations for children. Here is what you need:

jumbo balloons, waterproof oil-based felt-tipped pens, envelopes. Blow up the balloon and pinch the end closed with a rubber band. Hold in one hand and with the other write your invitation on the sides of the balloon. After the ink dries let the air out. Place the balloon in an addressed, stamped envelope and mail. The guest blows up the balloon, reads the message and has a party favor before the party starts. Or make your invitation in the form of a rebus that the child has to figure out. Invitations are not essential, but they help make the day special. They are an easy way to record the date, time, and place of the party. Explain the meaning of R.S.V.P. to the kids and encourage them to answer the invitation themselves on the telephone. Adults, however, should be contacted to confirm, to avoid possible confusion.

Having explained my general philosophy (paramount being "never act like a general") I offer the outlines for a handful of the many delightful children's parties I have hosted.

The Children's Great Sunday Sundae Event

This really was an event with a divine *raison d'eat-re*. It was for eight boys and girls in ages ranging from eight to ten. (I think it would have been a disaster if they had been any younger.) The invitation—a drawing of a sundae to be colored in—read: "Come to the first annual Great Sunday Sundae Event on Sunday, June ——from 2 to 4:00 P.M.(eat a light lunch so you won't be too full for the you-know-what). Please bring a bathing suit and a towel."

When the children arrived they went immediately to change for the main activity of the day, an "Olympic" swimming competition. I began the event by reading the official Olympic Code in my most stentorian tones. "May I open our contest with the stirring words which traditionally opened the Olympic games in Greece in the eighth century. The eyes of the world are upon you, your cities love an Olympic winner. From Olympus the Gods look down upon you; for the glory of your city; for the joy of your fathers and for your own good name I exhort you to do your best." The races, themselves, however, were conducted more in the spirit of fun and the prizes certainly reflected that. The Mark Spitz Award (first prize) was a bag of seven very large gold-foil chocolate-covered coins and a fake mustache.

After our day at the races, everyone changed back into their clothes and reconvened at the party table. At each place setting were a sundae (parfait) glass, a tall spoon, and the biggest napkin I could find with the child's name written on it in glitter. The napkins were the party favors.

Lined up in the center of the table were: chocolate, vanilla, coffee, cherry vanilla, strawberry, and butter-pecan ice creams, each with a scoop in them; chocolate and multicolored sprinkles; chocolate and butterscotch chips; maraschino cherries; real whipped cream, ("there are some things," to quote Winston Churchill, "up with which I will not put"); marshmallow, hot fudge, raspberry, strawberry, and walnut syrups. After each child completed his or her masterpiece, I took a Polaroid picture of the artist and creation as a souvenir of the momentous event. The party was such a great success that it has become an annual event as predicted in the original invitation.

The Children's Fall—All

The invitation to this party was a Xerox picture of a tree with ten leaves on it. Each leaf contained a name of one of the ten guests. The specific child's invitation had the leaf with his or her name outlined in gold. On the tree trunk was written: "Come to a Fall-All, blue jeans required." When the children arrived they took turns raking leaves together (I have more than a little Tom Sawyer in me). When we had gathered an enormous pile I scattered pennies and penny candy in the pile and the children buried themselves in the leaves trying to unearth them. Our next project was to gather the prettiest leaves we could find and use them to make beautiful collages. On the long table near the kitchen fireplace I laid out several pairs of scissors, colored construction paper, crayons, pastels, sparkles, glue, doilies, and Saran wrap to cover the collages with when they were finished. Then we all sat down at the table, decorated with shiny red apples and brown pipe-cleaner trees hung with crepe-paper leaves in red and gold and brown, and had warm cider with cinnamon sticks and freshly baked apple-and-banana bread.

The Children's Winter Carnival

This party really does require snow, so it has always been a last-minute telephone invitation event. The children are instructed to dress warmly and to plan to stay for an early dinner. Since they arrive dressed like the children of Nanook, I always plan an outdoor event to begin with. I line a long log with soda cans with rocks in them, if it is at all windy, and play the Arctic version of carnival toss ball. In this case the balls are snowballs. Each child gets a chance to knock off as many cans as he or she can. The prize—a kewpie doll or a stuffed toy with a muffler around its neck—goes to the one with the highest accumulated score. Next comes the snowman-sculpture contest. The children are paired off into teams and provided with a small bag of coal, given a time limit of between thirty minutes to an hour, depending on the wind-chill factor. The winners of this event are traditionally awarded a box of colored clays. By the time the army of snowmen has been constructed, both the light and our energies have begun to fade so we set about collecting apple-tree (sucker) branches and gather together around an outdoor fire (if it is too cold we retire to one of the indoor fireplaces) and roast frankfurters and marshmallows.

The Children's Easter Plant-Off

This is another party where my Tom Sawyer self comes into play. The invitations each contain a seed package with a note explaining that it should be brought to the party along with an old pair of cotton gloves and a shovel. We usually begin with the traditional Easter-egg hunt, although I dispense with the decorated eggs (floral-covered chocolate ones). After this event I gather the children together for the planting. I divide the garden into sections which are marked off by stakes, each bearing one child's name. That is his or her planting area. The nicest part of this activity is that whenever the children return to the farm they go to check on their flowers. They take an enormous pride in the visible results of their efforts.

After the gardening, it is inside to wash up and eat lunch. The table is decorated with baskets of flowers and Easter eggs. In the center is an enormous mason jar filled to the brim with jelly beans. At each child's place is a setting of colored felt pens, the party favor, and a placecard ballot. They use their pens to fill in the ballot, guessing the exact number of jelly beans in the jar. The winner has a corner on the jelly-bean market for life.

Just a word about kids and rain. They will not take cancellations as lightly as adults. If you see that you are going to be rained out, create an alternate activity that can be done indoors. Try to preserve the original flavor of the party. If you were going to fly kites outside, then switch to making kites inside. (As the host you will have to supply the necessary supplies.)

Summer: The Picnic-A Pleasure Party in the Open

There is something about a picnic that is extraordinarily satisfying. A picnic that is worth the trouble requires careful planning and preparation—and a picnic to be any fun at all requires good food.

Under most circumstances picnics are generally reserved for days uncomplicated by work or usual routine. The picnic should be planned so that it is truly relaxed.

I don't recommend that anyone rise at dawn on the day of the picnic and carry on into exhaustion before you even get started.

I really feel the only work that should be done on the day of the picnic is athletically to wave your pencil across a check list just to be sure the right condiments, utensils and gadgets have not been forgotten.

All the major carrying-on should be done before picnic day. If you are going to have sandwiches then get the materials all prepared and assemble them just before picnic time or they may get soggy. A crisp fresh sliced tomato allowed to lie around for too long becomes a messy and tired experience.

My two favorite times for picnics are the spring and the fall. I don't like the beach for picnics because the sand, with unerring instinct, will find its way into almost everything.

I suppose that where you go must be personally solved. The perfect picnic setting for me is an area that is semiwooded and has a stream nearby. We all know that endless equipment has been developed for picnics in the form of ice chests and ice bags, but as technically wonderful as all that is, nothing is as spiritually satisfying as pulling the drinks, whether they be soft, diet, or a casual, but correct, chablis, dripping from an ice-cold stream.

Picnic guests really have to be picked very carefully. Even when you can produce a picnic as smoothly run as a highly staffed informal dinner, there are people who are not amused by picnics.

I do think one should divide one's picnics between family picnics and picnics for other friends. Outsiders are often left feeling sentenced to the event if there are children to cope with. Any party that includes children, in my opinion, should be a children's party. Grownups may well feel like kids at picnics. There is something timeless and extraordinarily romantic about picnics, and grownups should be allowed to act whatever age pleases them without being reminded by the presence of real children that they are not.

The outdoors seems to be a world of galloping informality, but that is not an alibi for poor menu planning.

What about Picnic Sandwiches?

Although the usual tunafish salad, salmon salad, egg salad, or bacon, lettuce, and tomato are all good eating, it is a better idea to use the picnic as grounds for some new directions.

—How about a selection of the following?

a. Black bread with crabmeat, lobster shreds, capers, pimentos, green peppers, mayonnaise, and a good squeeze of lemon.

b. Thin white bread—wafer slices of tongue, Swiss cheese, Bermuda onion, sliced hard-boiled egg, and all held together by a generous spreading of chopped mustard pickle.

c. Thick brown bread (and an equally thick digestive system), a base of cold mashed baked beans, baked ham, Swiss cheese, and a substantial slice of onion all coated with a good French mustard.

d. White bread with rare roast beef, thinly sliced pickled walnuts, and shredded cheese.

e. Thinly sliced pumpernickel with curried eggs (it is just egg salad with a little chopped celery and curry added to taste). However, if you add drained chunk pineapple and toasted sesame seeds to the top of the salad, you will set up a new sandwich for your guests.

f. White bread and Waldorf salad combined with diced chicken (one cup of salad to one cup of chicken). Bind it with a half cup of mayonnaise. Just butter the bread.

g. Whole-wheat toast with sliced tomatoes, fresh basil, and chopped clams combined with mushroom slices and a half cup of mayonnaise.

h. Italian crisp loaf, garlicked and then filled with Italian tuna spread. (In a bowl mash with a fork two 7-ounce cans of tuna in oil and one stick of butter which is softened until it forms a paste. Add four tablespoons *each* of drained and chopped capers and lemon juice, one tablespoon of minced onion, salt and white pepper to taste.)

i. Rye bread spread with chicken livers chopped up with onions, olives, hard-boiled eggs, and wetted down with madeira.

j. White bread with cold breaded scallopini and bound together with cheddar cheese and anchovy paste.

k. Whole-wheat bread filled with egg salad made with cucumber, smoked salmon, celery, and dill. (Chop 3 hard-boiled eggs. Peel and half 1 large cucumber and with a small spoon scoop out the seeds. Mince the cucumber, put it into a colander, and sprinkle with ½ teaspoon salt—let it stand for 1 hour. Squeeze out the excess moisture, put the cucumber in a towel and squeeze out the remaining moisture. Add the cucumbers to the mashed eggs with ¼ cup minced smoked salmon, 1 tablespoon minced celery, 1 teaspoon minced fresh dill. Bind the mixture with 2 tablespoons of mayonnaise and 1 tablespoon heavy cream and season it with salt and pepper.)

1. Brioche filled with pâté. Your local French bakery will have brioche on hand. They do freeze effectively and can be thawed the day of your picnic. A charming idea is to make this a "do it yourself" sandwich. You purchase at the gourmet department of a major department store very good and relatively inexpensive (about $4.00 a can) pâté de foie gras. To give this additional dimension, add to the pâté a mashed portion of liverwurst. Blend this mixture by hand and place in a separate interesting dish, pot, or pan. A bag of chopped onions and a fresh ground pepper gives you the makings of this superb, untraditional sandwich. You slice off the top of the brioche. Scoop out the inside and fill it with pâté garnished with the onions and coarse pepper.

A Patchwork Picnic

Do you have the courage to involve your friends in a patchwork picnic?

All it takes is to get all your friends to come to your selected site with the food. Get them to provide the food and, hopefully, to compete with each other in producing from their kitchens the greatest delicacies and the special gourmet secrets of each kitchen. If you are having young men and women who have no facilities for providing cooked dishes or cold salads, make a positive out of that limitation. Encourage them to bring a bottle of champagne, some fabulous fruit, or a quart of the best ice cream or sherbet.

Surprise your friends by arranging either a live concert or a cleverly taped one with some introductory remarks that include reference to the personalities, habits, and relationships of the guests.

Set up a site for hot dishes and one for cold dishes. Another area for desserts. Be prepared to keep on ice quarts of ice cream and sherbet. Be sure that you have the necessary utensils for scooping out ice cream, cutting fruit, or serving cakes and pies.

One of the things I have done to amuse my guests was to have some Polaroid cameras in the hands of people who could handle them to take pictures of groups. It is so easy for people to relate in the shared experience of being "caught" by the camera. It also makes a charming souvenir for the guests to take with them.

Do's and Don'ts for Picnics

Let's go back to the checklist I referred to earlier. There is nothing that can destroy the pleasure of a picnic faster than discovering that one of the unglamorous essentials is missing.

What *does* one do without—
Can opener
Bottle opener
Corkscrew
Fruit knife
Paring knife
Carving knife
All-purpose (Boy Scout–type) knife
Cigarettes and Matches (I have given up smoking but I recognize that some of my best friends are nicotine addicts and if they run out—watch it!)
Forks and spoons
Glasses
Salt
Pepper
Other spices that go with your menu
Paper toweling
Dish cloths
Garbage bags
Insect repellents
One of the prepared wash clothes to wipe one's hands
Extra blankets
Extra pillows
A table cloth—and listen to me carefully—I take this very literally. I want a cloth—not a plastic (they always smell funny) cloth and not a paper cloth

I loathe the idea of a paper cloth but don't mind paper napkins. They are particularly effective if they are the folded dinner size that look like the extra-large double damask dinner napkins that one always inherits but no longer uses at the table. If you

— 180—

have any of the real thing, why not treat the picnic grandly and take the cloth napkins along. The tableware can be all the odds and ends that one accumulates—everything certainly does not have to match. There is a lot of very attractive and colorful tableware sold these days that's perfect for casual dining at home as well as picnics. Stainless steel is ideal. If your picnic is small enough you may want to take china plates. I don't if there are more than eight of us. For any larger groups I find it impractical because of weight to use the real thing, as much as I love it. But there are quite good plastic plates on the market that happily do not look like what they are—and they are very light and easy to transport.

I do have one firm rule that cannot be broken. *You cannot serve wine in anything but glasses.* The plastic, the styrofoam, the anything else will not do. I get thin glasses and pack them exactly as though I were moving them. I have yet to break one.

This is not empty pretension, but hard fact. Wine in anything else but glass tastes awful.

I have found no difference in taste of any hot drink—tea, coffee, or cocoa when taken from the insulated foam cups that are available everywhere.

I transport everything in plastic containers. It has become almost a game to shop in cities I visit around the world to find interesting as well as attractive plastic containers of different shapes and sizes. They are perfect for picnic use. The trick here is that you can pack everything securely in separate containers and they fit easily into baskets or boxes. I always tape the tops down so that there is no spillage.

Years ago I bought one of the great picnic baskets with all its fittings at Harrod's in London only to discover that our very own Abercrombie & Fitch had something quite similar. Today, even after their sad demise, there is an enormous choice of insulated bags, coolers, picnic baskets, and insulated boxes available in most department stores.

They come in every size and you do get the feeling that if you wanted to keep a guest hot or cold right up to the peak picnic moment someone has an insulated box in just the right size.

Now, if you are going to bring things in a casserole to heat over your open fire, be sure to check the container's qualifications. There are many things marked "ovenproof," but this does not mean they will not embarrass you if exposed to direct heat.

One of the tricks I learned in England was to keep all the foods involved in any one course together so that they can be opened at the same time. Color-coded plastic containers make this sublimely simple.

We all know what it is like to see a great picnic blanket woven and painted on an enormous museum tapestry but we do not see what happens to the food that has been unduly exposed to the air, dirt, and insects.

I listed extra blankets and pillows because I have learned from experience that when you combine the general tone of leisure at a picnic with vast quantities of good food and fresh air, even the liveliest "life-of-the-party" guest has been known to grow subdued. The blankets and pillows are simply for after-eating relaxation—sometimes referred to as just being "out."

People will get thirsty—often very thirsty—at a picnic, so here are a few suggestions:

1. Don't forget to bring plenty of plain cold drinking water unless you know that your picnic site affords it. No matter what else you have to drink, when you want a cold drink of water there is nothing else that can really take its place.

2. The variety of drinks can be related to your menu or to your knowledge of your guests' taste—there should be enough of both alcoholic and nonalcoholic drinks so that no one will feel deprived.

3. Serving seafood or poultry, there is chablis, sauterne, Rhine wine, and lots of others in the white- wine family.

4. Serving red meat—burgundy or claret.

5. Never forget that both cold beer and ale are very popular in the open air.

6. Serving casseroles and cheeses—a chianti or a California Pinot Noir will be more than a happy choice.

My own personal vote goes to iced tea as we do it at the farm.

TOLLGATE TEA

To 2 ½ cups of strong tea add ⅔ cup sugar. Cool the mixture thoroughly and add 5 cups of citrus-fruit juice; 10 oranges and 8 lemons seem to do it. Before serving add a small bottle of club soda and plenty of ice. Garnish tall glasses with orange and lemon slices.

I solved the picnic ice problem by buying one of those supermarket styrofoam chests. You fill it up with ice cubes and use the whole thing as a portable bar.

I bought another one to be used as my cold salad bar. Obviously all the usual salad fare is included, such as tuna, salmon, chicken, lobster, and potato—and then you can go creative with happy abandon.

Be sure you have a couple of large-size vacuum jugs and a few thermoses. They come in handy on a big-time picnic by allowing you to serve a first course of delicious cold soup. In the spring, fill your jug with borscht, sorrel soup, or vichyssoise. In the fall, start with double consommé, green turtle soup, clam chowder, or corn chowder.

Just remember that there is nothing as charming as the old-fashioned wicker basket, so be sure you have at least one to play picnic.

A Check List of Last Reminders

a. If you take a roast, keep it whole and slice it at the picnic site so it doesn't dry out.

b. If you take a roast chicken or duck, carve it at home—it's easier. Just wrap each slice separately.

c. Juicy salads should be drained at home so that they are not too soggy at serving time.

d. Tossed salads should be assembled on the spot.

e. The salad dressing should be canned in a screw-top jar so that the salad can be dressed at serving time.

f. Cheese should be in hunks—not sliced; so should bread.

g. The best picnic crackers are the English cheese bisquits that come in those handsome tall tins.

h. Fruit that doesn't squash or bruise easily is the best kind of dessert.

i. Take 6 extra lemons—I have never known them not to come in handy.

j. You know those people who "need" something sweet later in the day and try to hustle a sugar "fix" from everyone. This can be awkward away from the candy box, so take it with you in the form of a jar of hard candies and a couple of sheets of the popularly known "apricot leather"—dried apricots rolled out on transparent sheets, which is available in Middle Eastern–supply groceries.

k. Whether you are serving hot tea or coffee, take the milk, coffee cream, and the sugar separately to be added when needed.

l. I always (and I must admit, secretly) take "alternates and/or emergency fill-ins" just in case something drops and is covered with dirt, etc. These are cans of pâté and tins of caviar and a dozen extra hard-boiled eggs. You can always make some sandwiches or a spread or dip on the spot if you have to.

m. Take extra drinks in the form of tinned fruit juices. They can be chilled in the cans and opened when needed.

n. If you don't want to come on as a vintner—and lots of us would like to drink just lemonade (freshly squeezed lemons, of course), the best all-around picnic drink is champagne. You don't have to unlock the Dom Perignon, but you don't want anything just a grape above ginger ale, either. Just a good champagne—tell your wine seller you want something that can be joggled a bit without going into a neurotic fizz. You should figure on a bottle per person for the drinkers at the picnic. You will only open it as you need it, anyway.

o. About chilling the wines in the stream—if you have not learned the proper knots, you may, with romantic flourish, pull up the wine and be faced with a very wet piece of string rather than the bottle. I always take a fisherman's net with me to do the job, but a good, sturdy pillowcase does as well. Just be sure the net and the case are properly anchored to the bank or the wine celebration may drift away.

I have had Tollgate for fifteen years so here are menus and recipes for nine picnics given down at the pond.

Picnic One

CHILLED TANGERINE JUICE
CHAMPAGNE
CELERY, RADISHES, AND SCALLIONS
COLD FRIED CHICKEN
COLD BAKED HAM
SMALL BOTTLES OF PICKLED LAMB'S TONGUES
RUSSIAN SALAD—POTATO SALAD
BREAD STICKS AND RUSSIAN BLACK BREAD
BEER—SOFT DRINKS—ICED TEA
ANGEL FOOD CAKE
TAFFY APPLES AND A BAG OF MARSHMALLOWS

RUSSIAN SALAD

Depending on the number of guests, you can judge the proportions by what flavor and direction you want to emphasize in this salad. Mix diced potatoes, cold diced veal, cold diced beets, and diced apples in a large bowl. Add chopped pickled herring, hard-boiled eggs, capers, parsley, tarragon, salt and pepper to taste, and a large amount of mayonnaise.

Picnic Two

COLD BEET BORSCHT WITH SOUR CREAM
CUCUMBER AND DILLED MAYONNAISE
UNCRUSTED WHITE BREAD SANDWICHES
CREAM CHEESE AND RED HORSERADISH ON THIN
RYE BREAD SLICES
COLD ROAST BEEF—LOBSTER SALAD
TOMATOES STUFFED WITH DEVILED EGGS
ICED TEA
CHOCOLATE BROWNIES
CHILLED WATERMELON—CARVED ON THE SITE
HOT COFFEE

APRICOT NECTAR—CHAMPAGNE
A CASSEROLE COLLECTION:
LA CALADE CHICKEN
SPAGHETTI AND SHRIMP CURRY
VEAL AND HAM CASSEROLE
FRESH BREAD—WHOLE WHEAT ROLLS
ASSORTED FRESH FRUIT
BROWNIES
ROQUEFORT CHEESE—CRACKERS
COFFEE—LIQUEURS

A CASSEROLE COLLECTION

LA CALADE CHICKEN

3 whole broiler-fryer chicken breasts, cut in half

½ teaspoon salt	2 zucchini, cut in ½-inch slices
¼ teaspoon paprika	
½ cup butter	3 large tomatoes, peeled and cut in pieces
½ cup chopped onion	
1 clove garlic, chopped	¼ teaspoon Tabasco
1 green pepper, cut in strips	¼ teaspoon thyme
1 medium eggplant, cut in ½-inch slices	¼ teaspoon oregano
	2 tablespoons chopped parsley

Sprinkle the chicken with salt and paprika. Heat butter in skillet. Brown chicken breasts on both sides and remove. Add onion, garlic, and green pepper and cook until tender but *not* browned. Remove. Brown eggplant slices on both sides, a few at a time, in the skillet. Add zucchini and tomatoes to the skillet and cook rapidly until tomatoes are cooked down and part of the liquid is evaporated. Add cooked onion, garlic, and green pepper with remaining herbs.

Mix well and spoon half of the mixture into a 4-quart casserole.

Arrange the chicken breasts over the vegetables. Spoon

remaining vegetables around the chicken breasts. Bake uncovered in a 375° oven for 45 minutes. Baste several times with liquid from vegetables.

SPAGHETTI AND SHRIMP CURRY
(Serves 4)

1	package spaghetti (elbow)	½	cup chopped walnuts
1	teaspoon salt	½	cup chopped onions
2	teaspoons curry powder	½	cup chopped apple
¼	teaspoon freshly ground pepper	1	pound raw shrimp, cooked, cleaned, and chopped
⅛	teaspoon ginger	1	can (10½ ounces) cream-of-celery soup
½	cup seedless raisins		
½	cup flaked coconut	¾	cup water

Cook spaghetti in boiling salted water until tender. This will take about 7 minutes. *Do not overcook.* Add the salt, curry powder, pepper, ginger, raisins, coconut, walnuts, onion, apple, and shrimp. Toss lightly to mix. Blend soup with water and stir carefully into spaghetti mixture. Pour into buttered flat 2-quart casserole and bake in a 350° oven for 30 minutes or until lightly browned and bubbly. You can do most of this in advance. Just mix the cooked spaghetti with the seasonings and shrimp and then refrigerate. Just before baking, stir in the soup and water. Add another 15 minutes to the baking time.

VEAL AND HAM CASSEROLE

1½	pounds boneless veal shoulder	1½	teaspoons salt freshly ground pepper to taste
½	pound smoked ham		
4	tablespoons butter	½	teaspoon rosemary
12	small white onions	3	tablespoons flour
2	cups canned tomatoes	3	tablespoons water
2	cups chicken broth	6	small cooked potatoes
1	cup sliced celery	1	cup cooked peas, drained

Cut veal into serving-size pieces—and ham into strips. Brown the veal in butter and transfer to buttered 2-quart casserole. Brown onions and put in casserole. Combine tomatoes, broth, celery, and seasonings in skillet. Heat and scrape brown drippings from skillet. Pour mixture over the veal in casserole. Cover and bake in a 350° oven for 1 hour.

Mix flour and water into a thin paste. Stir into the stew. Add the potatoes and peas—cook 15 minutes longer.

BROWNIES

2 eggs	1 teaspoon vanilla
1 cup sugar	pinch of salt
2 squares bitter chocolate, melted	½ cup flour
	1 cup nut meats
½ cup butter	

Beat eggs, add sugar, beat again. Add melted chocolate and butter, vanilla, salt, and sifted flour—mix until smooth. Add the nuts. Pour into a greased 9 x 12-inch pan. Bake in a moderate oven at 350° for 30 minutes. (Yields 24)

Picnic Four

TANGERINE JUICE
ASSORTED SALAMIS
ASSORTED CHEESES
SPINACH FRITTATA
CHEESE STUFFED MUSHROOMS
FRESH ROLLS—BUTTER
CHERRY TOMATOES
GLAZED APPLE BARS
ICED TEA—COFFEE
RED WINE

SPINACH FRITTATA

I make this about three hours (no more) ahead of serving time. It takes very little time and is an unusual experience for most people. I went to a picnic just above Firenze near Settignano and was delighted with this Italian treat. For a picnic you cover and chill it. Cut in wedges to serve.

4	tablespoons olive oil (or salad oil)	1	package (12 ounces) frozen chopped spinach, thawed
1	medium-size onion, chopped	8	eggs
1	clove garlic, minced or mashed	¾	teaspoon salt
		¼	teaspoon pepper

In a well-seasoned frying pan or a Teflon one heat 2 tablespoons of the olive oil over medium-high heat. Add the onion and garlic and cook, stirring until onion is limp. Add the spinach and cook until the moisture evaporates.

Reduce heat to low. Stir the eggs, salt, and pepper together until blended and pour the mixture all at once over the vegetables in the pan. As egg sets around the edge, push the cooked portion toward the center, allowing uncooked eggs to flow underneath. When the bottom is lightly browned, carefully invert pan, turning frittata out onto a plate.

Add the remaining 2 tablespoons of olive oil to the pan and return pan to low heat. Slide frittata, browned side up, back into the pan. Cook until bottom lightly browns. This will take about three minutes. Serve cold like a pie.

CHEESE STUFFED MUSHROOMS

1	pound small mushrooms	cheese, softened by keeping at room temperature.
1	cup fresh lemon juice	
1	small round herb and garlic-flavored Boursin	

Remove the stems from the mushrooms (save them—they are perfect for soup!). Dip the mushrooms into the lemon juice completely to prevent discoloration. Put the mushrooms on a paper towel to dry. Fill the cavity of each mushroom with a little of the cheese.

(Other variations, of course, are to use your own formula for spicing up cream cheese with Tabasco, onion juice, garlic, dill, etc.)

Put the mushrooms in a dish, cover with plastic wrap, and chill. They are a superb accompaniment to the frittata.

GLAZED APPLE BARS

12 medium-sized cooking apples	2 teaspoons lemon juice
1½ cups chopped walnuts	2 packages of pastry mix
2 cups granulated sugar	4 tablespoons butter
2 teaspoons cinnamon	3 tablespoons lemon juice
⅛ teaspoon nutmeg	1½ cups powdered sugar

Peel and slice apples; add ¾ cup of the coarsely chopped walnuts, the granulated sugar, cinnamon, nutmeg, and the 2 teaspoons of lemon juice. Stir lightly until well-mixed.

Roll out half of the pastry and line the bottom and sides of a 10 × 15-inch jellyroll pan. Spread the apple mixture over pastry and dot with butter. Roll out the second package of pastry mix to cover the apple mixture; pinch edges to seal; prick the top.

Bake in a 350° oven for 1 hour. Mix together the three tablespoons of lemon juice and the powdered sugar; spread over hot bars, add remaining nuts, cool. Cut into bars. Yields 18 bars.

Picnic Five

ORANGE JUICE—WHITE WINE
SPANISH OMELET PICNIC LOAF
WHITE BEAN SALAD
GREEN BEAN SALAD
ASSORTED CHEESES
ASSORTED FRUITS (PEACHES, APRICOTS, CHERRIES)
TOLLGATE BUTTER CAKE
ICED TEA—COFFEE

SPANISH OMELET PICNIC LOAF

1 large round sourdough
French bread (about 12
inches in diameter)
4 tablespoons olive oil
10 ounces chorizo sausage
1 large new potato, cooked
1 medium sized onion,
chopped finely
1 clove garlic, minced or
mashed

1 medium size green
pepper, chopped
1 medium size red bell
pepper, chopped
9 eggs
¾ teaspoon salt
¼ teaspoon pepper

Use a long, serrated knife to split the bread in half horizontally. Partially hollow center of halves, leaving a 1-inch border. Brush cut surfaces with about 1 tablespoon of the olive oil. Reassemble loaf, wrap in foil, and keep warm in a 300° oven while preparing omelet.

In a 10-inch omelet pan, crumble chorizo sausage, *discarding casing* and sauté until lightly browned. Remove sausage with slotted spoon and drain; discard drippings. Peel and thinly slice potato. Heat 1 tablespoon of the olive oil in pan over medium heat; add potato, onion, and garlic and cook, turning often, until nicely browned—about 3 minutes. Add green and red peppers and cook for one minute longer, stir in the sausage and shut off the heat.

With a fork beat the eggs with salt and pepper. Return the omelet pan to medium heat and push the potato mixture to one side, drizzling 1 tablespoon olive oil over pan bottom. Redistribute vegetables in pan and pour in the eggs. As the edges begin to set, push toward center and shake pan vigorously to allow uncooked egg to flow underneath.

Cook omelet until top is just set but appears moist, and the bottom is lightly browned. I find that it takes about 5 minutes.

To turn the omelet, run a wide pancake turner around edge and under it to loosen. Invert a plate or try a baking sheet over the omelet while keeping one hand on the plate or sheet, the other gripping the pan handle; quickly invert pan, turning the omelet out onto the plate. Add remaining tablespoon oil to the pan, return to medium heat, and return omelet back into the pan.

Cook until lightly browned on the second side—about 3 minutes—then shut off heat.

Remove the bread from the oven and open out. Invert bottom half of loaf over top of the omelet, then quickly invert pan, turning the omelet out onto the loaf. Replace the top of the bread and wrap in several thicknesses of foil to keep warm up to 4 hours.

Now, this can be done in advance. Just refrigerate the wrapped loaf and reheat in a 400° oven for 30 minutes.

WHITE BEAN SALAD

4 cups cooked or canned white navy beans
1 medium onion, thinly sliced
1 garlic clove, mashed
1 tomato, peeled and coarsely chopped
⅓ cup minced parsley
⅓ cup olive oil
juice of 2 lemons
¼ teaspoon dried basil or marjoram
salt
freshly ground pepper

Drain the beans and put them in a deep bowl. Add the onion, garlic clove, tomato, and parsley. In a separate and smaller bowl, combine the olive oil, lemon juice, basil (or marjoram), salt and pepper to taste. Mix thoroughly. Pour over the beans. Toss gently, for you don't want to break the beans.

GREEN BEAN SALAD

1½ pounds green beans, trimmed
6 tablespoons olive oil
juice of 1½ lemons
1 garlic clove, mashed
salt
freshly ground pepper

Cook the beans until they are just tender. I do this in 3 inches of water brought to the boil. Then put in the beans under a tight cover and let them steam until tender. Drain them and while still hot mix with the oil, lemon juice, garlic, and salt and pepper to taste.

TOLLGATE BUTTER CAKE

1 pound butter at room temperature	grated rind of 1 orange
1 cup white sugar	1 teaspoon mace
1 cup dark brown sugar	½ teaspoon nutmeg
4 eggs	4 cups sifted flour
grated rind of 2 lemons	1 teaspoon baking powder

Use your electric mixer for this one. Cream the butter until light. Beat in the sugars, slowly, a tablespoon at a time, while the electric beaters continue. Beat the eggs one at a time. Then beat in the lemon and orange rind, the mace and the nutmeg. Be sure that the mixture is thoroughly blended.

Sift together the flour and the baking powder and beat it, a little at a time, into the batter. Spoon the batter into a well-buttered and floured 12½ × 6½ × 3-inch loaf pan. Bake in a preheated oven (325°) for about 1¾ hours. Cool in the pan 15 minutes before unmolding. This is a fine-grained and very solid loaf. It should be cut at the picnic site into very thin slices. It keeps for weeks if sealed carefully.

Picnic Six

COLD CREAMY WATERCRESS SOUP—WHITE WINE
RIPE OLIVES—CHEESE-FILLED CELERY
SANDWICHES:
PORK AND APPLE
CHICKEN AND CHUTNEY
CHILLED NIPPY ASPARAGUS
COLD WESTPHALIAN HAM (TINNED)
CHEESE-POTATO SALAD
GENOISE
ICED TEA—COFFEE

COLD CREAMY WATERCRESS SOUP

2 bunches of watercress	freshly ground pepper
8 cups chicken consomme	1 cup heavy cream
salt	

Cut off the greater part of the stalks of the watercress. Combine the watercress and the consommé and simmer, covered, for about 10 minutes. *Do not overcook* or the delicate flavor will be lost. Puree the soup in a blender. Season with salt and pepper. Add the cream and heat thoroughly but *do not boil*. Chill and carry in a thermos jug.

SANDWICHES

PORK AND APPLE SANDWICH:

Thin slices of brown bread spread with thick applesauce and a slice of cold roast pork between them.

CHICKEN AND CHUTNEY SANDWICHES:

Equal parts of chopped, cooked chicken, cream cheese, and chutney mixed and spread on thin slices of white bread.

CHILLED NIPPY ASPARAGUS

Trim the tough ends from 6 pounds of asparagus. In a wide uncovered shallow pan cook fresh asparagus in boiling salted water just until tender.

Pack these in a separate basket. I just cover them with Saran wrap.

THE NIPPY SAUCE:

1 cup prepared salad dressing (do not use mayonnaise)	2 tablespoons prepared mustard
	2 tablespoons lemon juice

Carry this sauce in a screw-top jar and pour at serving time.

CHEESE-POTATO SALAD

1 pound natural Swiss cheese, cut in ¼-inch cubes	½ cup chopped green onions
	½ cup sliced radishes
	¼ cup chopped green pepper
4 cups cooked, peeled, diced potatoes	basic French dressing
3 hard-cooked eggs, sliced	2 tablespoons chopped parsley for the top
½ cup chopped celery	

Mix together the cheese, potatoes, eggs, celery, onions, radishes, and green pepper. Blend in the basic French dressing, top with parsley, and refrigerate.

BASIC FRENCH DRESSING:

Blend together ⅔ cup salad oil, ⅓ cup basic white wine vinegar, 1 tablespoon lemon juice, 1 mashed clove garlic, ¾ teaspoon salt, ½ teaspoon basil, and a dash of pepper.

GENOISE

4 eggs at room temperature	¾ cup flour
¾ cup sugar	¼ cup melted butter, cooled

1. Preheat oven to 325°. Lightly grease and flour the bottom of two 9-inch layer pans.
2. Break the eggs into the bowl of the electric mixer. Beat at highest speed until soft peaks form. Do not underbeat the eggs. While beating the eggs, pour the sugar in a fine stream over them.
3. Lower the speed and sift the flour over the surface of the mixture as the bowl turns. Add the butter. Scrape the sides of the bowl and beat at lowest speed for one minute.
4. Pour the batter into the prepared pans and bake for 40 minutes. Let the cake cool at room temperature before removing from the pans.

CREAM OF ALMOND SOUP—WHITE WINE
CHICKEN LIVER AND MUSHROOM PÂTÉ
DIJON CHICKEN
TOSSED GREEN SALAD
FINGER ROLLS—FRENCH BREAD
FRESH FRUIT AMBROSIA
BRIE CHEESE

CREAM OF ALMOND SOUP

2	cups of blanched almonds, finely ground in an electric blender	2	bay leaves
		¼	cup butter
		¼	cup flour
6	cups chicken consommé	1	cup milk
1	small onion, grated	2	cups light cream

Combine the almonds, consommé, onions, and bay leaves in a saucepan. Simmer, covered, over the lowest heat for about 30 minutes. Remove the bay leaves and keep the soup warm. In a saucepan, melt the butter. Stir in the flour. Cook, stirring constantly, for about 3 minutes, but do not let the flour turn golden. Stir in the milk gradually. Cook over low heat, stirring constantly, until the mixture is smooth and thickened. Stir this sauce into the almond mixture and blend well. Continue to cook over low heat, stirring constantly for about 5 minutes. Remove from the heat and stir in the cream. Return to the heat and heat through but do not bring to a boil. Serve this sinfully good soup chilled.

CHICKEN LIVER AND MUSHROOM PÂTÉ

1½	cups butter	¾	cup dry white wine
2	pounds of chicken livers, cut in half	¼	cup brandy
		2	garlic cloves, mashed
1½	pounds mushrooms	10	drops of Tabasco sauce
1	teaspoon salt		freshly ground pepper
⅔	cut green onions, minced		

Take ¾ cup of the butter and heat in a deep skillet. Add the chicken livers, mushrooms, salt, and onions. Add the wine, brandy, garlic, and Tabasco. Simmer, covered, for 10 minutes or until the chicken livers and the mushrooms are very tender. Cool for five minutes. Puree in a blender until smooth. Beat in the remaining butter, one tablespoon at a time. Add pepper to taste. This should be chilled overnight before using.

DIJON CHICKEN

3 broilers, cut in half	jar of Dijon mustard
olive oil	tarragon
bacon grease	dry bread crumbs

Cut the broilers in half and cover them as though they were about to attempt to swim the English Channel with a mixture of olive oil and bacon grease. Set in a shallow pan and bake for 50 minutes at 350°. This does require some attention, for you should turn and baste the chicken about every 15 minutes.

Then—cover the chicken pieces with a thick crust of Dijon mustard and crumbled tarragon. Shower the chicken generously with very fine dry bread crumbs.

Set the chicken under the broiler until the bread crumbs brown lightly—it takes about 8 minutes.

Turn the chicken and repeat the mustard, tarragon, and bread crumbs.

Serve it cold in your picnic basket.

FRESH FRUIT AMBROSIA

3 large oranges	dash salt
1 fresh, ripe pineapple	2 additional oranges
1 cup shredded coconut	maraschino cherries
¾ cup sugar	mint sprigs

Peel the oranges with a sharp knife. Remove sections by cutting close to the membrane. Peel, core, and dice the pineapple. Combine the fruit with coconut, sugar, and salt and toss lightly. Chill overnight.

In a separate container place 2 oranges peeled with maraschino cherries and some fresh chopped mint.

Just before serving at the picnic site, combine the 2 containers and toss gently.

Picnic Eight

TOMATO JUICE—CHAMPAGNE
SANDWICHES:
CUCUMBER AND MAYONNAISE
CHIVE CREAM CHEESE AND HORSERADISH
COLD ROAST BEEF—LOBSTER SALAD
TOLLGATE DEVILED EGGS
PALACE ALMOND CAKE
ICED TEA—COFFEE

SANDWICHES

I slice the cucumbers and salt and pepper them in one plastic container. Take the jar of mayonnaise along in its conventional state.

Slice the crusts off thinly sliced white bread at the site and have the guests put together their own sandwiches.

I cream the horseradish with the chive cream cheese and place it in a container. Thin slices of black pumpernickel make this a taste treat.

LOBSTER SALAD

1 cup diced freshly cooked live lobster or cooked frozen lobster
2 tablespoons French dressing
1 tablespoon Dijon mustard
1 cup thinly sliced celery
1 tablespoon chopped capers
1 tablespoon chopped anchovies
1 tablespoon chopped chives
1 cup of mayonnaise thinned with tarragon vinegar

Season the lobster with the mustard and French dressing and chill. Then soak the celery in ice water for 1 hour. Drain, dry thoroughly and slice. Combine the celery, capers, anchovies, and chives. Coat the salad lightly with the mayonnaise thinned with tarragon vinegar.

In a separate container I place a mélange of stuffed olives, capers, pimento, and hard-boiled eggs. This is put on the individual servings of the lobster salad at the picnic site and should always be thought of as optional because this salad requires no help at all but is not displeased if help is offered.

TOLLGATE DEVILED EGGS

6	hard-cooked eggs	3	teaspoons mayonnaise
3	tablespoons of red caviar	3	teaspoons chopped
5	teaspoons lemon juice		parsley

Cut the hard-boiled eggs in half lengthwise. Remove the yolks and mash very finely. Combine the egg yolks with the caviar, lemon juice, mayonnaise, and parsley, mixing well. Then fill the cavities of the egg whites with the yolk-caviar mixture.

PALACE ALMOND CAKE

	butter for greasing the pan	1½	teaspoons grated lemon peel
1	cup sliced almonds	4	egg yolks
2	tablespoons sugar	3¼	cups sifted cake flour
1	cup butter	4	teaspoons baking powder
2	cups sugar	1½	teaspoons salt
2	teaspoons vanilla	1½	cups milk
½	teaspoon almond extract	4	egg whites

Lavishly butter the bottom, sides and tube of a 10-inch tube pan. Sprinkle with sliced almonds, rotating pan, until sides and bottom are coated. Sprinkle 2 tablespoons of sugar over the almond-coated sides and bottom.

Cream together the 1 cup butter with the 2 cups sugar until light and fluffy. Add vanilla, almond extract, and lemon peel.

Beat in egg yolks until light and fluffy. Sift together flour, baking powder, and salt. Add to creamed mixture alternately with milk, beating thoroughly after each addition. Beat egg whites until stiff but not dry. Gently fold into batter. Carefully turn into prepared pan. Bake at 325° for 1 hour and 20 minutes. Let the cake stand in the pan for 15 minutes, then invert onto a wire rack to complete the cooling.

Picnic Nine

CHILLED DOUBLE CONSOMMÉ—CHAMPAGNE
CURRIED CRABMEAT PÂTÉ
RYE BREAD—FRENCH BREAD
ROAST LEG OF LAMB
RATATOUILLE—ONION SALAD
PEAR TART
ICED TEA—COFFEE

CURRIED CRABMEAT PÂTÉ

1 cup fresh crabmeat or an
   8¾-ounce can of
   crabmeat
½ small onion, coarsely
   chopped (about ¼ cup)
¾ cup heavy cream
6 tablespoons stick butter,
   softened

1 teaspoon curry powder
¼ teaspoon salt
1 teaspoon fresh strained
   lemon juice
6 drops Tabasco sauce

If you are using canned crabmeat, drain it. When you think it is completely drained, drain it again. Discard any cartilage or pieces of shell from the crabmeat. Shred the meat by hand and place it in an electric blender. Add the chopped onions and ½ cup of cream. Blend at high speed for about 1 minute. Now turn off the blender, take your rubber spatula and scrape down the sides of the inside of the blender jar. Turn on the blender again, adding the remaining cream.

Continue to blend until the crabmeat becomes a smooth puree (don't worry if the mixture seems too fluid—it will firm up later).

Cream the butter with the curry powder by mashing it against the sides of a bowl with a large spoon until smooth and fluffy. Beat this mixture, little by little, into the crabmeat puree; then stir in the lemon juice, salt, and the Tabasco.

Taste the pâté and add any additional seasoning that your taste demands.

Spoon the pâté into a crock and chill, covered with plastic wrap for at least 3 hours or until firm.

NOTE: I find that you can use classic custard cups to house the pâté.

The very same recipe is valid for shrimp or lobster pâté. An interesting idea is to make all three and offer a pride of pâté to your guests. All you do in the basic recipe is substitute 1 cup of shrimp or lobster meat instead of crabmeat.

ROAST LEG OF LAMB

1	leg of lamb, about 6 pounds	½	cup ground almonds
1½	cups yogurt	1	teaspoon saffron
1	teaspoon ginger	1	teaspoon salt
1	teaspoon powdered chili	¾	cup butter
5	cloves garlic, finely minced		

Remove most of the fat from the leg of lamb and prick the entire surface with a fork.

Combine the rest of the ingredients *except* the *butter*. Rub the mixture thoroughly into the meat. Cover loosely and let stand overnight (or at least 12 hours) at room temperature.

Place the lamb in a roasting pan; dot with butter. Roast uncovered in a preheated oven at 350° for 15 minutes. Then reduce the heat to 300° and roast 4 hours more or until tender. You should baste the roast frequently during the roasting period.

Let cool and take whole to the picnic to be carved at the site.

RATATOUILLE

1 medium eggplant	2 large zucchini, sliced
salt	kernels from 2 large ears
½ cup olive oil	of corn
2 large onions, thinly sliced	1½ cups fresh okra, sliced
1 garlic clove, mashed	salt
3 each red, green, and	freshly ground pepper
yellow sweet peppers,	¼ cup minced parsley
seeded, cut into thin strips	½ teaspoon ground thyme or
4 large tomatoes, peeled	marjoram
and chopped	

Peel the eggplant and cut it into slices ½-inch thick. Sprinkle the slices lightly with salt and put them into a colander. Weigh them down with a plate placed on top of the eggplant. This presses the excess moisture out of the eggplant. Let stand for 30 minutes. Drain and dice. Heat the olive oil in a deep, heavy casserole. The oil must not smoke. Cook, do *not* fry the onions, the garlic, and the peppers in it until they are soft. Add the tomatoes, the zucchini, the corn, okra, and eggplant. Season with salt and pepper. Go easy on the salt, since the eggplant is salty. Add the parsley and the ground thyme. Simmer, covered, over very low heat for 30 minutes. Uncover and simmer 15 minutes longer or until the liquid is absorbed.

Ratatouille should never be dry and never be chilled. It should be soft and cold.

ONION SALAD

½ cup olive oil	¼ teaspoon ground cloves
30 small onions, peeled	¼ teaspoon ground
3 garlic cloves, mashed	cinnamon
½ cup vinegar	½ cup seedless raisins,
salt	dropped in hot water and
freshly ground pepper	drained
2 teaspoons Dijon mustard	

Combine the olive oil and the onions in a large deep skillet.

Cook, stirring constantly, until the onions are golden. Add the garlic, vinegar, a little salt and pepper, the mustard, cloves, cinnamon, and raisins. Simmer, covered, until the onions are barely tender. Check for the level of water; if necessary add a little hot water, 1 tablespoon at a time.

Chill before serving.

PEAR TART

FILLING:

1 dessert-spoon of flour	½ cup milk
5 ounces sugar	1 egg white
2 whole eggs	4 pears

PUFF PASTRY:

3 cups flour	½ teaspoon lemon juice
1 teaspoon salt	¾ cup cold water
1½ cups butter or margarine	

Sift the flour into a large bowl. Add the salt and mix it well. With a pastry cutter, cut the butter or margarine into the flour. Continue cutting until the mixture resembles bread crumbs. Add the water and lemon juice a little at a time, stirring with a knife as you do so, until you have a soft dough. Then roll it in an oblong on the pastry board and fold it in threes. Give the pastry a half turn. Repeat this rolling and folding three times. Put the pastry in a cool place for 30 minutes before using it. Bake it in a very hot oven.

Line a tart tin with the puff pastry. Mix the flour and sugar, add the whole egg and the milk slowly, beating the while. Add the egg white and beat to a creamy consistency. Pour this mixture into the pastry case. Peel the pears and cut them in two, lengthwise. Place seven halves, cut side down, in a circle in the pie dish. Put the remaining one in the middle. Bake in a hot oven for 30 minutes. Serve cool.

Fall: Thanksgiving-The Fast Feast

From Charles Dickens to Norman Rockwell, holiday entertaining is pictured as a three-generation family all seated at the dining-room table. The eldest carved and the drumstick was the prize for the kid with the most freckles.

Today, families are scattered all over the country and the holidays most often mean entertaining one's immediate friends. Dining rooms have almost disappeared and are replaced by an "L" on the blueprint labeled "the dining area." Trying to seat a large gathering is difficult. Everything seems less special if it is too crowded. Forks stab shoulders, glasses crash-land on teeth, and one is hard put to avoid stains.

I prefer a refreshing rebellion from the rigid tradition of the magazine-cover sit-down dinner, and serve my Thanksgiving guests at a Bountiful Buffet. Guests should be tormented by a mild excess of choices—a delicious torture—ham, turkey, many vegetables, farm stuffing, a bucket of creamy giblet gravy, and a separate dessert table.

The traditional holidays are not days for the blinding chic of pâté en croute and Dom Perignon. However, a splash of digestive chic—bottled mineral water along with the wine, cider, a pitcher of cold milk, and coffee—is a nice touch.

Compose an opera and you may be dead before it is sung publicly. Cook a holiday dinner and it's instant creativity. There is an extraordinary high in basking in the sensual pleasure of guests who are eating the food you have prepared.

Keep the menu simple and familiar. Don't dull the palates by sharp sauces. Guests should not be assaulted by spices. Let the flavors linger, but not loiter. Cooking with haute pretension should be practiced long before it is served to more than two.

Both your turkey and ham will come with specific directions that are foolproof and easy. The final buffet may look positively awe-inspiring but if, as on earlier occasions I've described in these pages, you preplan your work schedule, all the hassle of being both cook and host is eliminated.

The inexhaustible groaning board is a fine old American tradition, but only a compulsive purist has to do everything from the ground up. In planning the menu, remember that this is the twentieth century. Forget the cranberry bog and just open the can. Take advantage of the shortcuts that are made possible by prepared foods, such as stuffing mix, frozen and canned vegetables and fruits, bottled ham glaze, cranberry sauce, and assorted relishes.

Here is an advance working plan:
1. Assemble your recipes; read them carefully. Check the cooking equipment needed and don't forget the serving dishes and utensils.
2. Shop for the staple groceries.
3. Tell the market butcher the size turkey you will want. Ask him to set it aside for you. Follow defrosting directions and allow enough time for the defrosting to take place. If you have a personal relationship with your butcher, you may be able to avoid defrosting by arranging to pick up the bird already thawed the day before the party.

Timing information:
For a turkey over 12 pounds, allow about ¾ pound per person. If you're buying an extra large turkey (over 20 pounds), be sure it will fit in your oven with enough room for air to circulate around the bird and the pan.

Roasting:
Roast the bird unstuffed. Place the bird, breast up, on a rack in a shallow roasting pan. The pan should be big enough to hold the turkey without any overhang, and deep enough to hold drippings. If you do not have a roasting pan, you may be able to use the broiler pan from your range, or an inexpensive disposable aluminum-foil pan. Cook ar 325°. Time it according to weight-chart directions that come with the turkey and ham. Cook stuffing in a separate casserole and place in oven just 1 hour before serving.

Carving
Remove all skewers, clamps, and threads. Place bird on a large platter. Have ready a small, warm platter, carving tools, a towel for the carver's hands. Hold drumstick and slice through the skin and joint connecting leg and thigh to backbone. Remove the

piece to the small platter and slice through the leg/thigh joint. Slice meat off drumstick. Slice meat off thigh, cutting parallel to the bone.

Make a horizontal cut at the base of the breast meat, cutting to the bone. Then slice the breast in thin even slices, each ending at the base cut.

Baking

Bake away from scratch if you have the talent and time for it. Homemade mince meat or preparing your own pumpkin from scratch seem to belong to another era because they take so much time. I have wallowed in compliments as my guests bit happily into my mince and pumpkin pies. The mince and the pumpkin filling came from a jar and a can.

Don't hesitate to use a pie-crust mix. You can personalize the mince by adding brandy or sherry to it; the pumpkin by adding a little orange juice and a half cup of grated orange peel; the apple filling by soaking some raisins in madeira and eliminating the top crust and substituting shredded coconut. Combine a prepared package of custard and rice pudding and pour the mixture over freestone peach halves in a crystal bowl for people who prefer pudding to pie or just like both. Buffets allow guests to fill their plates as it pleases them, to return for seconds at their leisure, and to enjoy the sweets when they are ready.

Not all of us have a celebrated cellar or wine rack well stocked with noble labels of the best years. If chianti and spaghetti is the only wine and food combo of which you are absolutely sure, go to a specialist. Buy your wine from a wine dealer who is patient and enthusiastic with neophytes. These are good wines for all budgets (prices, of course, vary from month to month, place to place):

Domestic

Price	Vintage	
3.29	NV	Beringer Vineyards/north Coast country Pinot Chardonnay
3.89	1975	Sonoma Vineyards Chardonnay

Price	Vintage	
4.99	1976	Fetzer Vineyards Mendocino Chardonnay
5.50	1976	Calloway Vineyards Sauvignon Blanc Fumé
8.99	1975	Sterling Vineyards Pinot Chardonnay

Imported

2.99	1976	Macon Villages Blanc Cep de vin Sélection
2.99	1976	Pouilly Fuissé (Alfred de Montigny)
5.99	1973	Meursault (Charney Bellevue)
6.99	1975	Pouilly Fumé Ladoucette Frères
9.79	1976	Puligny Montrachet (Joseph Drouhin)
10.75	1974	Meursault Charmes (Prosper Maufoux)
29.95	1976	Montrachet Marquis de la Guiche

Full-bodied white wines are generally recommended for ham and turkey; however, red wine is, of course, acceptable to those who prefer it.

Champagne or white wine are the proper aperitifs; port preferably true vintage, would be the fitting classic end to the repast.

Recipes for the Fast Feast

A PLUMP, FULL-BREASTED GOLDEN TURKEY

(A 16-pound bird serves 12)

Preheat oven to 325°

After you have defrosted your turkey, remove the giblets and neck from the turkey, wash and set aside.

Many of the current crop come all trussed and ready for the oven. Fasten the wing tips to the body with poultry pins. Close the cavity with pins or twine. If the legs are not already trussed together you can easily tie them together.

Place the turkey on rack in shallow roasting pan. I brush the whole bird with butter and generously sprinkle salt and pepper on it. Make a tent of tinfoil and cover the bird. Shove it in the oven and go about your business. Give it 4½ hours and then remove the tinfoil. The turkey will brown quickly so keep an eye on it to prevent too much browning. Take it out of the oven and let it stand 30 minutes before carving. Use this time to make the gravy. Run a stick of butter or margarine over the bird, massage gently for a high gloss that doesn't do a lot to the taste but is great for the eye.

TOLLGATE FARM STUFFING

1   pound of chestnuts (about 2 cups) chopped
10   ½-ounce cans beef bouillon
¾   pound bulk pork sausage
¼   cup sausage drippings
1   cup butter, melted
10   cups finely crushed fresh bread or a bag of ground bread for stuffing
¾   cup onion, minced
1½   cups celery, chopped; I use the stalks and the leaves
1   tablespoon marjoram
2   teaspoons salt
½   teaspoon pepper
1   cup white raisins

With a sharp knife slit the skin on flat side of chestnuts. (You can save this chore by finding the dried chestnuts and soaking them in water overnight.) Place chestnuts in saucepan and cover with water. Bring to a boil. Remove chestnuts one at a time from water, remove shells and inner skins. Cook the shelled chestnuts in beef bouillon for 25 minutes or until tender. Drain. Chop nuts coarsely. Brown sausage in skillet, reserving ¼ cup of the drippings. Combine sausage drippings and butter. Add onions to butter-dripping mixture and sauté until onions are yellow. Stirring occasionally, mix in some of the bread crumbs, stirring to prevent excessive browning. Turn into a deep bowl and lightly mix in celery, marjoram, salt, pepper, and the rest of the crumbs. Add browned sausage, chestnuts, and raisins. Toss all ingredients together thoroughly. Bake in 350° oven for 30 minutes. Makes 3 quarts of dressing.

Be sure the gravy is on your buffet close to the stuffing.

Country giblet gravy and Tollgate stuffing combined provide moans and groans of satisfaction that surpass any compliment.

COUNTRY GRAVY

Use a 2-quart saucepan. Place the giblets and neck in 3 cups of water. Bring to a boiling point; reduce heat; simmer covered until the giblets are tender. Add the turkey liver and simmer another 15 minutes. Remove everything from the pan, let cool and chop. I do use the meat from the neck. Add giblets to 1 can concentrated chicken broth. Salt and pepper to taste.

When you remove the turkey from the roasting pan, pour drippings into a 1-cup measure and mix with the giblets and broth.

In a separate pan make a white sauce:

1 stick of margarine or butter	½ cup of flour
	2 cups of milk

Combine this with your giblets and add additional pepper to taste. Stir until smooth over very low heat.

FRUIT GLAZED BAKED HAM
(Serves 16)

10- to 12-pound cooked, bone-in ham	1 teaspoon dry mustard
½ cup light brown sugar	1 jar of ham glaze
¾ cup light corn syrup	1 jar of spiced peaches

Place the ham, fat side up, on rack in roasting pan. Bake it uncovered about 2½ hours. Meanwhile combine brown sugar, syrup, mustard. Cook over low heat, stirring occasionally, until sugar is dissolved, and mixture comes to a boil. In a medium bowl, combine the jar of ham glaze with the mustard mixture.

When you remove the ham, score the fat side into 1-inch diamonds with a sharp knife. Brush and cover the ham completely with the fruit mixture. Bake 15 minutes. Then repeat the glazing and bake for another 15 minutes. Remove from oven and surround with spiced peaches on a platter. Pass the remaining mustard sauce for the ham lovers.

BAKED SWEET POTATOES

Sweet potatoes or yams are a good choice with baked ham and turkey. I like the touch of sweet in a main course. This recipe serves 12.

2 *large cans of yams*	2 *teaspoons salt*
2 *4-ounce cans (No. 1 flat)*	2 *teaspoons nutmeg*
crushed pineapple	1 *box of diced dates*
½ *cup butter*	4 *tablespoons brown sugar*
2 *eggs slightly beaten*	4 *teaspoons butter*

Heat oven to 350° (moderate). Place all the yams with their juice in an ovenproof dish.

Combine yams, pineapples, ½ cup butter, eggs, salt, nutmeg, and dates. Sprinkle with brown sugar and dot with a tablespoon of butter. Bake uncovered 30 minutes.

LIMA BEANS WITH MUSHROOMS
(Serves 12)

Cook 4 packages of frozen green lima beans according to directions. Just before serving, toss with 1 pound of sliced fresh mushrooms sautéed in butter. It gives this basic bean an air of sophistication without a bit of arrogance.

KICKY CARROTS
(Serves 12)

Open 4 cans of whole baby carrots. Not many guests rush for seconds if you just boil them. You can guarantee their popularity if you sauté briefly with butter and salt and the juice of 1 lemon in a skillet until they are steaming hot but still slightly crisp. Add the most gossamer dusting of nutmeg and your guests will never believe that carrots are really good for them.

CONTINENTAL SQUASH
(Serves 12)

Use two large bags of frozen sliced zucchini squash. Sauté in ½ cup butter, melted, 2 teaspoons water, ½ teaspoon salt and ⅛ teaspoon pepper, 1 clove garlic, crushed.

Cook covered in saucepan with tight-fitting lid 6 minutes.

Serve the squash while still crisp. Keep your eye on this because overcooked squash becomes soggy, loses its shape, and will be ignored on the buffet.

TWO PROUD CAULIFLOWER HEADS

Just steam cauliflower until cooked but still crisp. Glaze it with a little melted butter. It's a vegetable that people either love or hate. I love it—both to eat and to look at.

PERFECT PEAS

I just boil the water, toss the peas in, and remove from the heat. Like the true beauties they are, they require very little else.

Winter: The Joy of Giving

Make the first party of the New Year very special by giving a New Year's Day Winter In-house picnic and dessert smorgasbord. After the galas and festive holiday gatherings I long for the simple directness of the sit-on-pillows-on-the-floor, or anywhere-you-like old-fashioned picnic. I toss big plaid blankets on the floor over my living-room rug and give my guests individual baskets of fried chicken, Russian eggs, French bread, wine, cheese, and fruit crudités. We skip the ants. When the "picnic" is over all is cleaned up quickly by putting everything back in the baskets.

Then comes the coffee, tea, hot chocolate, and milk. The dessert buffet ranges from cakes, pies, ice cream, individual French pastry tarts, assorted pastries, and cookies. Because this is the day after "Happy New Year," I don't do one bit of dessert preparation, I buy everything. I do, however, enjoy making my own fried chicken and Russian eggs.

FRIED CHICKEN
(Serves 12)

3 broilers (each about 3 pounds)	2 tablespoons pepper
1½ cups flour	2 cups bacon drippings and/or shortening
3 teaspoons salt	

1. Cut chicken into 8 serving-size pieces: 2 breasts, 2 wings, 2 thighs, 2 drumsticks. Wash chicken but do not dry. This is essential so that the skin will take on a thick flour coating.
2. Mix flour, salt, and pepper in a brown paper bag. Shake pieces, a few at a time, to coat evenly all over.
3. I use an electric skillet heated to 360°. Heat bacon drippings ¼ inch deep. Arrange chicken without crowding, in a single layer in hot fat.
4. Brown slowly for 15 minutes. Pink juices will start to show on top, turn and brown the other side 15 minutes. This slow cooking, plus turning just once, gives the chicken its crisp coating.
5. When pieces are browned I pile them into deep skillets and on top of the stove let the chicken cook 20 minutes longer—this will make it nicely golden and finger-lickin' good.

RUSSIAN EGGS

12 hard-boiled eggs	salt to taste
¼ cup mayonnaise	pepper to taste
½ cup thick sour cream	thin strips of pimento
1 tablespoon of finely chopped green onion	black caviar

Cut eggs in half lengthwise. Put the yolks through a fine sieve and blend with the mayonnaise, sour cream, and onions until a smooth paste is formed. Add the salt and pepper. You can use a spoon or pastry bag to stuff the whites with the paste. Top the egg with a pimento strip circle and fill the center with caviar. Fill the bottom of a white mug with a nest of parsley and watercress. Put two halves of the stuffed eggs leaning on a side of the nest. It stands easily in the "picnic" basket.

This New Year's Day party is my "gift" day to close friends. I don't mean I ignore the Christmas spirit with tree and presents. To me Christmas is a mixture of the sacred and the mundane, and it can be an exhausting and confusing experience. Yet I always try to remember that there is nothing else I know of that offers simultaneously the life-giving reward of nostalgia, hope, love, inspiration, strength, and warmth. How very good it is to know that whether or not we deserve it, we are given Christmas again and again.

A very real part of that renewal for me is sharing with people I love—my closest friends—on my annual first day of the year get-to-gether. I decided about ten years ago that I would give those people special gifts on that day, unlike Christmas, which makes people feel they must exchange gifts with you. This gift day is, instead, my own privilege, separate from the canned carols, the department-store displays, commercials, and mailing pieces of which the sole purpose seems to make you run around town buying more and more things in a compulsive frenzy. I revel in the joy of finding gifts for the special people in my life as an all-year-'round experience. Remember, their value cannot be measured in dollars and cents, so let your gifts sparkle with originality. There are few more challenging moments in a relationship than the one when you are forced to unwrap a gift in the presence of the giver who is smiling in expectation of your rapture and then, holding it in your hand, you all too obviously have to wonder what it is.

"To give is better than to receive" can ring true only with a little acquired skill in the art of gift-giving. The trick is to enjoy it as a genuinely creative experience.

Reach into your head, as well as into your wallet, and pull out an original idea. Think about what you would like to have that you don't have due to a lack of time or money. Then, think of your friends and family in the same way. Think about people and what they have said to you about their personal interests. You'll discover that if you really listen, you can do enormously creative gift-giving. Your doctor is also a camera freak—so haunt the secondhand book stores to locate an early book, magazine, or print about the field. Wrap it with a current foreign photography magazine or a lucite frame for his latest favorite photograph; perhaps your lawyer is a bread baker—so get the best Italian pepper bread in your town along with its recipe; your best friend is married to his foreign sportscar—give *him* the most expensive chamois for his car and a promise to help simonize it. For the gardener a handy new bulb planter and a dozen exotic bulbs; for a serious cook—research a divine sauce that demands shallots and then send the recipe, a quart of shallots, and the right wine to go with the dish. A wonderful gift for a salad lover is a basket filled with everything needed to make the most perfect salad dressing from a fine gourmet food shop: French olive oil, peanut oil, tarragon, vinegar, mustard from Dijon, a container of Telichenary black pepper, basil, dill, celery seed. Surround this with four to six heads of lettuce.

Give a theater lover a pair of tickets to an upcoming production. Add a limousine service to the package if you want to make the evening truly unforgettable; arrange a dinner for that young couple who are still on a tight budget, and have the bill sent to you, once or once a month.

Most people take pride in the personal style they have achieved. Be careful not to project what you *think* the person should be rather than what he *is*. Avoid the "why don't you change for the better" gifts, such as diet books and exercise guides. Your gift should declare your understanding of the person. If his most athletic activity is the signing of a check or the mixing of a martini, then don't assume that the surprise personalized hockey stick will precipitate him onto the ice. Give him a collection of belts for every occasion, hanging on an oversized saddle hook, or fill a big punch bowl with a cold-weather recipe for mulled wine, the ingredients, and a wardrobe of different-colored mufflers; if she is happy only when adding her voice to the shriek of chic at a celebrity cocktail party, you may please her enormously by giving her gloves (one pair or a complete wardrobe) that she can slip into as she kisses her way out.

Don't enter unchartered regions by making assumptions. If all his furniture is Museum of Modern Art–approved, don't rush to the nearest Williamsburg shop for an eighteenth-century reproduction because you feel the apartment needs warmth. Build on what you know about him. If he is a man proud of his Irish heritage, find a handsome old map of Ireland and have it framed appropriately for his own furniture. If she is into nutrition, give a jar of organic peanut butter with a card that says: "I watched this being made and was reminded that peanut butter is your soul food." A bachelor girl in an efficiency apartment would be elated with a tailored robe, but would be hard put to find space in the closet for one appropriate to the second act of *The Barretts of Wimpole Street.*

Gifts really are best when they are suitable to the life of the person. Acres of maribou may be glamorous for the moment, but do consider the upkeep of any clothing before you send it. If the gift will spend most of its life moulting in the closet, or at a cleaner's whose charges rank with major surgeons', don't give it. Don't let your gift complicate anyone's life. Dogs, cats, fish, and birds may seem charming, but when the receiver finds himself having to take care of them daily, there may be a lot of teeth gnashing. Avoid cute bug or animal items for your lady, unless you're sure of her feelings about them. Earrings in the form of a tiny spider in its web could send her hurrying back to the analyst.

Everyone is getting layered this season, but there is no use in giving the marvelous shirt, tie, sweater, jacket, and scarf to make up the layers if he is too fat to wear them. He may come off looking like a self-destructive shoplifter. If the commission of too many sins or gins has added substance to his middle, then it is kinder to find a bloused jacket cut loosely at the waist so no one can tell where he stops and the fabric begins.

There is an insidious concept that appears every season as a solution for the man who has everything. The idea of a man so rich and classy that nothing remains to give him that he doesn't already own, or wouldn't sneer at, has given way to the man so broken in spirit by the presents of seasons past that he will receive the most ridiculous gadget without a shudder of complaint. This theory is based on the curious assumption that if a gift is a gadget it has to have masculine appeal ipso facto—the more virile the guy, the more complex must be the gadget. So, even though you are a man who can't operate a pencil sharpener without getting a trifle confused, you are inevitably given a musical chronometer that can be made to play your alma mater. But, to make it work you need an engineering degree, ten years of experience in the field, and an assistant to help.

Eliminate all the so-called "masculine" gifts—is there anyone who really wants an elephant's-foot hassock? Forget the fun objects that hang in the car over the dashboard or the "conversation piece" such as a desk lamp shaped like an amoeba.

There is something marvelous to be said for gifts that are clearly meant to be shared by two. A china breakfast set with two bed trays, napkins and the most beautiful tea strainer you can find, a bottle of precious liqueur with two handsome glasses, an espresso machine, and a pair of cups, a lemon and a slicing knife, or a season's series of opera tickets and a diary with the dates marked off and the place you will be having supper written clearly.

The charm of the unexpected is always welcome. Go beyond the usual initial monogramming if you are giving a personalized gift. Remember that nicknames, secret words, bits of cherished poetry, the date you met, or notes of a favorite song are impressively original. How about a superb bottle of brandy, two snifters, one with your name and his or hers on the other, or a silver box with a quotation that expresses your feeling for her.

Don't be afraid to give money. It always fits, needs no alterations, and the color is never disappointing. But, dress it up, either with a very personal note and the crispest new bills accompanied by a small thoughtful gift, or slip the money into a handsome wallet. Nastrix packages its designer watch in a wallet as a double gift . . . add some money inside the wallet with a note: "I want you to have the time of your life."

People who collect and are hooked will appreciate nothing more than a fresh gift fix . . . the one musical-comedy album missing from their collection, the one copy of *Flair* magazine they could never locate, the Rhythm Boys and Paul Whiteman recording that gave Bing his start, the latest nonfiction book in a subject of deep interest.

Don't make gifts yourself unless you have mastered the art or craft required. If the needlepoint pillow looks as though it were made in the occupational therapy ward—or worse, by a preschool nursery child—don't force a friend to house and hide it. However, if you really have mastered your Cuisinart and can produce a perfect chicken liver pâté, don't hesitate to give it, accompanied by one superb rye bread and/or a box of Carr's best biscuits, with a sterling-silver spreader to complete the joy.

Make out a "gift certificate," a mock contract, or a promissory note with a "gift" of your time and talent: cocktail party to be catered by you for twenty people which will include enough of your famous succulent stuffed mushrooms for the guests; or "one herb garden to be planted (by you in the spring)."

A gaudy book to grace the coffee table (unread) is a cliché . . . a coffee-table book on the ballet with two tickets to a performance for a ballet lover is inspired gift-giving. Extravagant chocolates sinfully overpriced may be another cliché, but five pounds of good fresh jelly beans in an old tin box for a penny-candy freak is imaginative.

The concept of giving double and triple gifts no matter what the level or price is super-thoughtful. Just as a cold gift certificate may be interpreted as a confession of disinterest and/or a total lack of imagination. The exception is the gift certificate earmarked for a specific present . . . something that you might pick out together. It could be fabric and style for his new coat at a distinguished tailor, or the latest attaché case from a department-store catalogue.

This kind of gift-giving thinking is guaranteed to add sparkling originality to your choice of gifts, and make this New Year the happiest ever.

TEN: The Celebrities Celebrate

There are two kinds of celebrities. There are those who are known just for their "well-knownness," as Daniel Boorstin wrote in his book *The Image*. And there are those who actually worked for a living, got good at it, and became renowned. Most of my friends are of the latter variety: Angelo Donghia, Joyce and David Susskind, Polly Bergen, Margaret Whiting, Donald Brooks. Like these celebrities or not, somehow they have been imbedded in your consciousness, possibly even more permanently than your social-security number, because they've designed the patterned sheets you sleep on, implanted the idea of quiche as a glorious entrée in your head, or created a celluloid fantasy you still dream about.

Because we live in a star-oriented society, we toss glittering names around at dinner, wear their initials to bed, and succumb to their latest doings in the gossip columns. Gossip is definitely back. Suzy, Rex Reed, Liz Smith, Earl Wilson, Diane Judge, *People* and *Celebrity* and *US* magazines wouldn't exist if Americans weren't celebrity-crazy. Behind the image the stars feed us via the media and their press agents lurk people who actually have mothers, fathers, siblings, husbands, lovers, children, and friends. Like everybody else, they have to eat, drink, dress, and undress. Here's how Betsy Bloomingdale, the Oscar de la Rentas, Celeste Holm, Bill Blass, and a host of other celebrities feel about entertaining, etiquette, families, cocktail parties, and privacy.

Oscar and Françoise de la Renta

It was Diana Vreeland who was first, as she is with so many styles, to bring old society, new money, and the literary and show-biz crowd all under the umbrella "The Beautiful People." No couple I know symbolizes that set better—or entertains them better—than fashion designer Oscar de la Renta and his wife Françoise. Their Mediterranean confidence in mixing color, pattern, and *objets* (as well as a variety of guests, their European friends with American actors, journalists, and socialites)—in short, their European love of *luxe* you can see in every detail of their life.

"We've always lived extravagantly," Françoise admits. "To have our friends around and to share with them the comforts of life—flowers, servants—that's our luxury. Not jewels or paintings or furs. What I adore is the nineteenth century, when maids were so prettily dressed. I would love to have had masses of servants and to be able to leave guests in a room and know they were being taken care of."

As it is, however, Françoise, very much a woman of the twentieth century, takes time from what she calls her "hobby" (you and I would call her interior designing a full-time career) to do most of the planning herself. "I've always been careful about details," she explains, "because it amuses me. I enjoy making everything comfortable and attractive." You could think of it as her philosophy of entertaining as well as of decorating: "Good light, proper pillows and an environment where your eye is always resting on something pleasant."

For her table in the city, Françoise uses white linen with blue-and-white china, or batik tablecloths with solid napkins in red, orange, green, or yellow, with Chinese bowls and saucers on silver plates. In the country she's used tablecloths made from scarves in French Provincial fabrics, with brown-and-white pottery from the South of France and baskets full of bread and butter. She often serves wine in carafes ("so very practical and pretty," she points out). It might be Muscadet 1972 or, in the country, cold Beaujolais ("It has the coolness of white and the warmth of red"). The centerpiece might be a red amaryllis. (In the living room, she says, "I *never* have cut flowers—they last only two or three days. I prefer plants, which last much longer.")

"I absolutely hate long, narrow tables. I always make a point of putting ten people at a round table where you would normally have eight—the conversation is always better and people enjoy themselves more. I try to have one couple or two good friends—a man and a woman—and I say to them, 'Now, I'm counting on you to help me with the conversation and make the party go.' I could sit around the table all night when conversation is stimulating."

For dinner Françoise often serves fish, particularly striped bass—hot or cold—or scallops; and interesting vegetables—leeks, turnips, zucchini—or vegetables from near their country home—corn, tomatoes, asparagus. A weekend country lunch for guests might be shepherd's pie, a terrine of macaroni with olives, or gnocchi. Salads are watercress with endive or Bibb lettuce, served with a whole Mimolette (French cheddar) or Stilton and biscuits.

After dinner coffee and white liqueurs in icy balloon glasses are served in the living room. "I would absolutely never have music with dinner. That's a nightmare. And I don't like music in the living room because it makes a woman talk louder."

What Françoise does have around her house is fragrance. "It's indispensable," she says. She loves Guerlain's "Potpourri aux Plantes Marines" and puts baskets of Floris potpourri all over.

To ensure that her guests are comfortable when she's entertaining in the country, Françoise tells them to bring a pair of jeans, "so they won't pack their Saint Laurents or Balenciagas." And the de la Rentas built their house in the Dominican Republic near the airport, so friends could jet in to visit easily. It's only a forty-minute flight from the Bahamas. But if transportation there is not a problem, what to wear can be. "We decided to keep thirty or forty caftans for men and women in the guest rooms. That's all you wear. For swimming you just slip out of the robe and swim in the nude. It's simple and practical. All our guests need for a visit is a toothbrush." Anywhere a guest is entertained by the de la Rentas, he knows he will be taken care of—with style.

Earl Blackwell

Earl Blackwell has used his entertaining to build his unique business, Celebrity Service, which—for a fee—will tell you how to reach any star of show biz. And that business has helped him to throw some of the most fabulous parties of the century. In fact, "party of the century" is what the *London Times* called Earl's masked ball at the Palazzo Rezzonico in Venice in 1967. Earl himself dressed like a courtier paying homage to Elizabeth Taylor, dressed like a princess in a sparkling headdress. Richard Burton came, also paying court to his then-wife, and a real princess, Grace of Monaco, was there. Also among the 700 were Rose Kennedy and Aristotle Onassis.

Earl has been staging news-making parties since 1940, when he persuaded some of his friends to appear and promote the New York World's Fair. He dreamed up the birthday party in 1962 for President Kennedy at Madison Square Garden, where Marilyn Monroe sang "Happy Birthday," Israel's 25th anniversary celebration with Golda Meir; and the opening of Sonja Henie's art museum in Oslo.

Called "The Pearl Mesta of Show Business," Earl says, "Nowadays, I do just one big event each year, besides my own little parties." Those "little parties," he explains, are "two tables of eight and one of ten in my dining room. Afterward I'll have maybe seventy-five more people in for drinks and dancing." You don't need to worry about crowding when you have a ballroom forty feet long and thirty feet high, with parquet floors, chairs from one of the Vanderbilt homes and murals of the Venice Earl loves.

"The important thing," he says, "is to take care of every tiny detail beforehand, then relax and enjoy yourself once the party starts."

Buffy Cafritz

"Giving a party means having fun," say Buffy Cafritz, the wife of the Washington realtor. She has three rules to share that make entertaining more fun for her and for her guests.

First, those guests should be "a mixed bag—old, young, pretty, interesting. I don't like a predictable crowd." For invitations, she uses stiff, white cards, bordered and engraved in blue, or engraved ecru parchment. "I always indicate the cocktail hour as well as the dinner hour and I keep the cocktails short—forty-five minutes. I want good conversation at my parties, not guests leaning to starboard."

Second, the menu should consist of simple but superbly prepared dishes. For Buffy, they might be lobster or crab mousse with a vert sauce, crown roast lamb with mushroom stuffing, glazed baby carrots, maybe an apricot soufflé or baked fruit in custard sauce. The champagne is always Dom Perignon.

Third, the decor should be coordinated. If the party is for fewer than twelve, she uses ecru placemats instead of tablecloths. "I like the sheen of the table." She has a set of blue porcelain, a set of Limoges Lafayette, and another two dozen orange, gold, and white Limoges.

But Buffy has always known that Porthault tablecloths and vermeil candlesticks are only one facet of successful entertaining. "My mother taught me always to offer something to anyone who comes through the front door," she says. "A little tea, hot chocolate, maybe just cookies. Maybe that's Italian, but I always do."

In fact, her favorite entertaining was the party she gave for her daughter Pamela's sixth birthday. She presented all the youngsters with red crepe-paper capes and baskets of goodies and dressed her son, Sandy, as the big bad wolf. "I'll never forget how those children laughed while they were being chased by Sandy and seeing those twenty-two little red capes go flying by." Buffy has made the news with parties for hundreds of Washington's diplomatic, Congressional, White House, and social set, but she says, "I'd rather do a superb dinner for ten or a little Sunday lunch after a volleyball game on my back lawn."

Lorraine Percy

Just because Washington has filled up with Democrats and Southerners, Lorraine Percy, wife of Senator Charles Percy, Republican of Illinois, isn't going to fold up her tents. She has always liked to mix guests ("Not all Republicans, all Congress or all administration. I like to invite writers, artists, Democrats"), every bit as much as she likes to mix china ("The only matching sets I have are for Chinese dinners"). In sort of cloth-coat

Republicanism, she uses the same silver, green, gold, blue, and orange English ironstone dinner plates, and blue Imari dessert plates the Percys use every day.

Lorraine likes to seat between six and twenty (ideally eighteen), divided between the French mahogany table in the Sister Parrish blue-striped dining room and a round table in the yellow sunroom with the huge modern painting. If she has extra women, she seats them next to other women. "I don't think people really care," she says.

Cocktails are served by a waiter if it's black tie. "If not, we set up a tray in the sunroom. If we're six to eight people, we help ourselves; if more, I have someone there to help."

Lorraine can tick off her dinner favorites. "A homemade soup (mushroom, watercress, chicken with egg drop); caviar, sour cream, and paper-thin tomatoes on toast points; cornucopias of smoked salmon, or mousse with cucumber. Lemon chicken, beef bourgignon, saddle of lamb, duck with currants, filet of beef or an all-Chinese menu. We serve two or three vegetables—sautéed mushrooms, some form of potatoes or rice, plus anything in season. I like to use endive, Boston or Bibb lettuce, and watercress, with an oil-and-vinegar dressing, followed by a cheese platter with Euphrates water biscuits. Dessert is simple—a homemade sherbet, a lemon or cold chocolate soufflé, hot fruit or pears and ice cream with chocolate sauce."

Live music couldn't add to Lorraine's intimate dinners. "Sometimes during cherry-blossom time we have a guitarist in the garden for large groups, but generally we just play records," she explains.

In the air, with or without music, "I use thick Siromani Chadanbath sandalwood that I bring back from India. Nehru taught me about it. But remember: you can have all the incense, music, flowers, and food in the world, but the most important thing is your guests—fun people who get along well together, stimulate each other, and are interesting for their own sake."

André Oliver

"For me," says André Oliver, a designer for Pierre Cardin in

Paris, "everything is a reason for a party. If I can't find a reason, I invent one." His favorites are a seated dinner for twelve and a huge reception. "If I'm giving it for someone," he explains, "then I invite their friends *and any* people I think the guest of honor might enjoy.

"For a small sit-down dinner, I keep the food fairly simple. For a big buffet, it's better to have a big choice of entrées." He even builds his cornucopia around a theme, such as curries. "I make up my menus based on the season—if fresh asparagus is in season, then I'll serve that. I repeat the same menus from year to year; it's better than to try things that may not succeed." André has all the dishes made in his apartment except dessert (often coconut cake or ice cream or sherbet), which he buys at favorite stores.

For a small dinner, he might play records, usually pop music (American). For big buffets, he'd prefer to have a band. "It creates a climate of folly and gives even more gaiety to a party."

For the table, he likes to mix silver objects with low bouquets of small flowers, like anemones. "I am a maniac about flowers. I can go to as many as twenty different florists to find the flowers I want. I love potted flowers—primavera, hyacinths.

"I always have something in a perfume burner. It could be sandalwood or Jansens's Maple fragrance, or sometimes I mix several different scents. I change scents often because otherwise you become used to an odor and no longer smell it."

André keeps the cocktail meeting-and-greeting down to forty-five minutes, unless the party is a buffet, when he lets drinks go on for more than an hour. In any case, André's parties are often late-night affairs. If the hour grows *too* late, André says, "I suggest we all go on to a nightclub."

Mary Lasker

"I don't put my mind on entertaining," says Mary Lasker. Still, when she *is* wearing her hostess hat, she's as successful as when she's promoting one of her social-welfare projects. The fact is that her charming parties have won many converts to her causes.

"I think parties of a certain size go better than small ones," she says, "unless you're very sure of the interrelation of your guests. Dinner parties for eight or ten are not as much fun. I like a big party if the guest list is well-enough selected."

Mrs. Lasker prefers sit-down dinners ("You have more control"), preceded by cocktails for "not more than forty-five minutes. If guests are late, I just sit down to dinner. You can ruin a party if you wait too long."

Dinner might be a fish course, such as a sole mousse, followed by lamb or a filet of beef, and ending with an ice or ice cream made to look amusing. The dishes serve her philosophy: "A short dinner—only three courses—and not too much food."

The flowers pick up the color of her beautiful Impressionist and modern paintings. "I like gay flowers. I sometimes place several small vases with an anemone in each around the table. And rather than tall candles, I occasionally scatter vigil lights at random. I like solid colors—mostly white—for table linens or placemats because china always has flowers on it."

For all that, Mrs. Lasker is definite about what makes entertaining successful. "If it isn't a good mix of people, it isn't a good party. And you shouldn't invite people because you owe them something. Invite only the people you feel warm about."

Angelo Donghia

Angelo Donghia's party giving, like his interior design, is the orchestrated result of a trip through his fantasy world. Exquisite food served on linen that is pure, clean, white, starched; flowers as far as the eye can see, liquor from first-rate bottles, salted almonds in Baccarat crystal bowls, are visual dramatizations of inner life that glitters with magic. Never will a guest feel more special than when he descends Angelo's mirrored staircase in evening dress, knowing that he is about to partake of a Roman feast every bit as grand as Nero's. Pasta, meats, cheeses, salads, the moistest of cakes, sherbets, figs, and grapes abound. Coffee is served with Amaretti, pignoli cookies, and after-dinner drinks. Cigarettes are offered with paper-thin mints and Italian sugar-coated almonds. Diets be damned! Angelo wants to turn you into an addict.

The usual Donghia seating plan covers his entire house. Guests have options: perches, the library, Chinese tables with cushions, the bedroom, the garden in spring with café tables and banquettes. "I want my guests to make themselves at home and select the group that they are prepared to relate to. I don't want them to feel too challenged. That way they can come out of their shells at their own rate."

When Angelo opened Donghia West, his showroom in Los Angeles, he invited five hundred people and two thousand showed up. Although he used the same technique of making guests feel special, the logistics were different. Ten car parkers in identifiable T-shirts were on duty. They were not allowed to accept tips. There were twelve bartenders, lined up shoulder to shoulder, behind the bar; six "floaters" served instant drinks so that no one had to wait. Eight waiters in black offered crab claws, snow peas in sour cream and dill, pullet eggs stuffed with caviar, crudités—fennel, green pepper, and radish. The music was manipulated by remote control so that the guests would remain revved-up; as the voices rose, the music went down, and vice versa. "The secret of giving a large business party is to be creative, and people will call to be invited. Both my reputation as a decorator and host preceded me. I had to deliver! Even though there was a crunch, only a few left early. But even the ones who left early never stopped talking about it." Here are two of his favorite recipes:

ANGELO DONGHIA'S TWO ITALIAN COLD SALADS

1. Use a loaf of day-old Tuscan bread, which is hard and mealy, and soak it in water. Quickly squeeze it dry, and place a layer of bread to cover the bottom of a bowl. Alternate layers of peeled ripe tomatoes, fresh basil, red onion, olive oil, salt and pepper and a touch of vinegar. Place another layer of bread on top, and repeat the layers two more times. Chill for 4 hours. The juices will run through. Just when you're ready to serve, toss it. Serve with fettucine, which you've cooked, drained, and mixed with sweet butter and grated Parmesan cheese. Accompany it with a nice, cold white wine like a Soave Bolla.

2. Blanch thin string beans and chill with a touch of olive oil, tarragon, vinegar, and fresh mint.

Joyce Davidson Susskind

Thanksgiving and other holiday entertaining are largely family affairs at the Susskinds'. Joyce usually starts cooking three days before, and the menu always includes turkey, ham with blackberry brandy sauce, rice stuffing, and seven-layer cheese cake.

Joyce's favorite party this year was daughter Samantha's ninth birthday. The furniture was removed from the dining room and replaced by a tree, fake grass, and picnic lunches. The main course was hot dogs in baskets wrapped in red-checkered napkins. This delightful event made it possible for Samantha and her friends to celebrate spring in January. "Last year there were twelve kids, boys and girls. This year it's all girls," Joyce told me, "because Samantha is at the age where she doesn't like boys."

The Susskinds' dinner parties usually include an eclectic group of twenty-five or thirty people ranging in age from thirty to seventy. "We never introduce people by credits because we believe that our guests' own curiosity will help them discover who else is present." But Joyce is very careful about seating arrangements. She will place college student Suzanne Goodson (daughter of Mark Goodson of quiz-show fame) next to Lillian Hellman, and seat Victor Sukadrev, the Russian translator for Brezhnev, on Lillian Hellman's other side. Joyce's theory is that people relate best to those who are most different in background.

I was present at a most unique Susskind party, David's birthday. What made it atypical was that David was not present. He was in London, and I presided as his surrogate host. At midnight, David called and we all sang "Happy Birthday." Unfortunately, I had to relinquish all the presents at the end of the evening.

Six Notions for Centerpieces by Joyce Susskind
1. Samantha's dolls from around the world spread in front of every place setting.
2. Baccarat cigarette cups, filled with quince, freesia, tiny orchids. An almost Oriental feeling. Set a cup in front of each place.

3. Antique silver cars, a dozen or so, filled with tiny fresh flowers which stick out the windows.

4. Chinese acupuncture dolls,* laden with quince and apple blossoms, for a pale-pink garden effect.

5. Coral shells filled with flowers.

6. Beeswax candles in assorted lengths. They're beautiful and they don't drip.

*These are dolls used to demonstrate where the acupuncture needles are placed.

Here are the menu and recipes for Joyce's Thanksgiving feast:

CHALLAH (Egg Bread)

1	cake or package of yeast	2	eggs
2	teaspoons sugar	2	tablespoons salad oil
1¼	cups lukewarm water	1	egg yolk
4½	cups sifted flour	4	tablespoons poppy seeds
2	teaspoons salt		

Combine the yeast, sugar, and ¼ cup lukewarm water. Let stand 5 minutes.

Sift the flour and salt into a bowl. Make a well in the center and drop the eggs, oil, remaining water, and yeast mixture into it. Work into the flour. Knead on a floured surface until smooth and elastic. Place in a bowl and brush top with a little oil. Cover with a towel, set in a warm place and let rise 1 hour. Punch down, cover again, and let rise until double in bulk. Divide the dough into 3 equal parts. Between lightly floured hands, roll the dough into 3 strips of even length. Braid them together and place in a baking pan. Cover with a towel and let rise until double in bulk. Brush with the egg yolk and sprinkle with the poppy seeds.

Bake in a 375° oven 50 minutes or until browned.

Makes 1 very large challah. If you wish, divide the dough in 6 parts and make 2 large loaves, or make 1 loaf and many small rolls. You may also bake the bread in a loaf pan.

NOTE: ⅛ teaspoon saffron can be dissolved in the water if you like additional flavor and color.

DRESSING FOR 30-POUND TURKEY
(One cup for each pound of turkey)
(From *The Art of Jewish Cooking* by Jennie Grossinger)

Determine how much rice is required for the amount of dressing needed for the turkey (2 boxes long-grain and wild rice make about 6 cups of rice). This is doubled when other ingredients are added, but 12 cups is not too much of this dressing.

STEP ONE:

1	8-ounce package chicken livers	5	cups packaged chicken stock
	giblets from turkey or chicken (omitting gizzard)	½	teaspoon salt
		2	packages long-grain and wild rice

Chop chicken livers and giblets. Bring chicken stock to the boiling point with the ½ teaspoon salt. Drop chicken livers into the water and simmer for about 10 minutes. Remove chicken livers from stock and set aside. Stir in rice and cook according to package directions.

STEP TWO:

While rice is cooking, melt ¼ cup of butter or margarine in large skillet.

¼	cup chopped shallots		pepper
2	cups chopped onions	¼	cup chopped celery
½	cup chopped green	½	cup chopped mushrooms

Sauté gently until onions and celery are transparent.
    Add freshly ground black pepper to taste—salt to taste.
Add:

½	teaspoon thyme	¼	teaspoon rosemary
½	teaspoon sage		

Add:

1	cup chopped water chestnuts	½	cup finely chopped walnuts
2	jars pignole nuts (about 1 cup)		

STEP THREE:

Add hot drained rice and chicken livers and ½ cup tomato paste. SEASON TO TASTE. This is very important.

ROAST HAM, BLACKBERRY WINE SAUCE

1 teaspoon dry mustard	½ cup kumquat juice
a 10-pound ham	2 tablespoons apricot jam
4 cans papaya nectar	6 tablespoons brown sugar
1 bottle blackberry wine	1 tablespoon coarsely
1 cup orange juice	grated orange rind
1 teaspoon ground cloves	large whole cloves

Sprinkle mustard over bottom of deep roasting pan. Remove rind from ham with a sharp knife, and put ham on an adjustable rack in the pan. Pour nectar over the ham. Roast in 300° oven, basting every 10 minutes, for about 1½ hours. Turn ham over halfway through cooking time so underside browns.

While ham is roasting, put blackberry wine, orange juice, ground cloves, kumquat juice, apricot jam, brown sugar, and grated orange rind in heavy enamel saucepan. Bring to a boil.

When ham has roasted 1½ hours, remove from oven. Score the fat on top of ham and make design with the cloves. Roast another hour, basting with a little of the wine mixture every 10 minutes, until browned. If ham is not browning, raise temperature to 350°. Serve remaining wine mixture hot as sauce. When sauce cools, fat rises to the top, lift it off.

CHEESECAKE (5-layer)

5 eggs, separated	grated peel of ½ lemon
½ cup plus 1 teaspoon	¾ cup all purpose
granulated sugar	flour—sift first

Preheat oven to 350°.

Cream egg yolks, ¼ cup sugar, lemon peel until lemon-colored and creamy. Beat egg whites until stiff, but not dry. Add remaining sugar by spoonfuls. Fold whites and flour (sift first) alternately into yolk mixture. Use wooden spoon for folding.

Spread 5 8-inch circles (butter and flour baking sheets. Using an 8-inch layer pan as a guide, mark 2 circles at least 1 inch apart on each baking sheet).

Bake for 10–15 minutes—watch them, should be like big cookies. Remove immediately from pan and correct the shape of the circle. Cool. Fill each layer evenly with filling, cover the top and the side too. Place into the refrigerator hours before serving. This cake is better if used the next day.

Decorate top and side with grillage.

FILLING:

7 ounces sweet butter at room temperature
1 cup fine sugar
3 egg yolks
12 ounces fresh pot cheese or cottage cheese, forced through food mill twice

⅓ cup seedless white raisins
¼ teaspoon salt
½ teaspoon or more fresh imported vanilla beans in powdered form

Cream butter, sugar, and egg yolks. Add all the rest of the ingredients.

GRILLAGE:

3 tablespoons blanched almond slivers

½ cup granulated sugar cooked for caramel

Mix almonds into caramel. Cool on oiled plate. When cold, put through a nut grinder or blender. Press by hand all over top and sides of cake.

Polly Bergen

Polly Bergen's lifestyle has undergone a metamorphosis since her Malibu days. Polly now divides her time between New York, cross-country lecture and TV tours, and Beverly Hills. Polly's all-time favorite party was in 1965 when she and Freddie Fields, her husband of twenty years, had a house on the Pacific Ocean with fifty yards of beach plus a large swimming pool. The fête was designed to last from Saturday afternoon through

Sunday—and *that* it did! One hundred and seventy-five people had arrived with swimsuits by three in the afternoon; by six the crowd had swelled to over three hundred.

The scene would have done justice to a C. B. De Mille spectacular: The Firehouse Five played on the patio as the guests twisted everywhere from the ankle-deep surf to the driveway. Three separate bars were conveniently set up and hot hors d'oeuvres were passed. As the sun began to set, braziers were lighted on the beach and low Hawaiian tables were placed on the sand. At nine, dinner was served to the accompaniment of a string quartet that strolled among the guests in formal attire—and sneakers.

At midnight, the most incredible thing happened: the grunions ran. These are tiny silver fish which, in the wee hours of the morning, will now and then run to shore, turning the beach silver and glittering. By three in the morning, there were still over one hundred people remaining. Polly had arranged for the caterer to stay and serve them bacon, eggs, and bagels. At five in the morning, several of the guests dragged the piano out of the house and set it on the beach. Steve Allen played the piano, and Lucille Ball sang Helen Morgan's songs. It was Polly Bergen's most perfect party.

Polly's entertainment pattern has been cut down to the size of her New York apartment, but the glamour is still all there. She has a wide range of vibrant and famous friends including Barbara Walters, Charlotte Curtis, Kitty Carlisle, Andy Warhol, and Rex Reed. Her guest lists range in age from twenty-one to eighty. The younger people she often invites are Carrie Fisher, Candy Bergen, Dena Kaye, Stephanie McLuhan. Informal buffet dining is her new mode now that she has a more demanding schedule, and it is served from the kitchen. Drinks and the first course are taken in the living room, forty-five minutes before dinner. Polly does not believe in hors d'oeurves, but serves the appetizer from the sideboard: smoked salmon, cold moules vinaigrette, cracked crab or crudités. The guests then enter the breakfast room, pick up their plates, and proceed to the kitchen where their food is on the stove; the wine is in the sink packed in ice.

"Los Angeles and New York parties are different," Polly explains. "In Beverly Hills, entertaining is incestuous and more cliquish because the stars don't want to meet people who are awestruck by them. They don't want to sign autographs at parties, nor do they want tales about them carried away. They want a protective situation, which is understandable, but it's a drawback to giving an interesting party."

Eleanor Lambert

Eleanor Lambert, whose public-relations firm bears her name, is responsible for the "Coty Awards" as well as for compiling the annual "Best Dressed" list. When her husband was alive, Christmas was always a family sit-down dinner at a large table. It included her one son, who is now thirty-seven, a stepdaughter, who is now forty, and close friends who were considered "family." Every attempt to modernize Christmas and Thanksgiving failed because "people expected and looked forward to one big table with its pure white cloth. It was because our roots are German-English," Eleanor explains.

Now that her son is married, she doesn't spend Christmas with him. She doesn't want to be considered a "spongy" mother. "I don't have to be part of his life. He has his own life, with his wife and children." The last three Christmases, she has visited Ireland with Sybil Connolly, the designer, or gone to Acapulco where she has a house. "People shouldn't be emotionally ruled by holidays," she claims.

Her dinner parties now are more likely to be buffet, but her basic rule is that there be room for everyone to sit down. "Men don't like to eat off their laps." Although she finds music at dinner parties dull, she likes flowers all over the house. "The best investment is an orchid plant. Although they can cost up to seventy-five dollars, they bloom for six weeks and are much more beautiful than still arrangements."

Margaret Whiting

"Entertaining is people caring and looking *at* you, not over your shoulder. It's conversation with people from different fields with no pressure on."

Margaret, like Polly Bergen, entertains quite differently from the days when she had her Bel Air house and her Sunday-night parties included up to fifty guests. She now has apartments on either coast, and feels equally at home in both locations. Margaret attributes her ability to adapt easily to the fact that she has been on the road all her life and awakened in a different hotel every night. "I'll be fifty in July and I know my roots are in me and not in my possessions."

No matter where Margaret Whiting happens to be, informality is always the keynote. The fare usually consists of casseroles on warming plates, or barbequed steak, salad, and bread. Cocktails are usually served on the terrace, and in California the dining is done outdoors on glass tables set with beautiful placemats.

All the wines are carefully selected by Margaret for summer drinking. Here are the choices of the light, dry, and cooling ones. Her favorite choices are the Loire Valley whites like Pouilly Fumé and Muscadet, because they are perfect for seafood. She suggests you try a Gewürtz-Traminer with Roquefort or a sharp cheddar cheese. For a lovely touch, the popular singer likes to serve a chilled, Anjou rosé with a fresh strawberry in each glass. Margaret believes in light meals for summer. Her California casual suppers usually start with cold soup. If the weather is very warm, keep food preparation simple, says Margaret—the first course should always be something to lift your spirits and lower your temperature. Here are a couple of ways she does just that.

CREAMY TARRAGON SOUP

2 cups boiling water	2 eggs (yolks only)
2 chicken bouillon cubes	half lemon
tarragon (fresh or dried)	garniture of chopped ham
instant potatoes	

Boil the water and add two chicken bouillon cubes, simmer for 3 to 5 minutes, add ¼ teaspoon of tarragon. Add instant potato, 1 teaspoon at a time, until the soup thickens—it should be rich and creamy, but never pasty and thick. Keep the soup gently boiling the few moments it takes to put egg yolks in a bowl large enough to hold all the soup. Stir into the yolks 2 teaspoons of the hot soup and stir briskly. Repeat with two more teaspoons of soup and continue to stir. Then add the rest of the soup and stir. Add the lemon juice, use the chopped ham as you would croutons, leave the amount of salt and pepper up to your guests.

COLD CUCUMBER SOUP

Margaret's dad, Richard, wrote Shirley Temple's most saccharin song—the one about the lollipop. He personally wasn't into sweets—his favorite soup was this unsweetened one.

chicken bouillon cube	*dill (fresh or dried)*
1 onion	*yogurt (small container)*
1 cucumber	*salt and pepper*

Two cups of boiling water, drop in the bouillon cube, simmer until dissolved, let the broth cool. A tablespoon of chopped onions. Very thin slices of cucumber to use as garnish, the rest of the cucumber cut into chunks to fit the blender. Put the broth, onion, and cucumber into the blender. Add pepper and ½ teaspoon of dill. Blend and cool the liquid. Add the yogurt, salt and pepper, and serve garnished with thin slices of cucumber and a pinch or two of fresh dill, if you can find it. Margaret pours the soup into shallow glass dishes filled with crushed ice.

In New York, Margaret's apartment also has a terrace, but every time she attempts to barbeque, representatives of the Fire Department appear at her doorway—necessitating her setting two extra places for dinner.

Maggie says that she accomplishes more in New York in one week than she does in California in a year. "There are no roots in Los Angeles. They talk tennis, the weather. It's very low key. In New York, I love the madness of the streets. People talk about the news, opera. They are so aware. In California they are so saturated with sun and orange juice their brains have become atrophied."

Margaret has been married three times and has one daughter, Debbie. One occasion has become a ritual for mother and daughter: their birthdays. After champagne and presents at home, they go to a restaurant like Coriander's or Pronto for pasta. Maxwell's Plum is a favorite for dessert. Debbie's gift to her mother last year was a collection of *Star Trek* paraphernalia because Margaret is a *Star Trek* freak.

Margaret's parties are very open, and she doesn't mind her friends bringing guests. Whether the escort is a man or woman, straight or gay is of no concern to her as long as it makes them happy. She also believes in mixing people of different ages. "We're no longer youth-oriented. Besides, who the hell cares? We've only got so much time left. We shouldn't be rigid."

Bobby Short

Although it is difficult to fit entertaining into his busy schedule as an entertainer, Bobby Short manages to give some exciting parties. His favorite soirées? Groups of attractive people who amuse each other, whether it is a buffet for forty, a sit-down dinner for eight, or a lunch in the library for three or four. Lunch might be roast pork with baked apples oozing rum and sugar butter, Brussels sprouts, and ripe raspberries. At Christmas his open house usually includes Mabel Mercer, Marion McPartland, Cy Coleman, and other luminaries of the musical world. Homestyle cooking is Bobby's preference, and the menu includes Smithfield ham, biscuits, a wheel of Brie, a pot of chili, tossed green salad, mince pie, and Christmas cookies.

Donald Brooks

Even though Donald Brooks is famous on Seventh Avenue, he rarely invites fashion people to his parties. "They have no dimension. They are only what they do. I like creative people like college professors, screen writers, and stock brokers, people who think for themselves in inventive ways."

His dinner parties tend to be small sit-down affairs and he claims that he detects a trend toward this type of entertaining among his friends as well. Donald has a full-time houseman who also cooks, and dinner is likely to be filet of beef, cold fish mousse, and braised celery or spinach gnocchi. He admits to a sweet tooth and usually indulges in two dessert offerings: one rich, such as a chocolate roll, and the other more conservative, like raspberry or pineapple sherbet.

Donald is also partial to round tables because they are more conducive to conversation. Although he does not believe that centerpieces are absolutely necessary, he uses objects like a cachepot of shells or a pot of moules. "I love textures and patterns and colors like red, pink and black." The crudités which are served with cocktails are not nearly as important to him as the bowl, which might be pewter, clay, or straw. "I'm hung up about how food should look. I like to make it look appealing because, after all, everybody knows the flavor of a raw carrot or cauliflower." The gifts he gives are chosen with the same instinct. "I give animals, tortoise shells, theatrical manuscripts, out-of-print books. My eyes are always open because giving presents is an emotional, open thing."

Donald Brooks abhors parties where there are too many wines at dinner, too much flatware, and elaborate seating arrangements with pretentious placecards. "I like proper service, but when it is overdone, it is irritating and annoying." Cocktail parties are another one of his peeves, and unless one is being held directly across the street, he refuses to attend.

Summer entertaining at Donald's house in Roxbury, Connecticut, is an opportunity for him to cook himself. He has simplified lunch to a basic formula and style which makes it possible for him to carry it off easily. He starts with a cold soup: gazpacho, cold cucumber, watercress, or asparagus. The main dish and the salad are also cold: roast beef with horseradish and sour cream sauce, cold capon, or lobster brought from the city. Salads will be mixed greens with a decorative dressing of oil, vinegar, mustard, and dill. "Summer food is all cold because it is easy to take, and feels comfortable in the stomach. I like to serve it in chilled frosty bowls, or good-looking straw baskets with glass linings."

DONALD BROOKS'S GAZPACHO

8	cucumbers	1	bunch of parsley
10	tomatoes		salt, pepper, sugar (to
2	or 3 Bermuda onions		taste)
3	cloves of garlic		juice of three lemons

Peel, slice, seed, salt, and drain the cucumbers. Blanch and peel the tomatoes, slice the vegetables, and mince the garlic and parsley. Use an orange squeezer to squeeze the pulp of the tomatoes, then add the finely diced onion, cucumber, garlic,

parsley, salt, pepper, sugar (to taste) and lemon juice. Chill it.
Prepare all this the day before it's served. It takes the place of a
big salad. Serve it with very thick croutons. It is far more
delicate and lush when the flavors are left to meld overnight.
Serve it with a whole Brie, bread or crackers, and a fresh fruit
dessert. Making the soup takes a whole day out of my life.

Paul Kovi

Paul Kovi, owner of the Four Seasons, is a Hungarian
extraordinaire. Paul loves food so much that he is forced to go on
a diet every six months, in order to stay on an even keel. In
between these diets, he indulges himself on the richest gourmet
foods known to Western civilization. His palate knows no limits,
and when asked to name his favorite delights, he gleefully
laughs and rubs his hands together: "Pastas, soufflés, goulash
soup, pheasant with fresh foie gras and white truffles, stuffed
baby birds, crème fraîche sprinkled with caviar, zabaglione with
framboise or kirsch over fresh raspberries, chestnut purée with
rum, cinnamon, and chocolate." He takes a deep breath and
continues: "Fresh duck livers in spinach leaves served with
hearts of palm, tiny tomatoes, melon balls and white onion, and
Chateau Y'Quem, a sweet white wine to accompany desserts."
Taught to cook by his mother and his grandmother, he obviously
learned his lessons well, because his restaurant is a triumph of
elegant food and décor. It is my favorite lunching place, and an
ideal site for executives who demand style and panache in their
business lunches as well as at their tête-à-têtes.

Paul Kovi's Do's and Don'ts for planning formal dinners

Don't overcomplicate.
Don't try out new things on guests.
Don't improvise or try to outdo the great chefs. Escoffier had
much more experience, knowledge, facilities, and help!
Don't invite any more guests than you can handle comfortably.
Don't clog your kitchen with items which all have to be done at
the last minute.
Don't stuff your guests to death.
Don't underestimate your guests' culinary knowledge.

Don't boast about your triumphs until the dinner is over—if ever!

Don't ask your professional guests to entertain.

Do plan every step carefully.

Do discuss your dinner with your favorite wine merchant and order your wines well ahead of time.

Do have a good idea of your timetable for the entire dinner.

Do invite people who feel comfortable in each other's company.

Do invite some guests who are good mixers and can hold the fort.

Do have a surprise element injected into the most important phases of the dinner.

Do relax. It is your party.

Here are three of Paul's favorite recipes:

STEAK TARTARE CANAPES WITH CAVIAR
(Serves 24)

½ pound beef top round, freshly ground
1 egg yolk
1 tablespoon snipped chives
salt
freshly ground black pepper
softened butter or margarine
24 slices cocktail dark rye bread
1 jar (2 ounces) black caviar

Mix ground beef, egg yolk, and chives; taste and adjust seasonings. Spread butter liberally on rye bread slices; top each slice with about 1 tablespoon of beef mixture and ½ teaspoon of the caviar.

ROAST RACK OF LAMB WITH ROSEMARY
(Serves 6)

1 lamb loin double roast (4–6 pounds), bone in, tied
½ cup vegetable oil
1 carrot, pared, chopped (about ½ cup)
1 onion, chopped (about ½ cup)

1 clove garlic, crushed	1½ cups water
1 bay leaf, crumbled	salt
¼ teaspoon dried thyme	pepper
leaves	rosemary sprigs, if
1 cup dry white wine	desired
½ teaspoon dried rosemary	
leaves	

Heat oven to 350°.

1. Heat oil in heavy skillet. Lightly brown meat in oil on all sides, about 10 minutes; remove meat from skillet. Place meat fat side up in open shallow roasting pan. Combine carrot, onion, garlic, bay leaf, thyme, and wine; pour over meat. Insert meat thermometer so tip is in center of thickest part of meat, away from bone. Roast, basting every 10 minutes with pan juices, until thermometer registers 170°, about 45 minutes for medium. Remove meat to ovenproof platter. Sprinkle with ½ teaspoon rosemary leaves; return to oven 5 minutes. Remove platter from oven; keep warm.

2. Add 1½ cups water to pan juices; taste and adjust seasonings. Simmer juices over low heat 10 minutes: strain. Garnish lamb with rosemary sprigs. Pass pan juices.

FROZEN ORANGE SOUFFLÉS
(Serves 6)

6 large navel oranges	2 teaspoons grated orange
3 egg yolks	peel
¾ cup sifted powdered	¾ teaspoon orange liqueur
sugar	1 cup heavy cream,
¼ cup fresh orange juice	whipped

1. Cut top quarter off each orange. Remove fruit from shells. Dry insides of shells with paper toweling.

2. Beat egg yolks and sugar until smooth, about 1 minute. Stir in orange juice, peel, and orange liqueur. Fold in

whipped cream. Pour about ¾ cup of the soufflé mixture into each prepared orange shell. Freeze until firm, 4–6 hours.

Bill Blass

Like his preference in design, Bill Blass likes his food simple and first-class. Hominy-grits soufflé with Smithfield ham and cucumber sauce, pasta with sour cream and butter, or with asparagus, mushrooms, scallions, and Parmesan cheese are his frequent menu choices. So are new asparagus in vinaigrette sauce and shad-roe soufflé. His two pet peeves where entertaining is concerned are hosts who let you starve and those who cater their parties. "If you are going to have people over for dinner, for God's sake, don't cater it. If you can't cook, take your guests to a good restaurant. You can spot store-bought food instantly." The only dish that you will ever find in his home that comes from the outside is a chocolate mousse which he occasionally gets from Caravelle.

On one of his country weekends he went to a sumptuous place with twelve servants on Long Island and literally starved. "Fortunately, I had a Mars bar in my bag." His own new country home is in Washington, Connecticut. "South Hampton was a nightmare, much too social, like the *Discreet Charm of the Bourgeoisie*. Ten years ago, I was more active socially. The older you get, the more privacy you want." Although he invites a great many house guests to his home, he takes a dim view of staying at other people's homes.

Cocktail parties do not please him either; because there is no place to sit, too many people, too much smoke, and the same boring food. "It's simply uncivilized. The only cocktail parties these days are given by Josh and Nedda Logan. They've got a huge river view home, they invite a cross section of the world; fashion people, theater, politics, business people—somehow they pull it off."

Other negative views he holds include mixing business acquaintances and personal friends at parties, although sometimes it is unavoidable. Often he entertains by taking people to "in" restaurants like Mortimer's in New York, which is glittering and glamorous. San Francisco's restaurants appeal to him more than New York's because of the freshness of the food. In England, he adores the food at the Connaught, but feels that Milan has the greatest food in Europe, even better than in France. His secret passion—Red Poppy Ice Cream. Another Bill Blass favorite:

BILL BLASS'S HOMINY-AND-CHEESE SOUFFLÉ
(Serves 4–6)

1 cup water	1 teaspoon salt
1 cup milk	½ cup hominy grits

Combine water and milk in the upper part of a double-boiler. Bring to boiling point over direct heat. Add salt and the grits, stirring constantly, over low heat. Place over hot water, and cook for 45 minutes, stirring occasionally. Remove from the heat and set aside to cool for 15 minutes. Now prepare:

3 egg yolks	¼ teaspoon pepper
5 tablespoons grated Parmesan cheese	3 tablespoons butter, melted
½ teaspoon salt	4 egg whites
1 tablespoon chopped chives	

Beat the egg yolks in a bowl until light in color. Add the cooked grits, beating steadily until smooth. Add the cheese, salt, pepper, and melted butter. Mix well. Preheat oven to moderate, 325°.

Beat the egg whites until stiff but not dry. Fold them into the grits mixture carefully. Pour into a buttered 1½ quart soufflé dish. Bake 40 minutes.

Betsy Bloomingdale

Bloomingdale's is a tradition in New York, and, as you might expect, the Bloomingdales are a tradition-oriented family. Christmas is a well-tried formula that everyone loves and expects: mushroom soup, a huge turkey, two kinds of stuffing, a green vegetable, creamed celery and onions, candied yams, and persimmon pudding. David Jones, the florist, has designed Betsy's Christmas decorations for years. "He makes me three-foot Christmas trees in silver containers that are placed along the length of the table, interspersed with three beautiful old tureens that have been in the family for years. The look is red, silver, fir trees, and candles with the scent of Xmas."

While Christmas is definitely a family affair at the Bloomingdales', Betsy does include a few "strays," "but only those who fit. I won't have anyone who isn't loved by the whole family."

Anniversaries, with the exception of the "special" years, are private. It's a time for just the two of them. On their tenth anniversary the Bloomingdales gave a large and memorable party in the old Romanoff's. Loaves of bread were flown in from Paris by TWA, something quite unusual twenty years ago, but it was "absolutely necessary" to go with the French decor and the cassoulet!

While tradition is the keynote for family occasions, variety is what Betsy strives for at "secular" events: small "intime" dinners served in the breakfast room, more elaborate menus for a seated dinner for twenty in the dining room; and buffet with tables set atrium style for summer. "I like to have a different look in summer than in winter and use different locales: summer—cocktails in the poolhouse, dinner in the atrium; winter—cocktails in the library, dinner in the dining room. I used the barbeque house when the children were young. It was fun and all lit by candles. My big parties were held there too, but those California nights are always cool, and when you've worked madly to have a fabulous setting—candles in the waterlilies on the ponds, candles in the trees, and everyone wants coffee in the house, it becomes too much trouble."

Now her entertaining has been scaled down to the simplest functions possible for her lifestyle. Sometimes she will invite people over for tea or cocktails and then have dinner out. Her idea of an ideal evening is to fly to San Francisco for dinner in a couple of private planes. Once there, they partake of caviar and cocktails in an apartment high in the sky overlooking the bay, then go on to Ernie's, where a lovely dinner has been ordered. They wing it home via the same route and are in bed by midnight. "I think it is the only way to go. It beats the tent parties of yesteryear, or is it the tent parties of today?"

A Christmas Favorite recipe:

PERSIMMON PUDDING, ST. CECILIA SAUCE

2 cups of persimmon pulp
2 cups sugar
4 teaspoons soda
4 teaspoon baking powder
2 cups sifted all-purpose
   flour
½ teaspoon salt

1 cup blanched almonds,
   chopped
1 cup seedless raisins
2 tablespoons butter
1 cup milk
2 teaspoons vanilla

SAUCE:

4 egg yolks

2 cups powdered sugar

GARNISH:

1 persimmon
6–8 tablespoons brandy

1 pint heavy cream,
   whipped

Remove the stems from the washed persimmons and press through sieve or food mill.

Measure and sift the dry ingredients, add the almonds and raisins.

Melt the butter and stir into the persimmon pulp. Add the milk and the vanilla.

Combine the 2 mixtures and blend well.

Pour into a well-greased mold and cover with greased wax paper. Steam on rack in covered steamer for 3 hours.

For the sauce, beat the egg yolks until thick, add the powdered sugar and the brandy slowly, beating constantly. Fold in the whipped cream.

To serve. Unmold the pudding on a round platter. Garnish with fresh persimmon.

Arnold Weissberger and Milton Goldman

No guest list in the world has more glitter than you are likely to find when Arnold and Milton are the hosts. They are agent and lawyer to many of the brightest stars in the firmament: Rex Harrison, Robert Morley, John Gielgud, Alec Guinness, Patricia Neal, Rebecca West, Sybil Thorndike, and Luise Rainer. Arnold's late mother was not as impressed with his array of clients as he would have hoped. When he arrived home he asked her whether anyone had called. She answered, "A man called, one of your 'customers.'" "Who?" Arnold asked. "Somebody named Gielgud. He had an English accent." For her birthday several years ago, Arnold had his mother flown to London to vacation with them at the Savoy, where they've reserved the same suite for twenty-five years. All of Arnold's celebrated "customers" attended a buffet in his mother's honor—and Mrs. Weissberger never admitted that she had never heard of any of them.

"Our favorite parties are those where things begin and happen," Milton says. The show *Look, Ma, I'm Dancing* had its inception at a party which included Jerome Robbins, Hugh Martin, and George Abbott. "Jerry started talking about an idea he'd had for years, about satirizing a ballet. The musical was born at that moment, and the fact is even mentioned on the record album."

Recently they had a reunion of the Group Theater Project which, in the 'forties, had included Eli Wallach, Robert Lewis, Morris Carnovsky, Stella Adler and her brother Luther, and Arthur Miller.

International stars hug and kiss a lot when they meet at a Weissberger-Goldman party. There is a Tower of Babel of affection and sounds, and the hugs range from frigid English to frantic French with some gymnastic Greek thrown in. The group has professional dieters so their hosts have eliminated rich desserts from their menus. Whether it is an "A" dinner party (major stars in all fields, industrial achievers, and a few well-chosen political and cultural types) or a "B" party (featured performers, both fading and rising stars, and beautiful, young people with potential) these two star-makers adopt the European custom and serve dessert wines and cheeses. They offer a selection of wines attractively displayed in shining crystal decanters and a silver cooler that would be at home in Buckingham Palace. There is always a myriad of wines available, but at their recent at-home salute to Lillian Hellman this is what they served: creme sherry, maderia, muscatel, Tokay, port, sweet sauterne, and Angelica. After the first glass is poured it is acceptable to let guests help themselves for seconds.

Milton is almost dogmatic about the kind of glasses to be

used. He doesn't care if they all aren't matched, but he does insist that the dessert wine glass be stemmed and transparent. He points out that the stem is essential because it prevents your hand from warming the wine. Dessert wine must be served either chilled or at an energy-saving cool room temperature. All this is complemented by the choice of cheeses served on an enormous, circular, wooden platter, featuring Bel Paese, Blarney, bleu, Camembert, fontina, and Port Salut. The variety allows for the guests' varied tastes. Milton advises that one should select at least one each of a mild, a robust, and a spicy cheese. Each cheese is well separated on the board and each has its own knife. The cheeses are served at room temperature to bring out their true flavor. They should stand at least half an hour to two hours (for the harder cheeses) before serving time. Be sure to make a single cut on each cheese to encourage guests to slice away. When the party is over the cheeses should be refrigerated at 35 to 40 degrees. Hard cheeses may be covered tightly with foil or plastic to prevent drying out and stored in a cool dry place. Arnold is a hoarder, and after some experimentation discovered that natural Swiss, cheddar, Edam, and Gouda can be frozen, if done so rapidly, in small packages.

Jeffrey Butler

Jeff Butler, successful president and publisher of *East/West Network*, lives in California. Fortunately, he has not succumbed to some of California's more bizarre ways. Thanksgiving is still a formal sit-down family dinner served at 6:00 P.M. The evening, however, is an open house for a large number of friends who stop by for coffee, dessert, and after-dinner drinks. "It is a way of sharing family get-togethers because our friends are invited to bring fathers and mothers as well as out-of-town guests." There is a sumptuous dessert buffet containing a large array of pies—pecan, pumpkin, mince—and carrot cakes, cookies, candies, and nuts, as well as coffee served from a large urn with old Imari cups and saucers. On a side table, there is another silver tray with assorted after-dinner liqueurs as well as a regular bar set up in another room.

Perhaps his most famous event is his "August Moon" party which he has given every year since 1968. The idea was originated by Virginia Robinson, of the Robinson department stores, who is now over a hundred years old. The concept of entertaining on a summer night when the moon is full is now followed by many people in the Los Angeles area. "It's a wonderful idea because it sets the tone for outdoors, moonlight, and beautiful gardens. The theme can so easily be carried out in flowers, candles, and other decorations. It creates an enchanting mood for the entire evening's entertainment."

House guests are frequently invited to the Butlers'. One touch which makes the entertaining of weekend visitors relatively painless is that Jeff provides a car for his visitors. If their two cars are not adequate, they rent a car. This gives them schedule flexibility and takes the pressure off Jeff and his wife to play Mr. and Mrs. Taxi Driver. Another little gesture that gives their house guests much pleasure is having the breakfast table set with animated children's placemats. "Obviously ours say 'Jeff's Place,' 'Erin's Place'; we have others with the various names of our guests. It always arouses a surprised chuckle when they come down to breakfast; it makes them feel part of the family."

Beverly and Vidal Sassoon

"At the beginning of 1975, we made a resolution that our future Christmas gifts to each other and to our children would be the entire month of December, a holiday together in the snow and away from the normal trappings of our life and business. This became a reality and added a totally new dimension to our lives which brought us much inner peace and joy."

The Sassoons, for all their glamorous image, are devoted parents to their four children—ranging in age from three to seven. Thus, their holidays are largely child-oriented and wonderfully imaginative; the decorations for such occasions as Mother's day and Father's day are usually designed by the youngsters. Beverly and Vidal's most treasured gifts, as they are for most parents, are their children's art efforts—which are framed and hung with the rest of the Sassoon collection.

The Sassoon children usually entertain as many schoolmates as can be stuffed into a variety of sleeping bags, and party food is made as interesting as possible to compensate for the fact that hot dogs, french fries, and sugar are never included in the menu. "Instead of lots of sweet snacks, we put out bowls of nuts and raisins and baskets of fresh fruit. Our constant battle is to try to substitute carob for the chocolate in the children's diets—but they 'secretly' switch right back. Popcorn is a marvelous nibble: there are only fifty calories in a cupful, provided you don't douse it in butter. The kids don't care about the calories, but it is good for mothers and fathers to know while hosting these rip-roaring events."

Unlike many celebrity parents, the Sassoons try to participate in as many activities as possible with their children, working with them and guiding them to understand what life and living are all about. Catya and Elan, their two eldest, sometimes travel with them on their worldwide trek to shows and appearances. "It is a joy to watch them grow and share with us. It's also an important experience for us to see through a child's eye."

The irony of all this is that for all their tender, loving care, and their attempt to have their children develop both physically and psychologically into healthy adults, the children remain resistant to them when it comes to food. Despite the fact that Beverly and Vidal have written a book devoted to beauty and health and are apostles of diet and nutrition, their kids know the location of every McDonald's within a 100-mile radius.

Informality carries over into the Sassoons' personal entertaining, which usually takes place, like most California events, around their pool. While they are in easy reach of the ocean, desert, and snow, they are content to spend time in their own surroundings because they are away from home so much on business. Friends drop in, especially on Sundays, for cold cuts which are served do-it-yourself style. "Someday we are going to give a really fabulous party with elephants parking cars and pygmies serving drinks—or was it pygmies parking cars and elephants serving drinks?" That will probably have to wait until they can clear out the sleeping bags.

Some Sassoon favorite recipes:

PRUNE WHIP
Beat 5 egg whites till stiff. Fold in 1 cup pureed prunes with 2 tablespoons lemon juice. Chill.

BANANA SMOOTHIE

Combine in the blender 2 cups cold skim milk, ½ cup instant nonfat powdered milk, 1½ (or 2 small) bananas, ¼ teaspoon nutmeg. Blend. Serve in tall glasses.

Drink and encourage your guests to do the same.

PROTEIN DRINK FOR TWO

2 *tablespoons powdered protein* (from a health-food store or pharmacy)

1 *tablespoon granular lecithin* (from a health-food store or pharmacy)

1 *large banana*
1 *raw egg*
2 *cups low-fat or skim milk*

Toss everything into the blender and let it whip for 30 seconds. This recipe can be varied to suit taste. Bananas can be substituted for any fresh berries or fruit in season. For variety, fresh orange juice can be substituted for low-fat or skim milk. In other words, use your imagination and the combinations are endless.

Celeste Holm

Celeste is a very dear and long-standing friend, but since she is a very private person, she is willing to share only her recipes and her wit. "I keep my private life private, so how can I talk about it? It wouldn't be private." She does, however, admit to playing Scrabble at her country home and even a little backgammon—but hates bridge. "We don't entertain much in the country. My father is there. I taught him how to cook. Grandma cooked, but Mom didn't because she was a painter. I studied with her—painting, not cooking."

Although Celeste does not talk about her own dinner parties, she loves to talk about other people's. Once, she was invited to a huge soirée in California which was held in a magnificent rented house, by some people who'd recently come into their own money. They took the house to impress everybody and really succeeded. The dining room was huge and oval-shaped, with wonderful molding and corner cupboards which held Chinese teaboxes and shells. The wallpaper had gold running through it and it was obvious the decorator had done a glorious job. The main course was filet mignon, sliced and served by a butler at each end of the oval table. Suddenly, there was a pause in the conversation and a voice said, "Whatever happened to that little fairy who was married to so and so?" Silence. Then, another voice said: "Here I am." The first voice came back with great aplomb: "Well, whatever happened to you?"

But that was not the worst catastrophe of the evening. The butler got drunker and drunker, and when he brought out the dessert, a strawberry bombe, it slid off the tray and onto the lap of the hostess. She burst into tears as Celeste leaped up and scooped the bombe back on the tray. The butler disappeared, and so did the hostess for the rest of the evening.

"Classic good taste should be the norm both at the table and during introductions," Celeste feels. Her hostilities are directed at people who talk with their mouths full and at those who make personal remarks when they are introduced, such as "Oh, you color your hair," or "How's your weight?"

Celeste Holm's Entertainment Tricks
1. Plan ahead.
2. Enjoy yourself.
3. Listen to your guests.
4. Lead them into topics. Let *them* shine.
5. Serve very few hors d'oeuvres—they ruin the appetite.
6. Serve very little liquor—no more than two drinks before dinner.
7. Try to serve wine before and during dinner.
8. Invite people who know each other and two who don't.
9. Send the help home after the guests arrive. The help can come back the next day to do the dishes.
    Celeste's favorite recipes:
    My father, who lives down at our farm in Bucks County, hates Mexican food. He's never eaten it, but he's sure he hates it—anything hot. The other day I opened a can, thinking it was chili. It was tamales. So I figured I'd better disguise it.

—251—

MEXICAN FOOD IN DISGUISE
FOR THE SAKE OF DEAR OLD DAD

Take one can of tamales and peel off husks. Now you have messy broken bits of cornmeal and a whisper of meat. Pour boiling water over this mess to soften. Add:

4	eggs	½	cup Pet milk
1	tablespoon flour	2	teaspoons baking powder

Put everything into the blender. After the mixture has been blended, add ¾ pound grated jack cheese. Slice three zucchini. Sizzle separately ¾ cup bread crumbs in 3 tablespoons butter. Mix the cornmeal mush with the zucchini and put this in a baking dish, with the sizzled bread crumbs sprinkled on top. Bake 40 minutes at 350°. It comes out light and fluffy and should be served with cold ham, Carta Blanca, and a salad.

FINISH THE TURKEY SALAD

	shredded leftover turkey, boned and skinned	2	teaspoons honey soy sauce, to taste
2	cups torn-up lettuce	1	lemon
8	sliced scallions		white pepper
2	stalks celery		crisp Chinese noodles
6	slices bacon, cooked and crumbled	6	slices pineapple
¾	cup pineapple juice	¾	cup pecans

Drain off the fat from the pan in which you've fried the bacon. To this pan, add the pineapple juice, honey, soy sauce, juice of 1 lemon, and white pepper. Heat until the flavors meld. Pour over the salad and top with crisp Chinese noodles.

CELESTE HOLM'S SHORTCUT TO ELIZABETH DAVID'S CHOUCROUTE GARNIE

This is a twenty-minute version of Elizabeth David's two-hour minor production number, which is a perfect example of "much-to-do" over red cabbage.

1	head of grated, shredded or chopped red cabbage	½	cup currant jelly
¾	cup water	¼	teaspoon powdered cloves
3	tablespoons vinegar		

Put everything in a big pot, cover, and cook over a medium flame for 20 minutes. Cook until al dente. Serve it with left-over ham.

SHRIMP FIESTA

2 tablespoons oil or butter
2 tablespoons flour
1 cup chopped scallions
2 cloves garlic, pressed
½ cup green pepper, sliced
1 14-ounce can of peeled tomatoes
1 teaspoon pepper
¼ cup minced parsley
1 cup cream of mushroom soup (canned)
½ teaspoon sweet basil
2 cups cleaned medium-size shrimp, cut in half

Sauté everything but the shrimp in a pan until hot. At the last minute, add the shrimp and cook only 1 minute. Serve on a bed of rice.

My Fantasy Party—
A Melting Pot-Luck Million Dollar Gala

The aim of the party is that it should be enjoyed, give happiness to the guests, and even take them out of their own world into a different sphere that could excite them. When society first began to mix guests from many divergent worlds, it created the international set. My party will bring to life the supernatural set—from out of this world and heaven and hell.

The goal of the Fantasy Party would be to raise one million dollars (one million for Goodwill Industries to pursue its efforts to retrain the handicapped). The money would be raised by placing a $5,000 price on each share of the evening. The two hundred guests would be seated at twenty celebrity-decorated tables with a famous host and hostess at each one. The forty hosts and hostesses would each be responsible for a covered dish. Each dish would be reproduced by a world-famous chef in quantities for the total party. A corps of distinguished photographers would photograph each table, and a souvenir album would be given to each host, guest, and performer at the party.

Table Settings

People of style have a way of making everyone they are with change vividly via the impact of their own presence and personality. People with style have an energy that makes life overflow with fullness. This list represents a group of people with style. None of them would blindly accept fashion trends unless they delighted in them. Each of them is skilled in the practice of the unexpected. Each would create the table settings for one table. Each is unique in the ability to create a table of taste allied to an individual point of view. The personal touches at each table would ensure my guests of an original moment as they sat down. Each table would possess a sense of perfection to be enjoyed by the most sophisticated at the table. Each table, for each guest, would capture an expression of the beauty of living. Ladies and Gentlemen, be seated.

Each table would be decorated by a person of style: Billy Baldwin, Cecil Beaton, Christiaan Barnard, Charles de Beistegui, Salvador Dali, Angelo Donghia, Fabergé, Nicky de Gunzberg, Kenneth J. Lane, Rita de Acosta Lydig, Syrie Maugham, Lady Mendl, Richard Neas, Louise Nevelson, Paul Poiret, Cole and Linda Porter, Rex Reed, Millicent Rogers, Diana Vreeland, the Duchess of Windsor.

Photographers

In writing this book I realize how foolish I have been about photographs. I either did not have them taken or threw them away as I cleaned up my life with the change of seasons or address. From now on I will be more responsible. It would be very important to me to have a photographic memory of my Fantasy Party—the associations and the sense of nearness involved fixed forever. I should want all my guests to have a record of this extraordinary experience. The whole scene is to be imprisoned on film. Part of the wonder is that the camera will produce photographs that represent details, angles, nuances the eye doesn't see. What a joy to be able to relive the moment and share it with others who were not there. All these fabulous people will live in print as intensely as when the images were captured at the party. My choices to photograph my Fantasy Party—each photographer to use the camera as a third eye and to shoot everything and anybody: Diane Arbus, Richard Avedon, Peter Beard, Margaret Bourke-White, Matthew Brady, Cartier-Bresson, Louis Daguerre, Walker Evans, Robert Frank, Hiro, Horst, Moholy-Nagy, Muybridge, Hansan, Irving Penn, Paul Strand, August Sanders, Francesco Scavullo, Steichen, Stieglitz, David R. Taylor, Edward Weston.

The Entertainment

The longest list of unforgettable pleasures I have is as a ballet lover. The ballet is an art that moves with and reflects the times, and remains eager, youthful, and full of vitality, (with the exception of the purely classical ballets like *Swan Lake* or *Les Sylphides*). There is an anthology of images in my head: the exquisite Toumanova, the forceful Eglevsky, the elegance of Markova and Dolin, the agility of Massine, the rakish slimness of Lifar, the perfection of Fonteyn, the wit of Danilova, the mystery of Helpmann, Nureyev, and Barishnykov, Cynthia Gregory, and Gelsey Kirkland, Edward Villella, Eric Bruhn, Jacques d'Amboise, the Bolshoi, the American Ballet Theatre, the New York City Ballet, the Joffrey Ballet, in London, in Paris, in Russia, in Canada.

I have pursued dance in all its forms, Miss Ruth and Ted, Martha, Agnes, Len, Merce, Louis, Alvin, Judith, and Twyla. The miracle of Nijinsky leaping fifteen feet to the stage as the spectre of the rose and Anna Pavlova as the dying swan are missing from my album of memory. Both these originals should be an important part of the entertainment—a Fantasy Party Ballet Gala. The program will be produced by Diaghilev assisted by Balanchine. It will involve Sondheim and Stravinsky, assisted by Bernstein. The décor and costumes to be done by Benois, Sert, Leon Bakst, Karinska, Patricia Zipprodt, Bill Blass, Donald Brooks, Yves Saint Laurent, Pierre Cardin, and Ralph Lauren.

Curtains for the evening would be by Chagall, Picasso, Roualt, Cézanne, Kenneth Noland, Jackson Pollock, Georgia O'Keeffe, Jasper Johns.

Hosts and Hostesses for Fantasy Party

Isadora Duncan and Woody Allen
William Shakespeare and Lillian Hellman
Alice Cooper and George Sand
Marco Polo and Barbara Walters

Don Juan and Mae West
Tennessee Williams and Sarah Bernhardt
Oscar Wilde and Lily Tomlin
Catherine the Great and Warren Beatty
Carole Lombard and Mel Brooks
Cleopatra and John F. Kennedy
Louis XIV and Jackie O.
Queen Elizabeth I and Alistair Cooke
Thomas Jefferson and Diana Ross
Gloria Steinem and George Bernard Shaw
Garbo and D.W. Griffith
Alexander Woollcott and Nora Ephron
Gertrude Stein and Truman Capote
Noel Coward and Maggie Smith
Leonardo da Vinci and Candice Bergen
Barbra Streisand and Florenz Ziegfeld

Fantasy Party Chefs.

James Beard
Paul Bocuse
Mrs. Bridges—The Downstairs Fictional Cook
Robert Carrier
Julia Child
Craig Claiborne
Claude Deligne
Urbain Dubois
Escoffier
Michel Guerard
Jacques Maniere
Oscar of the Waldorf
Claude Peyrot
Fernando Point
Joseph Renggli
Brillat-Savarin
Albert Stolkli
Jean Troisgros
Marcel Troupiere
Claude Verger
Rene Venson.

And these are the dishes I've fantasized my hosts and hostesses and chefs might concoct.

ISADORA DUNCAN—BABA CAKES

Baba

4   eggs
½   cup granulated sugar
4   teaspoons baking powder
1¼ cups all-purpose flour

6   tablespoons butter
    (melted)
½   cup warm milk

Beat eggs with sugar until fluffy; add baking powder and flour sifted together. Mix mixture, then add butter and milk. Mix again vigorously. Pour into a buttered and floured pudding mold or individual molds. Bake the individual molds 25 minutes or the larger mold 35 to 40 minutes at 325°. After removing from the oven unmold. While hot pour rum syrup over the baba. Cool and serve with sweetened whipped cream.

RUM SYRUP:

½   cup granulated sugar
½   cup water

½   cup rum

Cook sugar in water until a thin syrup is formed. Remove from the heat and add the rum.

WOODY ALLEN—CHOPPED LIVER

1   small onion
½   pound liver or 4 chicken
     livers
2   hard-boiled eggs

1   stalk celery (if desired)
2   tablespoons chicken fat
     salt and pepper to taste

Saute diced onion in chicken fat. When soft add liver. Saute together until liver is done. Put liver, onion, egg, and celery through a chopper two times. Add salt, pepper—add more chicken fat if you desire a softer mixture. Mix thoroughly to form fine paste.

WILLIAM SHAKESPEARE—GRETE PYE

Make a forcemeat by pounding beef or mutton into a fine paste. Season with pepper and salt. Lay this inside a pastry case.

Parboil capons, hens, rabbits, mallards, woodcocks, teal, and any other birds. Place inside each of these salt and pepper and lay them inside the pie. Cover them with the remainder of the forcemeat, over which is strewn chopped marrow, hard yolks of eggs, mace, cinnamon, currants, prunes, dates, cloves, and saffron. The pastry is tightly closed and then baked in medium hot oven for 1 hour.

LILLIAN HELLMAN—SPICED PEACH COBBLER

In a saucepan combine 6 cups stoned and sliced peaches with 1 cup of firmly packed brown sugar and ½ stick butter. Cut this into small pieces and simmer the mixture, covered, for 5 minutes. Stir in 1 tablespoon of flour and ½ teaspoon vanilla and spread in a buttered baking dish (12 x 8 x 2 inches).

Into a bowl sift together 2 cups of flour, 2½ teaspoons double-acting baking powder, 1 teaspoon ground ginger, ½ teaspoon each baking soda and salt, ¼ teaspoon of nutmeg and ground allspice and ⅛ teaspoon ground cloves, add ½ stick plus 1 tablespoon butter, cut into small pieces, and blend until all is well combined. In a small bowl combine ⅔ cup buttermilk with ½ cup unsulfured molasses and stir into the flour mixture. Turn the dough out on a lightly floured surface and pat into a ½-inch-thick rectangle. Cut out rounds with a 1½-inch cutter and arrange on the peach mixture, leaving spaces between them. Sprinkle the top with 2 tablespoons sugar and bake the cobbler in a hot oven (425°) for 25 minutes, or until it is brown. Serve this cobbler with whipped cream.

ALICE COOPER—QUEEN OF PUDDINGS

2 cups soft bread crumbs	1 teaspoon vanilla
2 cups scalded milk	2 teaspoons butter
2 egg yolks	2 tablespoons raspberry
1 tablespoon sugar	jam

Pour the hot scalded milk over crumbs in a bowl. Allow this to stand for 10 minutes. Beat the yolks with the sugar; add vanilla and bread crumbs. Mix in soft butter. Turn into buttered 1-quart casserole. Place dish in pan of hot water and bake slowly in moderate oven (350°) for 45 minutes or until set. Remove from oven; allow to cool slightly. Spread the top with the raspberry jam.

MERINGUE:

¼ teaspoon salt	2 tablespoons sugar
2 egg whites	1 teaspoon lemon juice

Add the salt to the egg whites and beat until stiff. Slowly add the sugar and lemon juice and beat until stiff. Spread over the top of the pudding. Place in oven and brown slowly.

GEORGE SAND—BANANAS IN RUM

6 ripe, large bananas	3 tablespoons rum
½ cup olive oil	¼ cup powdered sugar
½ teaspoon vanilla	

Peel the bananas and cut across in thin slices. Fry them in hot oil. When browned remove and drain on brown paper. Cool and place in a shallow serving dish. Add the vanilla to the rum and sprinkle mixture over the bananas. Sprinkle the powdered sugar over the top and serve cold.

MARCO POLO—TAGLIARINI CON FEGATINI

½ cup butter	1 pound chicken liver
1 onion, chopped	½ cup Marsala wine
½ pound mushrooms, sliced	¼ cup water
¼ cup flour	1 pound tagliarini or
½ teaspoon salt	medium noodles
⅛ teaspoon pepper	

Melt the butter in a large skillet; sauté the onions and mushrooms in butter until the onion is transparent. Combine the flour, salt, and pepper. Cut chicken livers in half, cover with flour. Add chicken livers and all the flour mixture to the skillet. Cook until the chicken livers are a light brown. Stir in the wine and water. Cook over a low heat, stirring, until chicken livers are cooked (5 to 10 minutes). Cook noodles, drain well. Serve the chicken livers over the noodles.

BARBARA WALTERS—RED SIMMERED PORK

½	pound dried Chinese squid, cleaned (optional)	1	garlic clove, minced
¼	cup Chinese lily buds (optional)	3	slices ginger root, sliced
		6	tablespoons soy sauce
3	pounds pork	1	tablespoon sherry
2½	to 3 cups water	1	teaspoon salt
		3	teaspoons brown sugar

The squid and the lily buds give this dish an unusual character. But the pork will taste marvelous on its own. Soak squid in warm water. Cut the body in half, lengthwise. Score the inside with a sharp knife. Soak the lily buds in warm water for about 1 hour. Rinse with cold water and drain. Remove all the tough portions. Cut the pork into 1½-inch cubes. Place in a heavy pan or casserole, add water, and bring to a boil. Add garlic, ginger root, soy sauce, sherry, and salt. Bring to a boil again. Simmer for ½ hour. Add the squid, cover and simmer 40 more minutes. Add lily buds and the brown sugar. Cover and simmer for another 30 to 40 minutes.

DON JUAN—OSSOBUCCO ALLA MILANESE
(VEAL SHANKS)

6	veal shanks, 2½ inches thick	1	teaspoon dried marjoram
½	cup flour	½	cup dry white wine
½	cup salad oil	1	can tomatoes (1 pound)
1	onion, chopped fine	1	cup beef bouillon
1	carrot, grated	1	tablespoon chopped parsley
1	finely chopped stalk celery	1	teaspoon grated lemon rind
2	garlic cloves, minced		

Cover the veal shanks with flour. Heat oil in a large Dutch oven. Brown veal in the hot oil; then remove. Add onion, carrot, celery, 1 garlic clove, and marjoram. Cook over medium heat, stirring, 3 minutes. Add wine, cook until wine is reduced by half. Place the veal shanks again in oven; add the tomatoes and bouillon. Cover. Simmer 1 to 1½ hours. Stir in remaining garlic, parsley, and lemon rind, cook 1 minute.

MAE WEST—STUFFED BREAST OF VEAL

1	3½-pound breast of veal with pocket for stuffing	2	eggs
			pinch paprika
½	teaspoon salt		dash salt and pepper
⅛	teaspoon pepper	¼	cup margarine
¾	cup onion, cut fine	½	cup water
	chopped parsley	1	tablespoon cornstarch
4	slices bread, cubed	¼	cup currant jelly
2	tablespoons half-and-half	1	teaspoon lemon juice
2	tablespoons salad oil		

Sprinkle inside pocket and outside of veal with salt and pepper. Mix together onion, parsley, bread cubes, half-and-half, oil, eggs, paprika, salt and pepper. Fill pocket with bread mixture. Skewer shut. Melt margarine in Dutch oven. Put meat in margarine; add water. Cover. Cook over medium heat until veal is tender, about 1½ hours. Turn meat once after 45 minutes. Remove veal; keep warm. Measure any liquid in pan; add water to make 1 cup. Stir in cornstarch and replace in pan. Cook over medium heat, stirring and scraping up browned bits until thick. Add jelly and lemon juice; stir until jelly is dissolved.

TENNESSEE WILLIAMS—CHICKEN SAVANNAH

4	tablespoons butter	2	cups cooked chicken
4	tablespoons flour	1	can mushroom slices
2	cups chicken broth	¼	cup slivered almonds
½	cup light cream	½	cup Parmesan or Gruyère cheese, grated
¼	cup dry sherry		butter
8	ounces fine noodles, cooked and drained		

Melt butter in a saucepan, add flour, and stir until mixture is smooth. Add the chicken broth and the light cream and cook until all is thick and smooth. Then add the sherry. Place the noodles in a buttered casserole and add the chicken, mushrooms, and the cream sauce. Sprinkle the top with almonds, cheese, and butter. Bake in 350° preheated oven until bubbly and the nuts are browned.

SARAH BERNHARDT—STUFFED GOOSE WITH APPLES

1 pound pork sausage meat	1 teaspoon sage
1 onion, chopped fine	1 egg, lightly beaten
1 stalk celery, chopped	1 5-pound roasting goose
½ cup walnuts, chopped	2 tablespoons butter
1 apple, peeled, cored, and sliced thin	1 jar small unpeeled red apples, drained
1 teaspoon salt black pepper	1 pound fresh chestnuts, boiled, peeled

Cook pork sausage and drain off the fat. Heat 2 tablespoons butter in a skillet and sauté onions, celery, and nuts for 3 minutes. Add and cook apples 3 minutes until softened. Remove from heat and stir in sausage meat. Season with salt, pepper, and sage. Stir in the egg. Fill dressing into the goose and skewer the cavity. Brush goose with melted butter. Place on a roasting rack and roast uncovered at 375° for 2¼ hours. Simmer cooked chestnuts in boiling water for 5 minutes. Place goose on a serving platter. Arrange apples and chestnuts around the goose and serve hot.

OSCAR WILDE—CASSIS SOUFFLÉ

1 package plus 1 teaspoon unflavored gelatin	1¼ cups crème de cassis red food coloring
¼ cup water	1 cup heavy cream, whipped
4 eggs, separated	
½ cup sugar dash salt	3 egg whites crystallized violets

Soak the gelatin in the water for 5 minutes. Fold a strip of aluminum foil in half lengthwise. Secure it with string around the outside of a 1-quart soufflé dish so a collar is formed above the dish. Oil the dish and the inside of the foil collar lightly. Place the egg yolks, sugar, salt, and soaked gelatin in the top of a double-boiler. Set over hot water and beat with a wire whisk over medium heat until the mixture is creamy, thick, and light. The gelatin dissolves and the mixture resembles thick zabaglione. Don't let this boil.

Remove top of double-boiler from stove and beat in the cassis. Add three drops of red food coloring to give a rosy color. Put mixture into a large bowl and chill until it begins to thicken—stir several times. When it is the consistency of thick custard sauce, fold in the whipped cream. Beat the 6 eggs until stiff. Do not allow them to become dry. Stir ⅓ of the whites into the cassis mixture. Fold in remaining whites. Spoon mixture into the prepared soufflé dish. Chill a few hours or overnight. Remove foil collar and garnish with crystallized violets. Serve with a tablespoon of cassis poured over.

LILY TOMLIN—POTAGE PAYSANNE

½	pound cubed lean bacon	½	pound cubed carrots
6	small sausage links	1	teaspoon salt
1	onion, finely chopped	1	teaspoon pepper
3	medium sized onions, halved	6	cups beef broth
		½	pound fresh green peas
2	pounds potatos, cubed	½	pound fresh green beans

Cook the bacon and sausage until crisp and brown, then drain the sausage links on paper towel.

Strain the fat from the pan and add the onions, carrots, potatoes, salt and pepper to the bacon and combine thoroughly.

Cover and simmer for approximately 20 minutes. Add the broth, peas and beans, and drained sausage links, bring to boil, then cover and allow to simmer for another 20 minutes.

Skim the fat from the top, and add a sausage link and onion half to each serving. Serves 6.

CATHERINE THE GREAT— BABY PHEASANT SOUVAROFF

6	baby pheasants, 1 pound each	1½	cups brown sauce
		½	cup heavy cream
3	tablespoons butter, melted	4	tablespoons foie gras
		1	tablespoon diced small black truffles
3	tablespoons cognac or brandy		
¼	cup dry sherry		

Roast pheasants for about 30 minutes at 350°. Baste every 10 minutes with melted butter. Remove pheasants and keep hot. Pour drippings from roasting pan into a skillet. Add cognac and flame it. Add the sherry, brown sauce, and heavy cream. Bring to a boil. Place pheasants in an ovenproof tureen, spread with foie gras, sprinkle with truffles, and pour gravy on top. Cover and bake at 300° for 10 minutes.

WARREN BEATTY—APPLE STRIPS
WITH WHIPPED CREAM AND STRAWBERRIES

3	eggs, separated	1 apple, peeled, cut in thin strips
1¼	cups milk	
1	envelope unflavored gelatin	½ pint whipped cream
		1 pint whole strawberries
½	cup plus 1½ tablespoons sugar	

Beat the egg yolks until they are foamy. Add the milk, gelatin, and sugar and mix. Cook in small saucepan over low heat, stirring. When thick and custardlike, remove from heat and cool. Beat egg whites until they form soft peaks. Fold beaten egg whites and the apple into the milk mixture. Pour into an oiled 1-quart mold and refrigerate until it has set. Unmold and garnish with whipped cream and strawberries.

CAROLE LOMBARD—ORANGE FRITTERS
WITH ORANGE SAUCE

Combine in a saucepan ½ cup water with ½ stick butter, cut into bits. Boil the water over high heat and add ½ cup flour all at once, stirring with wooden spoon. Reduce heat to moderate and cook until it forms a ball and pulls away from the sides of the pan. Transfer the mixture to an electric mixer and beat in 2 eggs, lightly beaten. (The mixture should hold soft peaks. Beat in part of a third egg to achieve the proper consistency, if necessary.) Beat in the grated rind of 1 orange, 2 tablespoons orange-flavored liqueur, 1 tablespoon sugar, and ½ teaspoon baking powder. In a separate bowl beat in 2 egg whites with a dash of salt until they hold stiff peaks and stir ¼ of the whites into the orange mixture. Fold in remaining whites gently but thoroughly and chill the mixture for 1 hour. Cover the mixture.

In a deep fryer drop the batter by ½ teaspoon a few at a time into hot deep oil (365°), fry the fritters, turning them for 3 minutes or until they are puffed and golden brown. Place on paper towel to drain. Transfer fritters to serving plate and sift confectioner's sugar over them. Serve with orange sauce.

ORANGE SAUCE:
Combine in a saucepan 1 cup orange marmalade with ⅓ cup orange-flavored liqueur and 2 tablespoons lemon juice. Heat over moderately low heat until the marmalade has melted. Place in a small pitcher.

MEL BROOKS—BAVARIAN APPLE STRUDEL

1	tablespoon oil	2	tablespoons dark rum
1	egg	3	tablespoons sugar
⅓	cup water, warm	½	teaspoon cinnamon
¼	teaspoon salt	¼	cup chopped almonds
1½	cups sifted flour	¼	cup seedless raisins
⅓	cup butter		Confectioner's sugar or
6	tablespoons dry bread crumbs		whipped cream (optional)
8	cups apples, thinly sliced, peeled and cored		

Beat together oil, egg, water, and salt; add flour while beating until a firm dough which pulls away from bowl is formed. Knead several times until smooth and elastic. Cover and let stand for 30 minutes. Cut with sharp knife into 2 equal parts. Roll out each piece on floured cloth to a 12 x 18-inch rectangle. Brush with melted butter. Sprinkle evenly with bread crumbs. Spread 4 cups of the apples on each portion, lengthwise down the center of the dough. Sprinkle with 1 tablespoon rum, 1½ tablespoons sugar, ¼ teaspoon cinnamon, 1 tablespoon almonds, and 2 tablespoons raisins. Fold dough over apples on one side, then the other. Put rolls on greased baking sheet. Brush with melted butter. Bake in a hot oven (400°) 45 minutes. Cut each roll into 2-inch slices. Serve warm or cold, sprinkled with confectioner's sugar or with whipped cream.

CLEOPATRA—
EGGPLANT AND GROUND BEEF CASSEROLE

1	onion, large	½	cup water
¼	to ½ cup butter		dash salt
1	pound beef, ground	⅛	pepper
½	cup tomato sauce	1	medium eggplant

Cut onion in small pieces and sauté in 2 tablespoons of the fat until yellow. Add ground beef and cook until brown. Mix tomato sauce and water, salt, and pepper and pour over meat mixture. Bring to a boil and cook for 5 minutes. Remove from heat, lift meat from sauce with a perforated spoon. Slice the eggplant and brown lightly in remaining butter. Place a layer of eggplant in 1½-quart casserole, then a layer of meat, another of eggplant, and another of meat. Pour the sauce over all. Bake uncovered at 350° for 20 to 30 minutes or until eggplant is done.

JOHN F. KENNEDY—VIRGINIA HAM

1	14- to 16-pound Virginia ham	1	bay leaf whole cloves
2	slices onion	1	cup brown sugar or molasses
2	carrots, sliced		
1	stalk celery, chopped	1	cup vinegar
1	teaspoon thyme quartered apricots or peaches (about 12 whole apricots or peaches)	2	quarts brown sauce
		¼	cup sherry

Soak Virginia ham according to packer's instructions. After soaking, place ham in a large steam kettle or deep pot and cover with cold water. Simmer for about 15 minutes per pound. Add more hot water to keep the ham covered. When ham is cooked, remove from water and allow to cool. Remove the skin by lifting the skin around the edge of the butt end with a sharp knife. Using a clean cloth in each hand, grasp the hock bone in one hand and, starting at the butt end, pull the skin toward the hock, do not tear fat. Leave 4 inches of skin on the hock bone. Trim excess layers of fat with knife.

Place ham in a large roasting pan. Spread a layer of onion,

carrot, and celery around ham and season with bay leaf and sprinkle thyme. Cut a diamond pattern in ham fat. Decorate crown of ham with quartered apricots or peaches secured with whole cloves. Cover ham with brown sugar or molasses. Roast at 375° until glazed and heated through. Baste as necessary. Remove from roasting pan and put in covered pan to keep hot. Add vinegar, brown sauce, and sherry to the pan. Cook slowly for 10 minutes. Strain the sauce and skim off grease. Serve hot.

JACKIE O.—RACK OF LAMB JACQUELINE

Recipe by Rene Verdon

1 half rack of lamb	1 garlic clove, chopped
salt and pepper to taste	1 tablespoon dry bread
1 branch fresh rosemary, or	crumbs
1 teaspoon dried	mint sauce or mint jelly
rosemary	
1 tablespoon chopped	
parsley	

Preheat oven to 375°. Season lamb with salt and pepper and bake with the rosemary for 30 minutes or until tender. Combine parsley, garlic, and bread crumbs. Sprinkle on top of lamb and cook for 5 minutes more. Serve with mint sauce or mint jelly.

LOUIS XIV—ESCALOPE DE VEAU ARLESIENNE

2 tablespoons butter	pinch thyme
1 tablespoon chopped	1 teaspoon chopped
onion, fine	parsley
3 tablespoons green	salt and pepper to taste
pepper, diced	4 veal cutlets (5 ounces),
8 tomatoes, seeded, peeled,	thinly sliced and breaded
and diced	4 thin slices Swiss cheese
1 garlic clove, chopped	

Melt butter and sauté onion and green pepper for 5 minutes in a saucepan. Add tomatoes, garlic, and thyme and cook for 5 minutes more. Add parsley, salt, and pepper. Remove the vegetables from the pan. Brown cutlets on both sides in butter remaining in pan. If necessary, add more butter. Place in a baking dish. Spread vegetable mixture over the cutlets, add the Swiss cheese on top and bake at 400° until cheese melts.

QUEEN ELIZABETH I—LONDON PYE

40	chestnuts	18	larks or sparrows
1	pound sweet potatoes	¼	ounce peppercorns
2	slices lemon	½	ounce cinnamon
12	hard-boiled egg yolks	½	ounce whole cloves
3	artichokes	½	ounce mace
	a pot of oysters	¼	pound currants
2	ounces lettuce stalks		

All mixed together with 1 pound of butter in a pastry case.

ALISTAIR COOKE—BEEFSTEAK AND KIDNEY PIE

1	pound steak (chuck or round)	¼	teaspoon pepper
		3	tablespoons fat
2	lamb kidneys	1	slice onion
1	tablespoon flour	1	pint cold water or stock
½	teaspoon salt		flaky pastry for topping

Cut steak into 1-inch squares and kidneys into slices. Dip into flour blended with salt and pepper. Sauté until brown in the fat. Add slice of onion and water or stock. Simmer 30 to 40 minutes. Cool and pour into casserole. The liquid should come nearly to the top of the dish. Cover the casserole with pastry, brush with egg or milk. Bake in 425° oven until brown or about 20 minutes. Reduce heat to 350° and cook further for 45 minutes.

PLAIN PASTRY FOR BEEFSTEAK PIE:

1	cup flour	2	or 3 tablespoons cold water
½	teaspoon salt		
⅓	shortening		

Sift together flour and salt. Cut in shortening with pastry blender or two knives until mixture is the size of small peas. Sprinkle water, tossing mixture lightly with fork. Gather dough together and press firmly into a ball. Roll out to fit top of baking dish; cut air vents in crust.

THOMAS JEFFERSON—CHICKEN BRUNSWICK STEW

Combine in a kettle 6-pound stewing chicken, quartered, with 8 cups water, 4 stalks of celery, and 1 teaspoon salt and bring water to a boil. Skim froth as it rises to the surface. Reduce heat and simmer chicken, covered, for 2 hours. Remove the chicken, skin and bone it, and cut it into 1-inch pieces. Strain stock and return to kettle. Add 5 canned tomatoes, 3 cups lima beans and butter beans (each), 2 potatoes, peeled and chopped, and 1 onion, thinly sliced. Cook over moderate heat 20 minutes. Add 3 cups fresh corn kernels, 1 tablespoon each ketchup, and sugar, salt, and pepper to taste. Simmer for 5 minutes. Add chicken and simmer the stew until it is heated through.

DIANA ROSS—ANGEL'S PIE

1	egg, separated	1	teaspoon vanilla extract
2	tablespoons sugar	1	baked 9-inch pie shell
2	tablespoons lemon juice	2	pints strawberries
8	ounces cream cheese	⅔	cup sugar for frosting
½	cup cream for whipping	¼	teaspoon cream of tartar
1	tablespoon confectioner's sugar	¼	cup water
			dash salt

Blend egg yolk, 2 tablespoons sugar, and lemon juice in the top of a double-boiler. Cook for 5 minutes, stirring, until mixture is thick. Remove from heat and slice in cream cheese, beating until no white remains. Beat cream with confectioner's sugar and ½ teaspoon vanilla extract until cream is stiff. Fold this into cheese mixture. Spread on pie shell. Chill for 30 minutes until set. Arrange strawberries, points up, in a single layer. Chill. Combine ⅔ cup sugar, cream of tartar, and water in small pan. Cover. Boil, uncover and cook rapidly until drops of syrup form soft balls in cold water. Beat egg white with salt until it forms peaks. Pour in the hot syrup in a fine stream, beating constantly until it stands in firm peaks. Beat in ½ teaspoon vanilla extract. Pile egg-white mixture in center of pie and chill 2 hours. Take from refrigerator 1 hour before serving.

GLORIA STEINEM—MS. CRABMEAT

1	pound crabmeat	1	teaspoon Worcestershire sauce
4	tablespoons melted butter		
½	cup heavy cream	½	cup grated Parmesan cheese
½	teaspoon mustard, dry		
1¼	teaspoons salt	6	crab shells
	dash white pepper	3	tablespoons bread crumbs
	dash cayenne pepper		

Flake the crabmeat, removing cartilage. Mix with butter, cream, mustard, salt, pepper, and cayenne, Worcestershire sauce, and 4 tablespoons cheese, and toss lightly. Divide among 6 crab shells or ramekins. Sprinkle with the remaining cheese and bread crumbs. Bake in 400° oven for 10 minutes or until browned.

GEORGE BERNARD SHAW—VEGETABLE HOTPOT

2	tablespoons butter or margarine	6	medium sized carrots (sliced)
½	cup mince	4	broccoli spears, separated
2	pounds potatoes, scrubbed and thinly sliced	2½	cups dark vegetable stock (boiling)
1	teaspoon salt		
½	teaspoon pepper	¼	cup grated cheddar cheese
6	ounces red lentils (soak in cold water approx. 3 hours and drain)	¼	cup dry bread crumbs
2	large onions, sliced into rings		

Dissolve 2 teaspoons yeast extract in 1¼ cups boiling water.

Preheat oven to 350°. Put the mince into a medium sized sauce pan and stir in the yeast extract liquid. Place over moderate heat (covered) for five minutes.

Cover the bottom of a greased baking dish with about one third of the potato slices and season with salt and pepper. Next, place about half of the lentils, onions and broccoli on top of the slices. Add a second layer of potato slices and more salt and pepper, then add the remaining lentils, onions and broccoli. Put the remaining potato slices over the top, and pour the stock into the baking dish.

Combine the bread crumbs and cheese in a separate bowl, and sprinkle the mixture over the top layer. Dot the top with the remaining butter or margarine, and bake for appromixately 1 to 1¼ hours, or until the potatoes can be pierced easily with a sharp knife.

Remove from oven and serve immediately. Serves 4 to 6.

GARBO—KOKT LAMM WITH DILL SAUCE

2	to 2½-pounds breast of shoulder lamb	12	sprigs of fresh dill
3	or 4 peppercorns	1	tablespoon salt for each quart water
1	bay leaf		pepper to taste

Place the meat in a kettle and cover with boiling water. Bring to a boil, skim, add peppercorns, bay leaf, few sprigs of the dill, salt, and pepper. Cover and simmer 1 to 1½ hours. Cut in pieces, place on hot platter and garnish with remaining dill. Serve with dill sauce and boiled potatoes or rice.

D. W. GRIFFITH—BISTECCA FIORENTINA

4	tablespoons parsley flakes	1½	teaspoons salt
1	teaspoon oregano		garlic salt
1	teaspoon basil		pepper
¼	teaspoon thyme	½	cup dry red wine
1	round steak	6	large mushrooms
4	tablespoons salad oil	2	tablespoons melted butter
		12	rolled anchovy fillets

Combine parsley, oregano, basil, and thyme, and mix well. Place the steak on a large piece of heavy duty foil. Rub 2 tablespoons of oil on one side of steak; sprinkle half the herb mixture over steak. Turn over, use remaining oil, salt, garlic salt, pepper, and herb mixture. Pour the wine on the steak. Secure foil. Let steak marinate in foil 3 to 4 hours, turn it once or twice. If marinated longer, place in refrigerator. Broil steak in foil, 10 minutes each side. Remove foil, brush mushroom caps with melted butter. Place on broiler pan for 3 to 4 minutes until desired doneness. Slice diagonally to serve. Garnish with broiled mushroom caps and rolled anchovy fillets.

ALEXANDER WOOLLCOTT—DUTCH APPLE CAKE

FILLING:

5	medium-size apples	3	eggs
½	teaspoon cinnamon		lemon rind, grated
⅓	cup brown sugar	1½	cups flour
½	cup butter	1½	teaspoons baking powder
½	cup sugar		

Peel, core, and slice apples and sprinkle with mixture of the brown sugar and cinnamon. Cream butter and sugar, add unbeaten eggs one at a time, stirring well, add lemon rind, add flour and baking powder, a little at a time. Fold carefully. Spread half of batter in an 8-inch square greased baking dish; cover with about half of the sliced apples; spread on remaining half of batter; arrange balance of apple slices in pattern on top. Bake 1 hour at 350°.

NORA EPHRON—FLOUNDER POACHED IN CIDER

1	teaspoon butter	1	tablespoon lemon juice
4	scallions, chopped fine	2	tablespoons butter
2	pounds flounder fillet	2	tablespoons flour
	dash salt	⅓	cup heavy cream
	dash pepper	4	tablespoons Parmesan
1	cup cider		cheese, grated
2	tablespoons apple brandy		

Butter baking dish and sprinkle dish with scallions. Arrange flounder fillets in a single layer. Season fish with salt and pepper. Add cider, apple brandy and lemon juice. Cover dish in a 350° oven and poach fish for 12 minutes. Strain off liquid. Melt the butter. Stir in the flour and cook for 1 minute. Add strained liquid and cream. Pour sauce back over the fish. Sprinkle with cheese and brown under broiler for 3 minutes.

GERTRUDE STEIN—BOUILLABAISSE ANTIBES

1½	pounds red snapper	1	pound halibut
1½	pounds sea bass	2	live lobsters (1½ pounds)
1½	pounds striped bass	1	pound mussels in shells

1 pound uncooked, peeled shrimp	1 stalk of celery, sliced
5 tablespoons olive oil	1 teaspoon saffron
1 onion, chopped	·1 quart bouillon
6 ripe tomatoes, peeled and chopped	1 bay leaf
1 tablespoon tomato paste	Dash of thyme
4 garlic cloves, chopped	1 cup Chablis wine
1 head fresh fennel, sliced thin	salt and pepper to taste
1 white leek, sliced thin	1 tablespoon Pernod
	French bread
	1 tablespoon chopped parsley

Skin, clean, and fillet all the fish into 3- or 4-inch pieces. Cut the lobsters into pieces, including the heads. In a large saucepan heat oil. Stir in onion, tomatoes, tomato paste, garlic, fennel, leek, celery, and saffron. Cook 2 minutes. Add bouillon, bay leaf, thyme, wine, salt, and pepper. Add fillets, lobsters, mussels, and shrimp. Bring to a boil and simmer 15 minutes. Add Pernod and mix. Toast bread, place in deep round platter. Pour fish broth over slices. On another platter arrange fish in attractive manner and sprinkle with parsley.

TRUMAN CAPOTE—
ROAST DUCK IN ASPIC WITH GRAPES

Trim loose fat from two 5-pound ducks, dry ducks thoroughly, and truss them. Prick fatty parts with skewer and sprinkle the cavities and skin with salt and pepper. Put ducks in a large roasting pan, pour ½ cup hot water over them, and roast at 425° for 1 hour. Put ducks in large dish, and pour off fat from pan. Return ducks to pan and roast them for 45 minutes more, or until crisp and well browned. Transfer ducks to dish and let them cool completely.

Skim fat from pan juices, deglaze pan with 1 cup Port, stirring in brown bits clinging to bottom and sides, reduce liquid over heat by half. Make 2 cups giblet stock, add to pan with 2 cups brown stock and cook for 15 minutes or until it is reduced to 4 cups. Season with salt and white pepper, strain into a bowl and let it cool. Chill the stock and remove the fat layer.

In a small bowl sprinkle 2 envelopes gelatin over ⅓ cup cold water for 5 minutes and transfer to a deep bowl. Clarify the stock, ladling it over gelatin and let the mixture cool. Put ducks on a rack over a baking pan and spoon a layer of the liquid aspic over them. Chill ducks for 10 minutes, spoon a second layer of aspic, and chill for 10 minutes more. Peel 2 pounds seedless green grapes and combine 20 of the grapes with ½ cup of the aspic. Arrange grapes along the centers of the duck breasts and chill the ducks until the aspic is set. Arrange each duck on a platter, spoon 3 or 4 more layers of aspic over ducks. Let the layers set before adding another.

Now combine the remaining grapes with 1 cup of the aspic and arrange them in clusters around the ducks. Pour remaining aspic into a pan large enough to make a ⅓-inch layer and chill for 1 hour. Invert aspic onto flat surface and cut into ¼-inch dice. Arrange diced aspic around ducks and chill. Remove from refrigerator 1 or 2 hours before serving—garnish with sprigs of watercress.

NOEL COWARD—VEAL AT THE MILL

2 tablespoons olive oil
1 3½-pound leg of veal, boned and rolled
1 large onion, thinly sliced
2 carrots, finely chopped
2 stalks celery, chopped
2 garlic cloves, minced
1 2-ounce can anchovy fillets
1 6-ounce can tunafish

1 cup dry white wine
3 sprigs parsley
1 bay leaf
Pinch thyme
pinch salt
pinch of pepper
1 cup mayonnaise
juice of half a lemon
3 tablespoons capers

Heat oil in large, heavy kettle with tight-fitting cover and brown meat on all sides. Add chopped vegetables, garlic, anchovies, tunafish, wine, parsley, bay leaf, thyme, salt, and pepper. Cover and simmer slowly for 2 hours. Remove meat and chill. Continue cooking the sauce until it is half its original quantity. Place in blender and purée it. Chill the sauce and then blend the mayonnaise, lemon juice, and capers. Remove strings from the roast and slice thin. Spoon sauce over the meat.

MAGGIE SMITH—PANCAKES

½ cup flour	2 tablespoons
½ cup milk	confectioner's sugar
2 eggs lightly beaten	juice of half a lemon
pinch of nutmeg	orange marmalade
4 tablespoons butter	1 can mandarin oranges

Preheat oven to 425°.

Mix the flour, milk, eggs, and nutmeg. Beat lightly. Batter should remain a little lumpy. Melt the butter in a 12-inch iron skillet. When the butter is nut brown pour in the batter. Bake in oven 15 minutes until golden brown. Sprinkle with sugar, marmalade, and mandarin oranges and return briefly to oven, Serve piping hot.

LEONARDO DA VINCI—LASAGNA VERDI AL FORNO

NOODLES:

3¾ cups all-purpose flour	2 eggs
½ cup plus 1 tablespoon cooked, drained spinach	3 tablespoons water
	dash salt

MEAT SAUCE:

¼ cup minced or grated carrots	½ teaspoon salt
	dash pepper
1 small onion, minced	1 tablespoon tomato paste
1 celery stalk	½ tablespoon water
1 tablespoon olive oil	½ tablespoon flour
½ pound ground beef	

Sift the flour, measure, and sift onto pastry board. Make a well in the center. Put the drained chopped spinach, eggs, water, and salt in it. Make a stiff dough. Knead for 20 minutes. Roll out to paper thinness. Let dry on board. When dry cut into oblongs 2 to 4 inches. Drop into a large kettle of boiling salted water and cook until tender, about 25 minutes. Drain.

While noodles are drying, prepare and cook meat sauce. Chop carrot, onion, and celery fine. Sauté in oil in skillet. Add beef, salt, and pepper. Cook on moderate heat, stirring. Blend in tomato paste to which water and flour have been added. Cook over low heat until meat is well cooked and sauce is thickened.

CREAM SAUCE:

For the cream sauce, melt butter in a saucepan. Blend in flour and salt. Add milk slowly, stirring. Cook, stir till thick and smooth.

Then, grease a 2⅓- or 3-quart shallow baking dish. Line baking dish with layer of lasagne. Cover with meat sauce, spreading it thin. Moisten with cream sauce. Cover with a coating of grated cheese. Continue alternating layers until all is used. Finish with cream sauce. Dot with additional butter. Bake 10 minutes at 300° and then 35 minutes at 450°.

CANDICE BERGEN—ORANGE PECAN PIE

Make pâté brisé. Roll the dough into a round ⅛-inch-thick on a lightly floured surface, drape it lightly over the rolling pin and fit it into a 9-inch pie plate. Prick the shell and chill for one hour. Line shell with wax paper, fill with raw rice, and bake in the lower third of a hot oven (400°) for 10 minutes. Remove rice carefully and bake the shell 10 minutes more or until golden. Transfer shell to a rack and cool.

Cream together in a large bowl 1 cup sugar and 2 tablespoons butter. Add 4 eggs, 1 at a time, beating well. Stir in 1 cup pecans, ¾ cup light corn syrup, and ¼ cup orange juice and grated orange rind. Pour filling into prepared shell and bake pie at 375° for 30 minutes.

FLORENZ ZIEGFELD—CHICKEN PAPRIKA

½ cup finely chopped onion	½ teaspoon black pepper
¼ cup shortening	3–4 pound chicken, disjointed
dash salt	1½ cups water
1 tablespoon paprika	1 cup sour cream

DUMPLINGS FOR THE CHICKEN PAPRIKA:

3 eggs, beaten	1½ cups flour
½ cup water	2 teaspoons salt

Sauté chopped onion in shortening until tender but not browned. Combine salt, paprika, and black pepper and stir into the onions. Add chicken and fry until all sides are lightly coated. Add water and cover. Cook for about 1½ hours or until chicken is tender.

Mix ingredients for dumplings, beating mixture until dough is not lumpy. Pour 6 cups of water into a 3-quart saucepan. Add some salt and bring to a boil. Spoon into this the batter, a teaspoonful at a time. Boil 10 minutes and drain.

Remove chicken and blend the sour cream into the liquid in the skillet. Pour dumplings into the sauce and serve hot with chicken.

BARBRA STREISAND—BOILED CHICKEN DINNER

	4-pound chicken	6	small onions
	White wine (optional)	4	turnips, white
1	bay leaf	3	leeks
	pinch thyme	12	carrots, small
	dash pepper	3	stalks celery cut in pieces
2	cloves, whole		and tied together
	dash salt		parsley
3	medium potatoes, peeled		

Cover chicken with water or white wine. Tie bay leaf, thyme, pepper, and cloves together and wrap in cheesecloth. Add to chicken and bring to a boil. Skim off any froth. Reduce heat and simmer for 45 minutes. Add salt and vegetables (not parsley). Simmer until chicken and vegetables are tender. Discard the cheesecloth. Serve chicken with vegetables and garnish with parsley.

Subject and Name Index

aperitif, 33
cooking, 96
table, 33–34
Winter carnival party, 175
Woollcott, Alexander, 7–8

Zaima, Chris, 145
Zipkin, Jerry, 43
Zipprodt, Patricia, 255

Recipe Index